Magic Moments

Photographs by Steve Wood

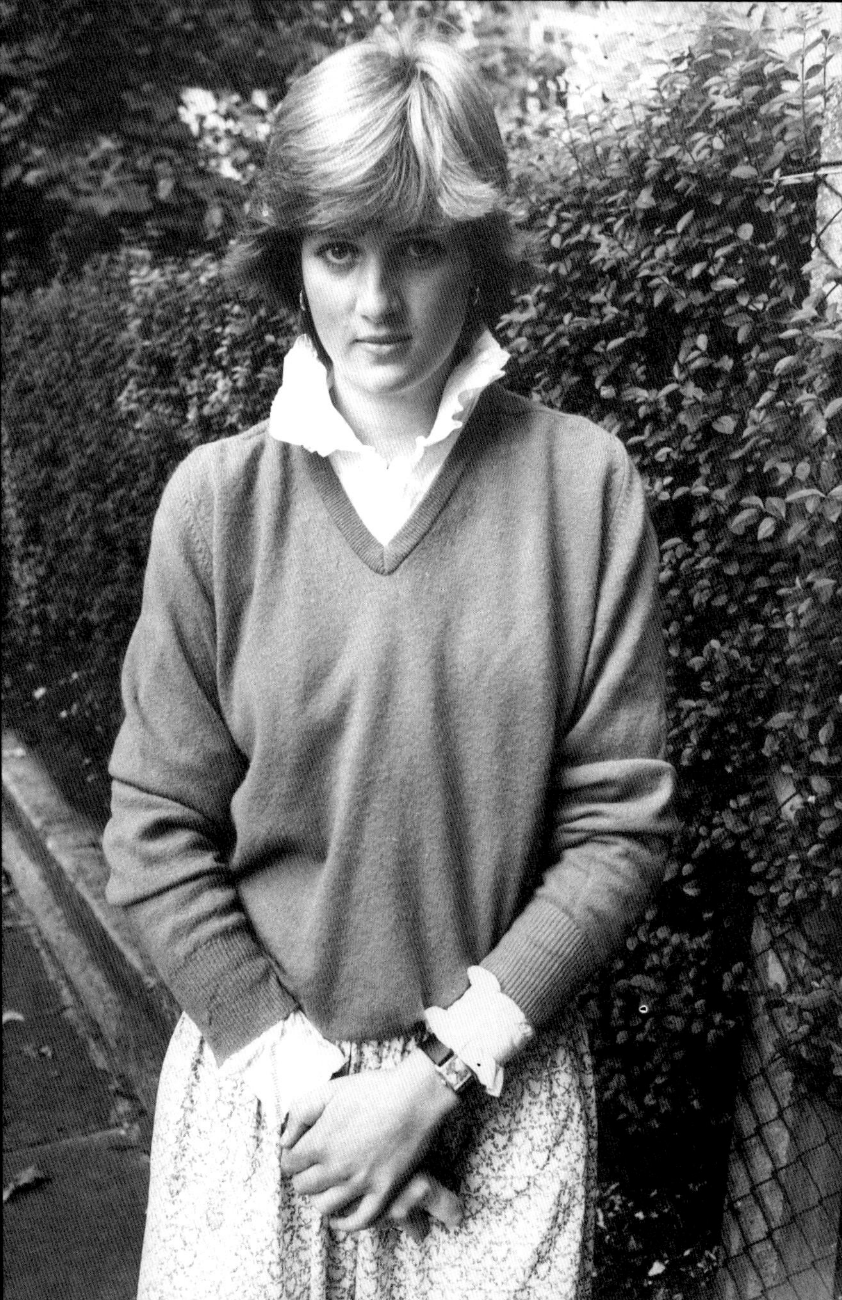

This is the moment the world first became aware of a teenager who would become the most famous woman in the world. Lady Diana Spencer, aged just 19, is waiting for a bus outside her flat in London's Earls Court. This is the first time Steve met the woman he would photograph many thousands of times.

MAGIC MOMENTS

PHOTOGRAPHS BY STEVE WOOD

Niche Publications

PO.Box 20988, 31 London Street, London W2 3GX
Telephone:+44 (0) 20 7402 1946;
email:info@nichepublications.co.uk

ACKNOWLEDGEMENTS

The publishers would like to thank the following for their boundless energy and invaluable advice in researching the information contained in this book: Express Newspapers, Rex Features, Ashley Walton, Sally Wood, Natalie Wood, Stephen Turnham, James Drury Desmond Robinson, Al Senter and Jennifer Watt.

Magic Moments
Was compiled and edited by Richard de Clare
published by: Niche Publications
PO.Box 20988, 31 London Street, London W2 3GX
Telephone: +44 (0) 20 7402 1946 email:info@nichepublications.co.uk

Printed by:
Nuffield Press England
ISBN 9 78095322 99 49

Contents

Introduction

By Ashley Walton

From the day Steve respectfully asked nineteen-year-old Lady Diana Spencer to pose with a kindergarten child in her arms, a superstar was born and the world just couldn't get enough of her.

He was always there, perched on a stepladder or behind a silken ceremonial rope, for all of her brief but triumphant public life. The pages with the 'Pictures by Steve Wood' tags were the ones Diana would turn to first thing every morning as she checked her public image in the tabloids.

From courtship, through the media madness of the engagement, to the joy of marriage and motherhood, Steve's unique talent to capture the magic moments of Diana's beauty captivated millions of Daily Express readers worldwide.

Steve was the Buckingham Palace accredited Royal photographer for the Daily Express, travelling the world with the 'People's Princess' covering her official tours in Australia, New Zealand, the US, Canada, Japan, Thailand, Bali and Africa. His trusty aluminium ladder allowed a unique view of a beautiful woman.

But he was also there whenever she met the people of Britain, in the crowd at an old folks home in Clacton, a school in St Albans, his lens told the same story of an icon loved by all.

That same camera lens also captured the trauma of the marriage break up and ultimately, the tragic aftermath in Paris. These photographs are a historic document of the happiest days of a teenager plucked from obscurity as she blossomed into a beautiful, elegant Princess becoming the most famous woman in the world.

Steve had photographed many of Prince Charles' girlfriends, from actress Susan George, heiress Sabrina Guinness, ironically the future Camilla Parker Bowles, and the stunning Anna Wallace, but he knew the moment he looked into the clear blue eyes of Lady Diana Spencer, then aged just nineteen, on the pavement outside her Earls Court flat, that she would be the future Princess of Wales. "She had an innocence that the camera loved and she was so delightful to know, 'says Steve. He knocked on the door of her Coleherne Court flat in London's Earls Court one evening, to be met by a flatmate who told him Diana was a little upset because her pet goldfish had died. 'I went out and bought a new goldfish and gave it to her', " said Steve. "She was so pleased that a few days later she agreed to do the school picture for me. 'I wanted her against the light because it looked so beautiful. I didn't realise at the time that we would be able to see through the skirt."

By default it became a very famous photograph worldwide. Prince Charles is said to have laughed when he saw it in the Daily Express. " What a lovely pair of pins, "he reputedly told an embarrassed Diana.

That fish served Steve well over the hectic following decades and was remembered with a laugh by the Princess when she met Steve at an informal (off the record) press reception at the beginning of her first ever foreign tour as Princess of Wales. A decade later Diana would begin to hate the papparazzi who followed her everywhere, firing their motor drive cameras right in her face. But back in 1980 the camera loved Diana and she adored the attention. Later on, with her marriage in tatters, Diana realised the power of the photograph, either to upstage Charles or just to get her on to the front pages. Diana often rang reporters and photographers herself, to give a tip on where she would be at a particular time,knowing the huge reaction she would get.

Over the years the once well rounded former Sloane Ranger, whose idea of a quiet evening was curling up in front of a television soap with a packet of wine gums and a cup of instant coffee, morphed into a super model with a tiny waist that looked as small as her Welsh gold wedding band. 'Shy Di' had gone forever but the beautiful Princess had become the most photographed woman in the world.

STEVE WOOD

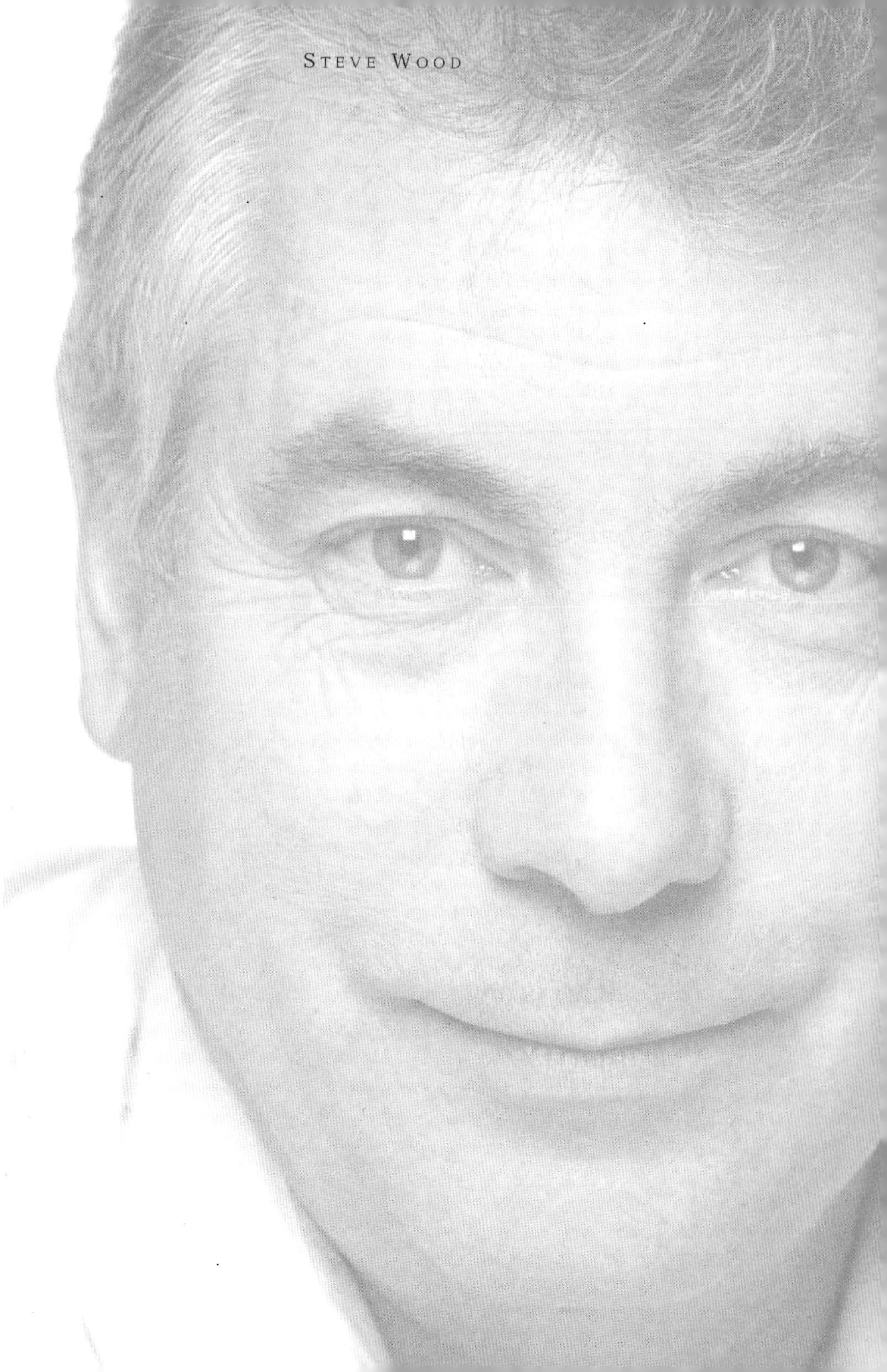

BIOGRAPHY

Publisher Richard de Clare battled for five years to convince the celebrated photographer Steve Wood that he should let the world see the fantastic images of Diana which he had captured over his professional life. Wood finally agreed that this book could be published a decade after the tragic death of 'The People's Princess'.

Steve was born into a photographic family in Southampton, Hampshire. His father Jim was a press photographer and both he and his brother Chris served their apprenticeships before moving to Fleet Street. Steve worked for the Daily Express for twenty years, covering Royals, wars, disasters and fashion.

When he left the Express, he moved full time into the world of haute couture and is now a renowned fashion photographer, a familiar face beside the catwalks in all the major shows around the world. Steve has a knack of becoming caught up in world disasters. He was in New York for a fashion shoot on 9/11 and witnessed the fate of the second tower. His photographs were used in most British national newspapers. He left the scene to send pictures to London and the building close to where he'd been standing collapsed, killing all the firemen gathered beneath it.

Then, on December 26th 2004, (Boxing Day) Steve was holidaying in Goa with his sixteen-year-old daughter Natalie, when the Tsunami struck all over the Indian Ocean. He immediately flew to the devastated area with his daughter.

Their photos were again used in all British newspapers. During those four harrowing days, Natalie learned and experienced a great deal about life. Will she be the fourth generation of 'Woods' to take up a press camera? 'We'll see.' said Steve. 'I believe that experience will shape her destiny.

'When Steve learned of Princess Diana's death, he flew to Paris. But it was just a knee-jerk reaction, he says. 'I felt I didn't belong there.' He was too upset to return to London for Diana's funeral. 'I didn't want my last photo of Diana to be her coffin' explains Steve.

These stunning, historic images are Steve's own tribute to a beautiful woman, ten years after her tragic early death.

Ashley Walton was at Steve Wood's elbow for the majority of these photographs. Ashley was the royal correspondent of the Daily Express from 1979 to 1992. He travelled with Steve to every continent covering numerous tours, not only of Charles and Diana but also the Queen and Prince Philip, the Queen Mother , Princess Anne and the Duke and Duchess of York. He was one of the first reporters to identify a young Lady Diana Spencer as a future royal bride and covered her last tour with Prince Charles to Korea. He was also among the first to reveal the romance between Prince Andrew and Sarah Ferguson.

He is the author of 'Charles and Diana', 'Charles and Diana The First Five Years' and is also the co-author of 'The Duke of Hazard' and 'What's In The Queen's Handbag'

He lives in Hertfordshire with his wife Joan and their two sons.

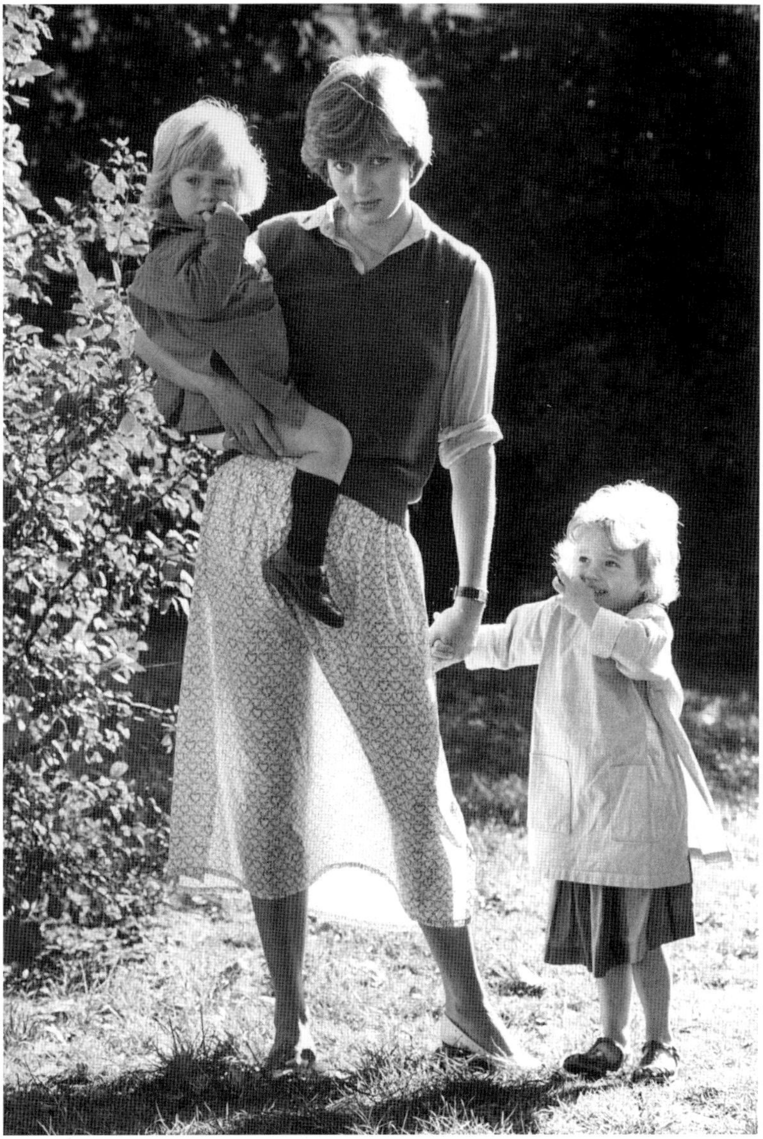

Diana at work in the garden of the New England Kindergarten in Pimlico, South-West London. She had agreed to pose for Steve and he asked her to stand with the sun behind her for what turned out to be a momentous photograph. He had not realised that the outline of her legs could be clearly seen but the resulting shot sparked off huge interest in Lady Diana, and earned her the nickname 'Shi Di'.

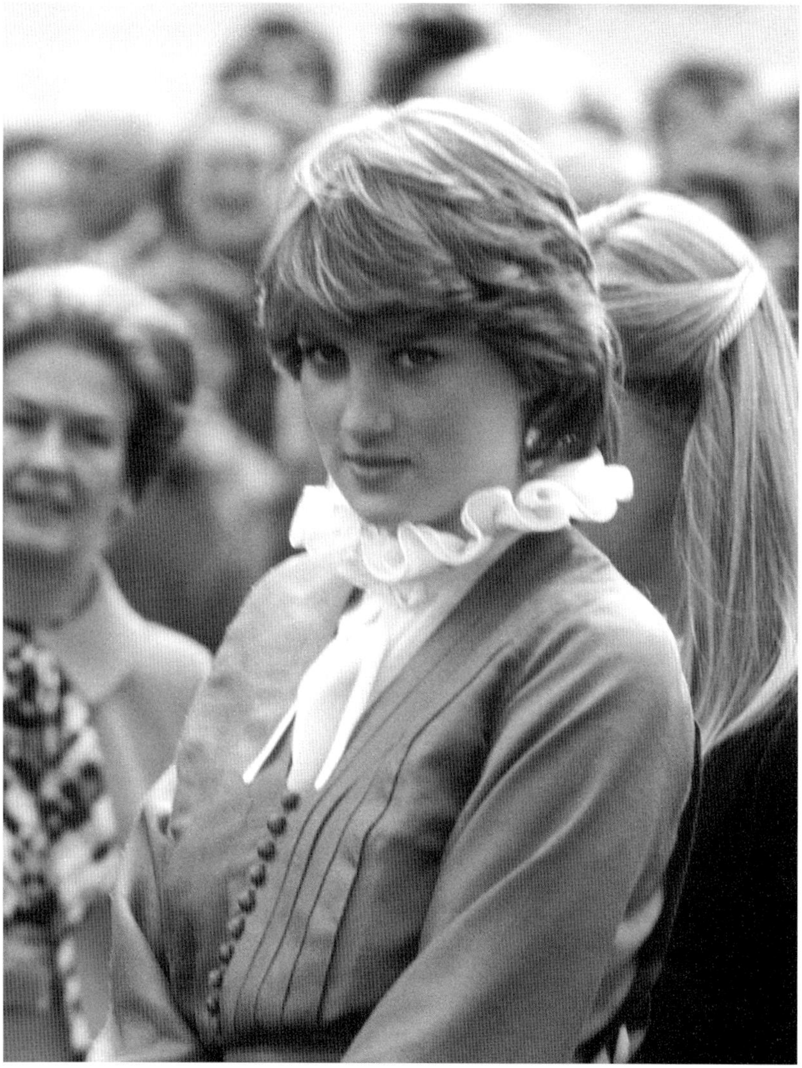

Still 'Shi Di' but she's beginning to gain confidence and learning fast how to get the best possible photos.

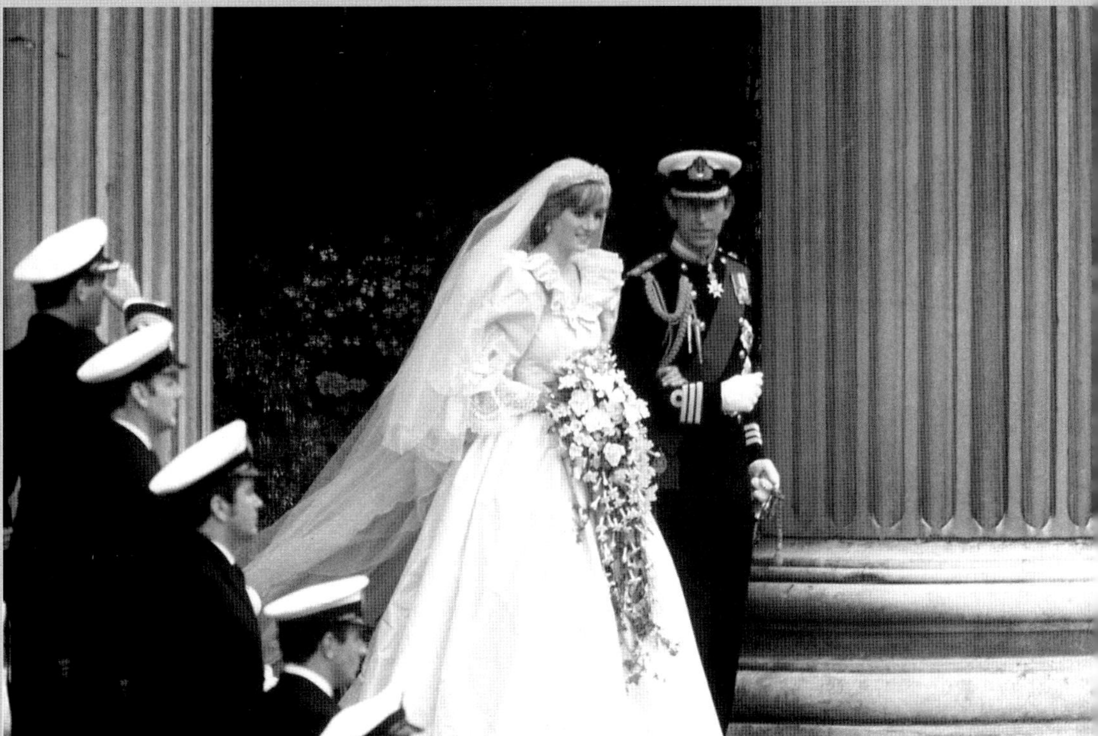

The steps of St Pauls Cathedral. Steve had a prime position in front of the main door and captured this sensational picture of a couple relieved that the huge tension and trauma of the ceremony was over at last.

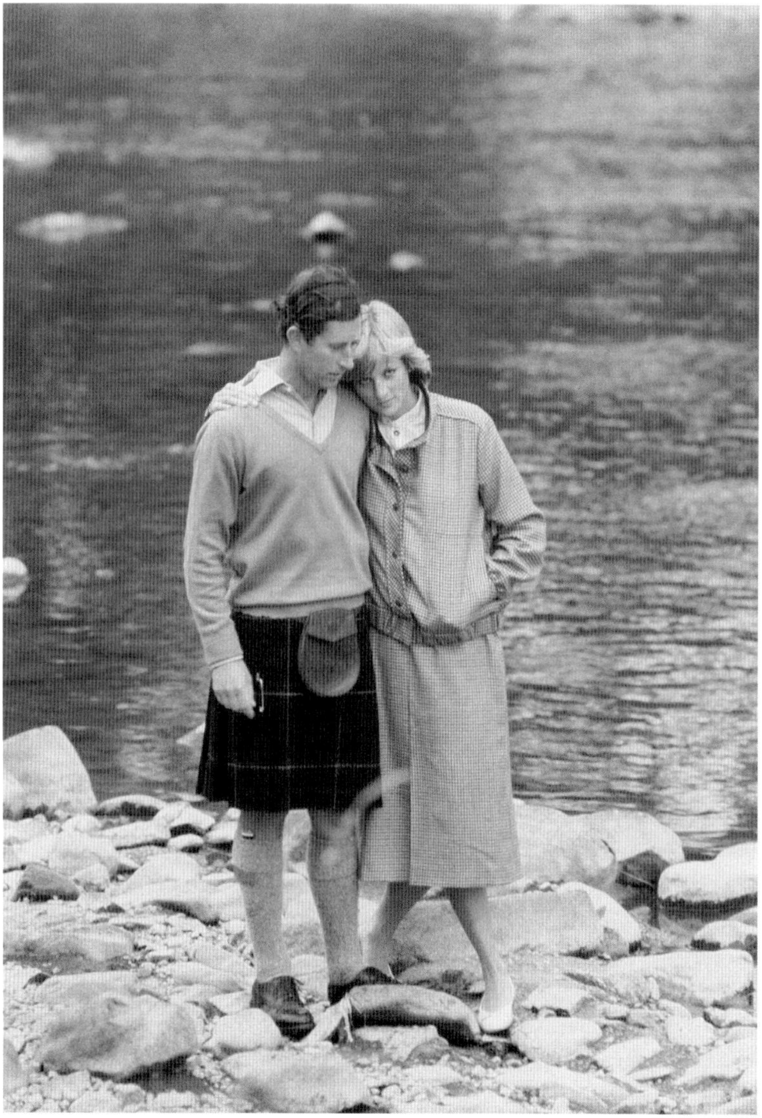

The official honeymoon portrait beside the River Dee on the Royal estate at Balmoral in Scotland. The world had seen very little of the new Princess of Wales since the wedding and this super relaxed, and very affectionate pose was a real delight.

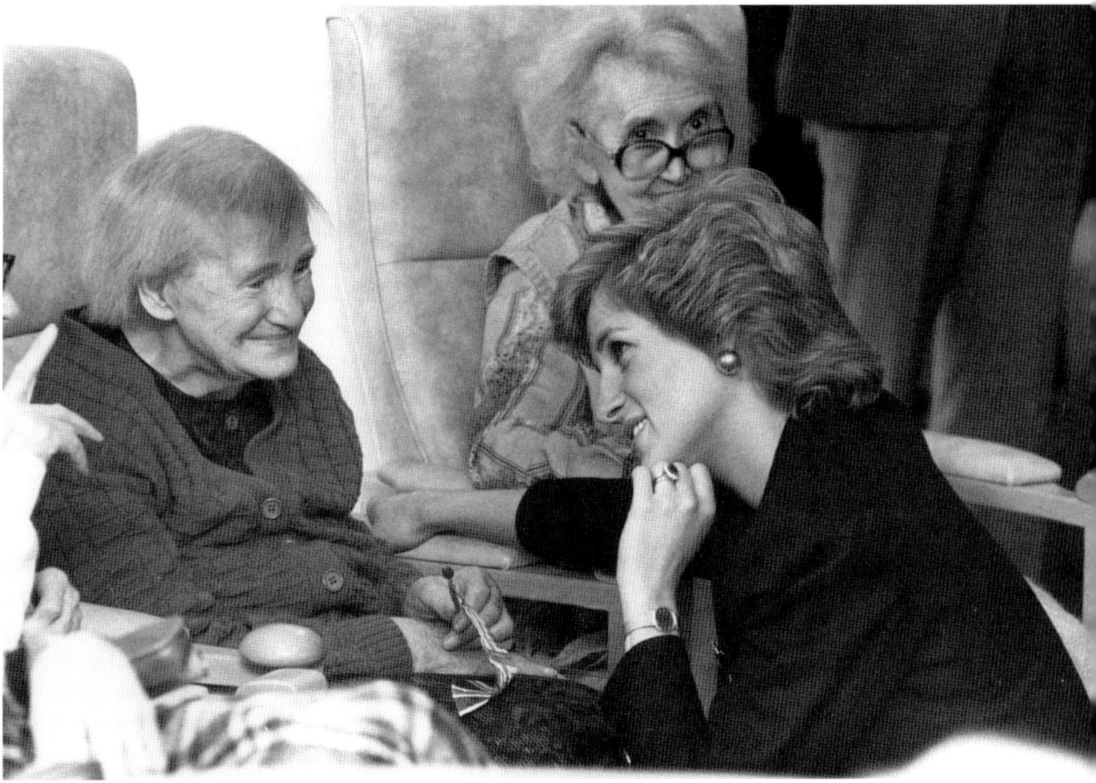

Diana is in thoughtful mood as she visits the residents of a home for the elderly in Colchester, Essex.

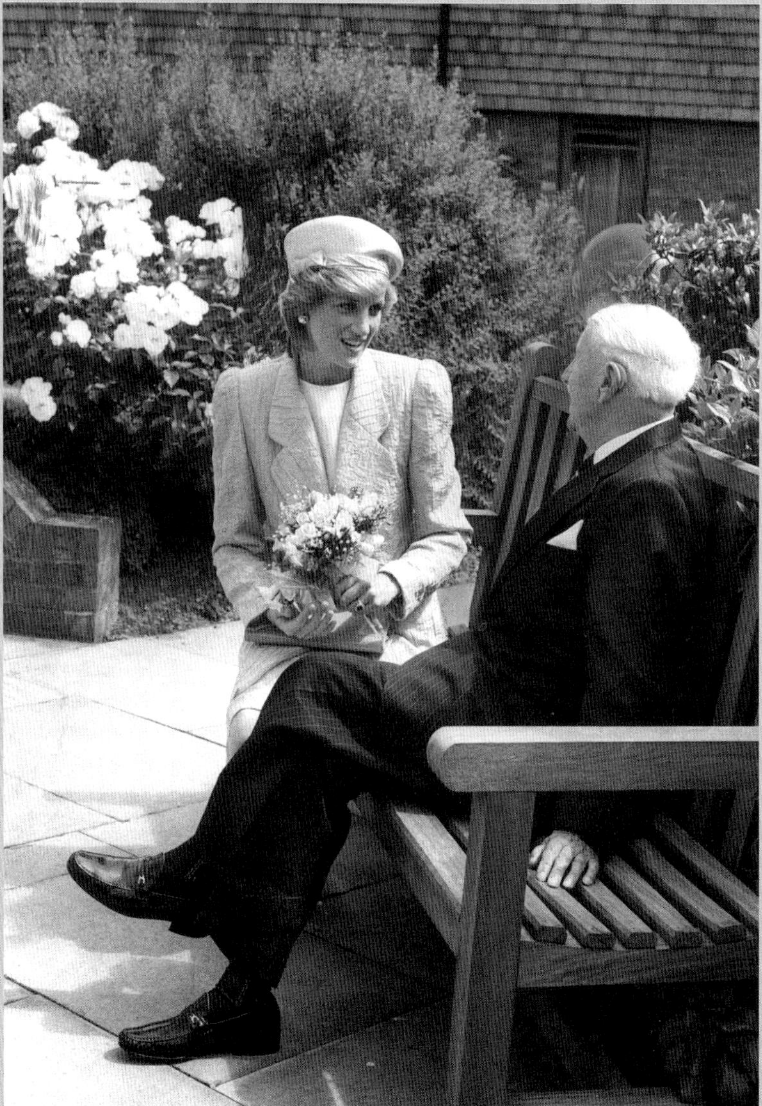

Diana is beginning to show the first signs of her future Royal superstar status. This was an era when Royals never actually engaged with ordinary people. Diana was able to change all that.

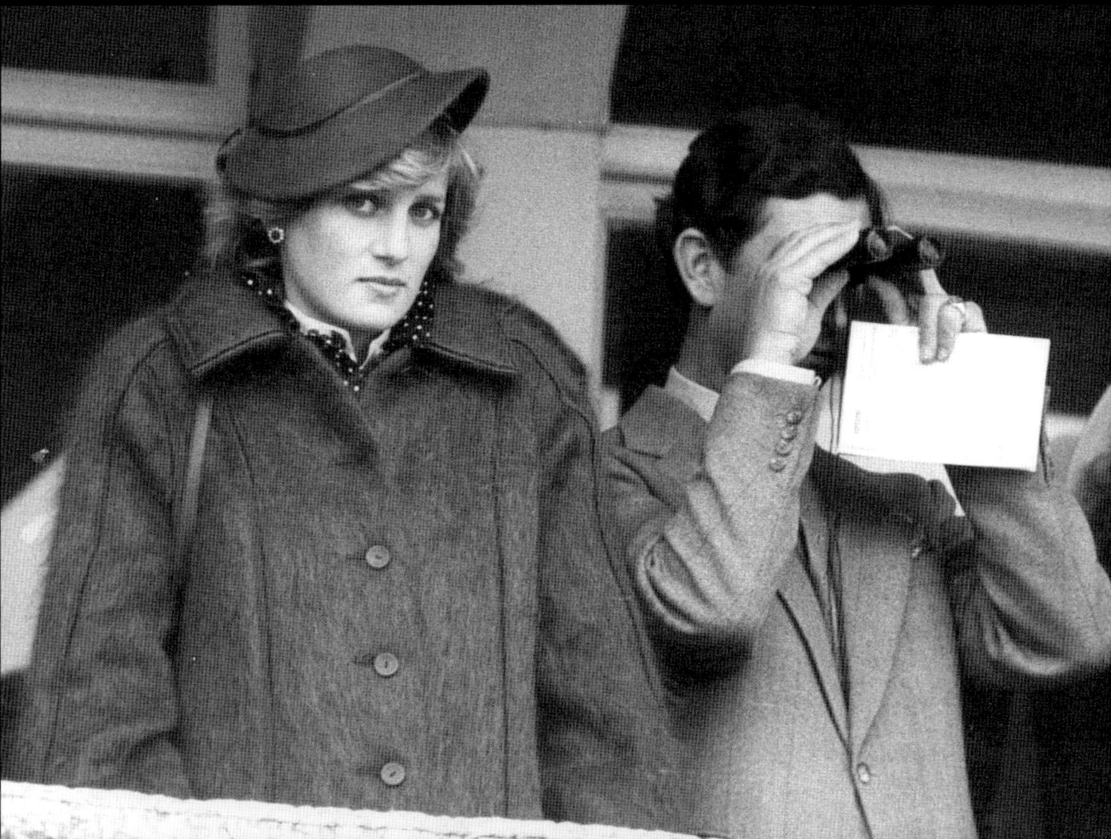

The Cheltenham Gold Cup. Charles dragged his new wife round racecourses as he pursued a brief fling with the turf. He fancied himself as a jockey, an idea which soon fizzled out after a bruising fall. But Diana was more interested in the cameras following her everywhere.

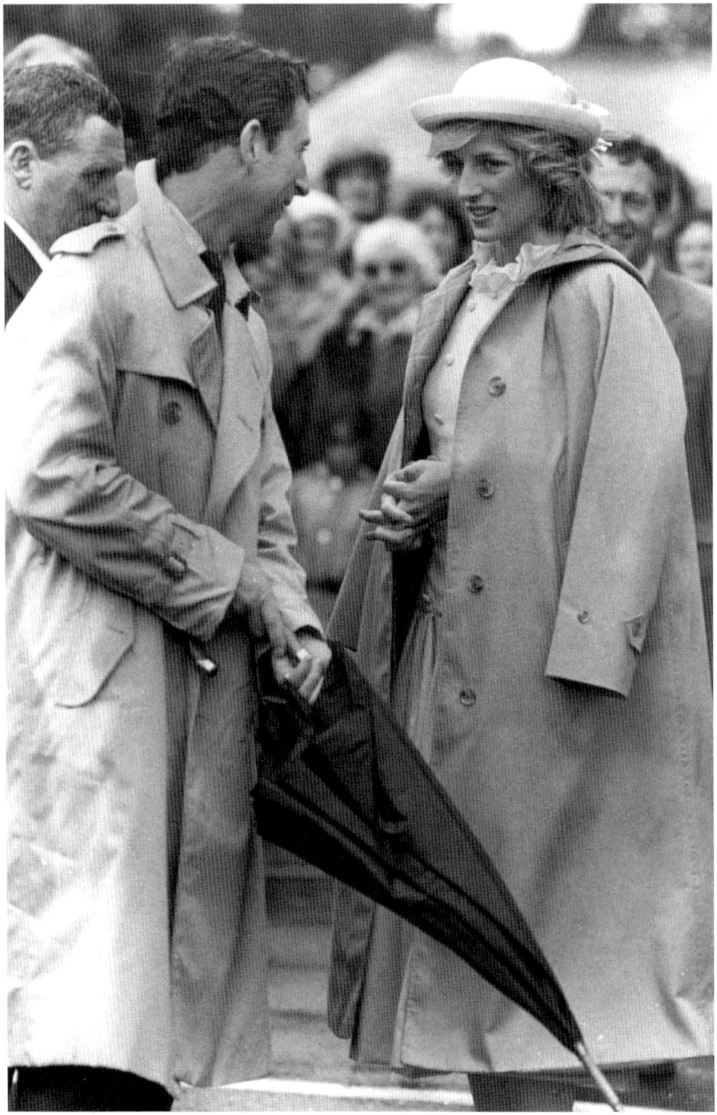

The first time the people of Wales saw their new Princess. Diana and Charles toured a very wet and windy Wales in the first autumn of their marriage. It was a busy few days as the young Princess tried to get used to the pressures of the public walkabout and the gathering media frenzy surrounding her.

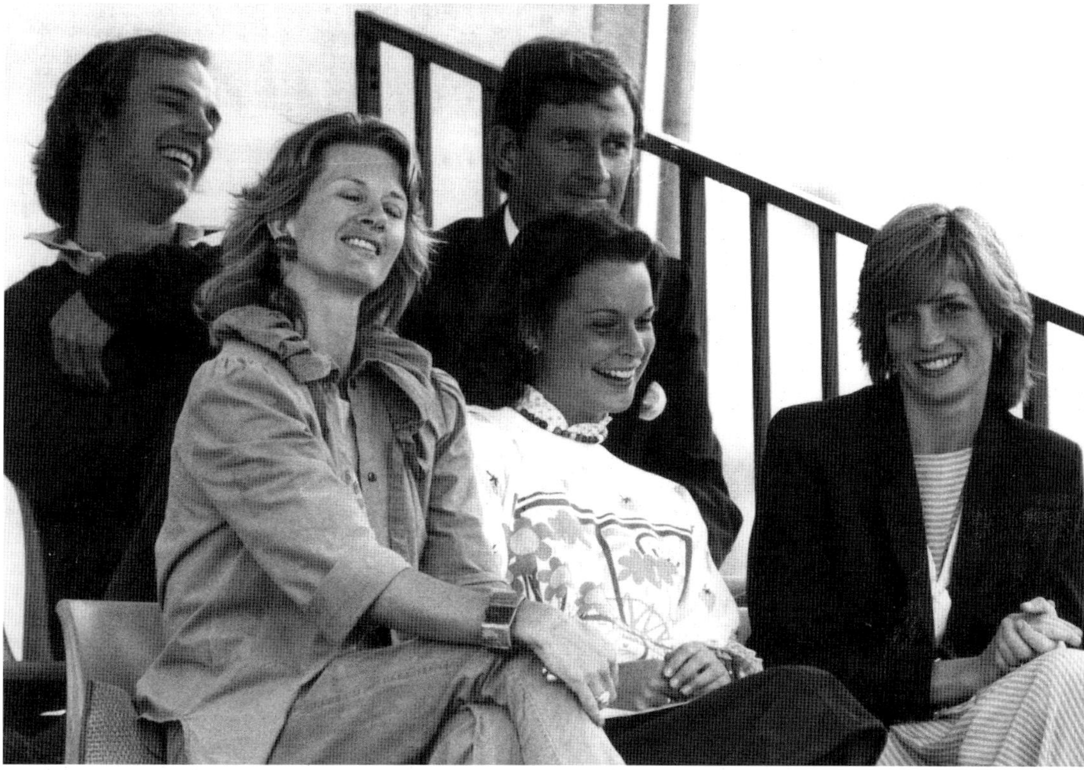

Diana never forgot her former Earls Court flatmates and invited them to a girl's day out to watch Prince Charles playing polo at the Guards Club in Windsor Great Park, accompanied by their husbands.

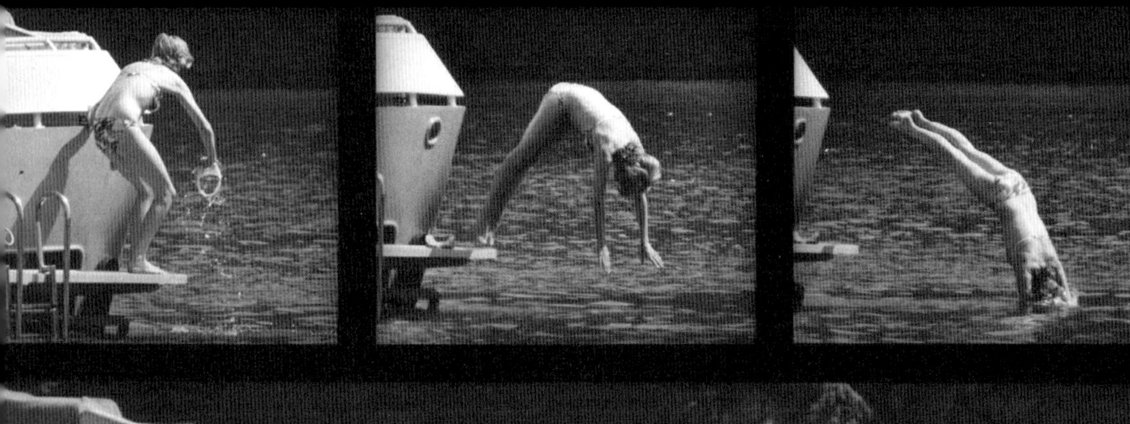

Royal holiday in Majorca with the King and Queen of Spain. Diana knew the press were in a nearby boat and put on this display of a perfect dive.

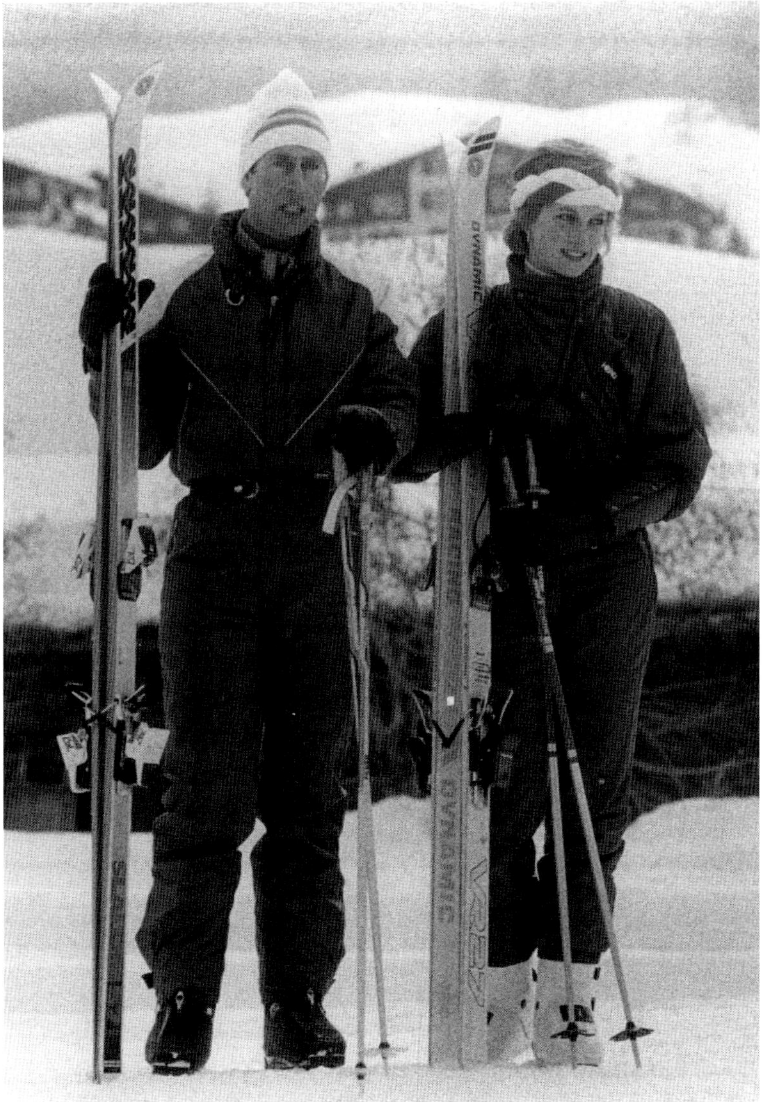

Official photocall with the Prince for a ski holiday in Switzerland. She made the Prince buy a new fashionable one piece ski suit to replace the, very unfashionable, outfit he had worn for many years as he skied in his favourite spot in the Alps.

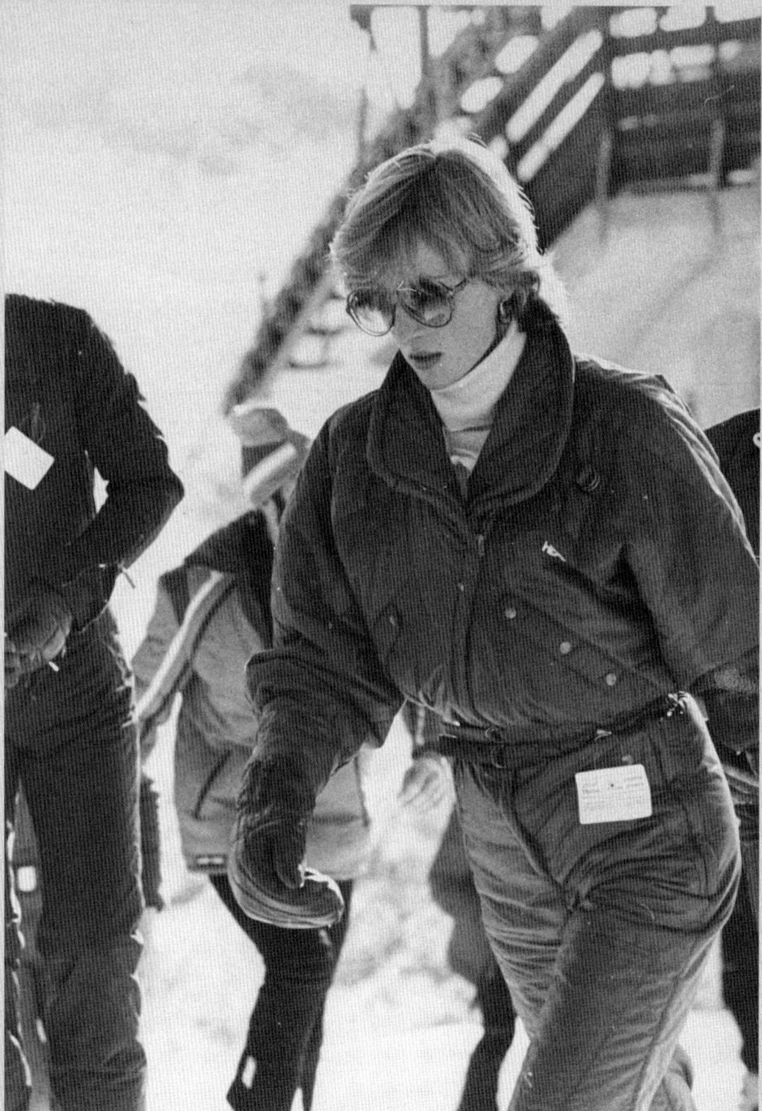

Still in Switzerland, Diana never liked the resort much preferring Lech in Austria in the years to come.

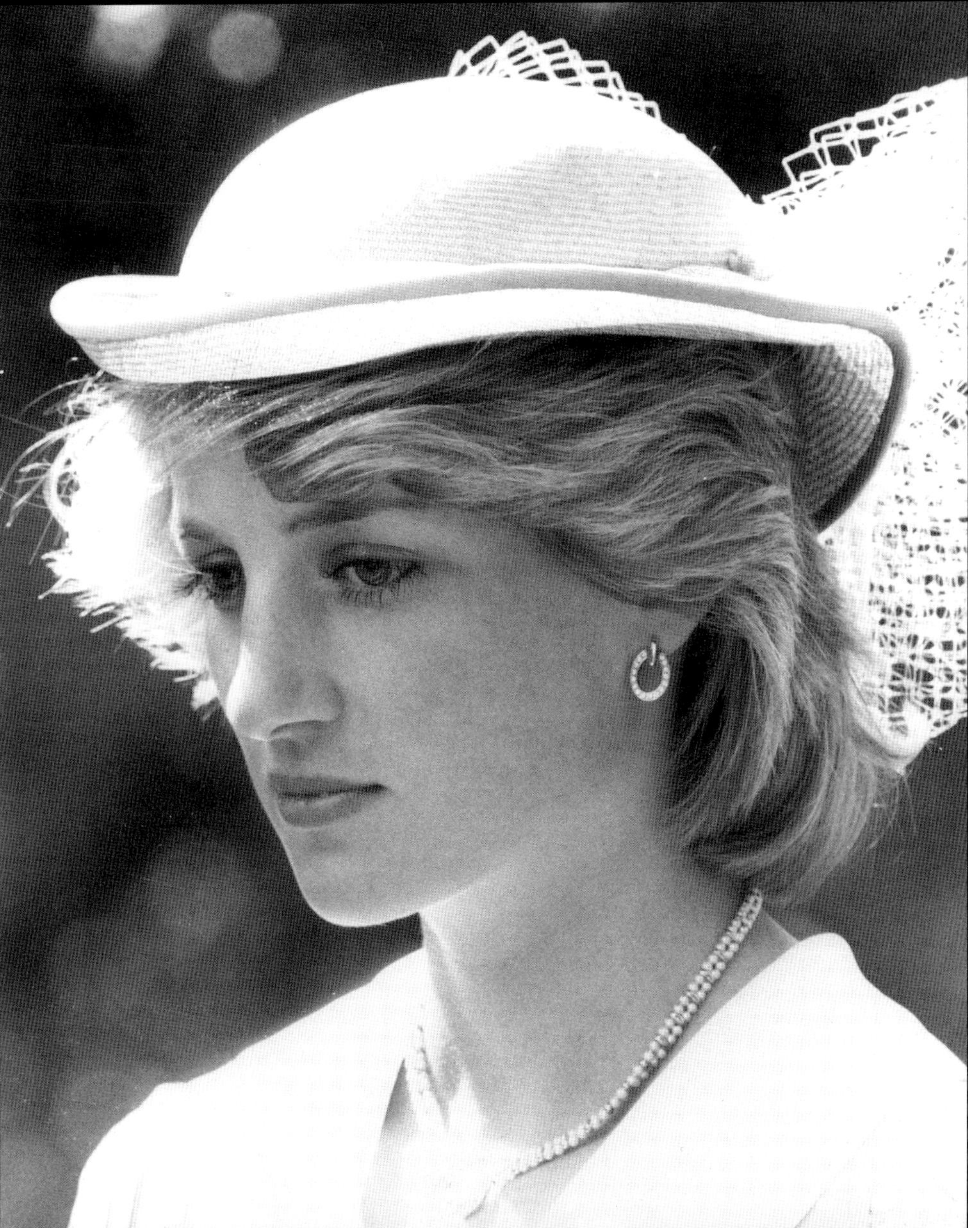

She still has the 'Shi Di' look as she visits a home for the elderly.

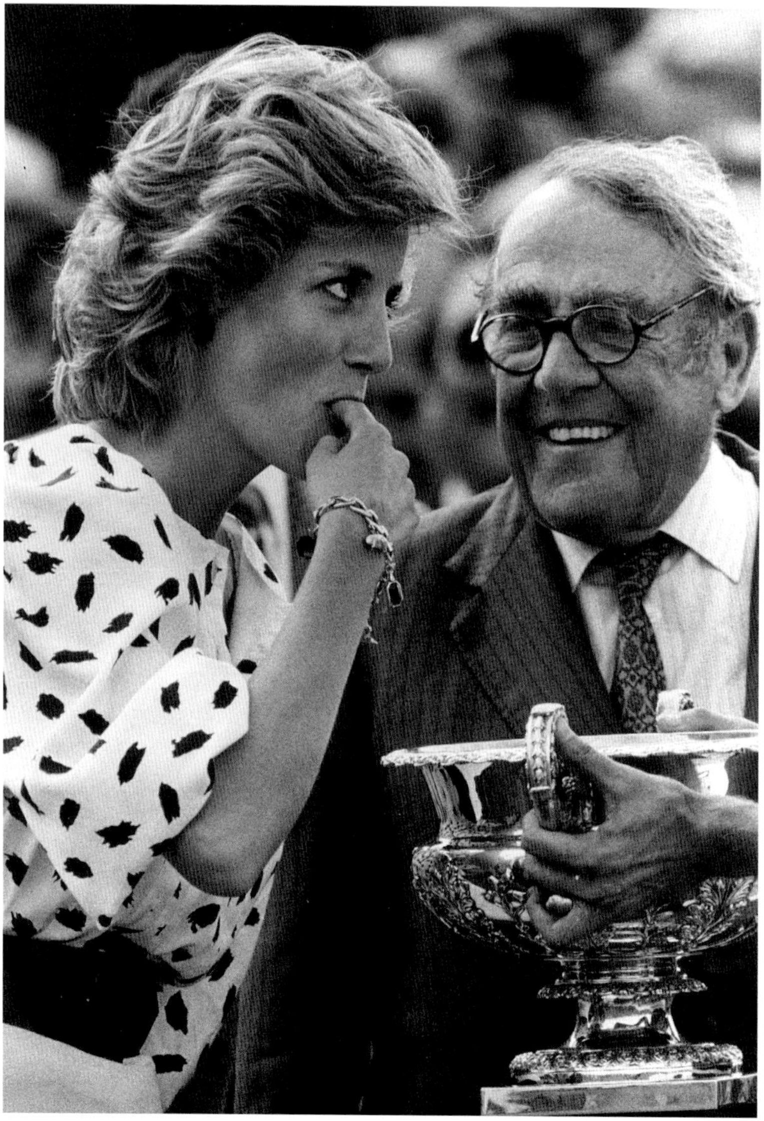

Polo at Cowdray Park in Sussex. The Princess was presenting a championship cup filled with the best celebration champagne and cheekily she couldn't resist dipping her fingers and then licking them. A break with stuffy Royal protocol which the crowd loved.

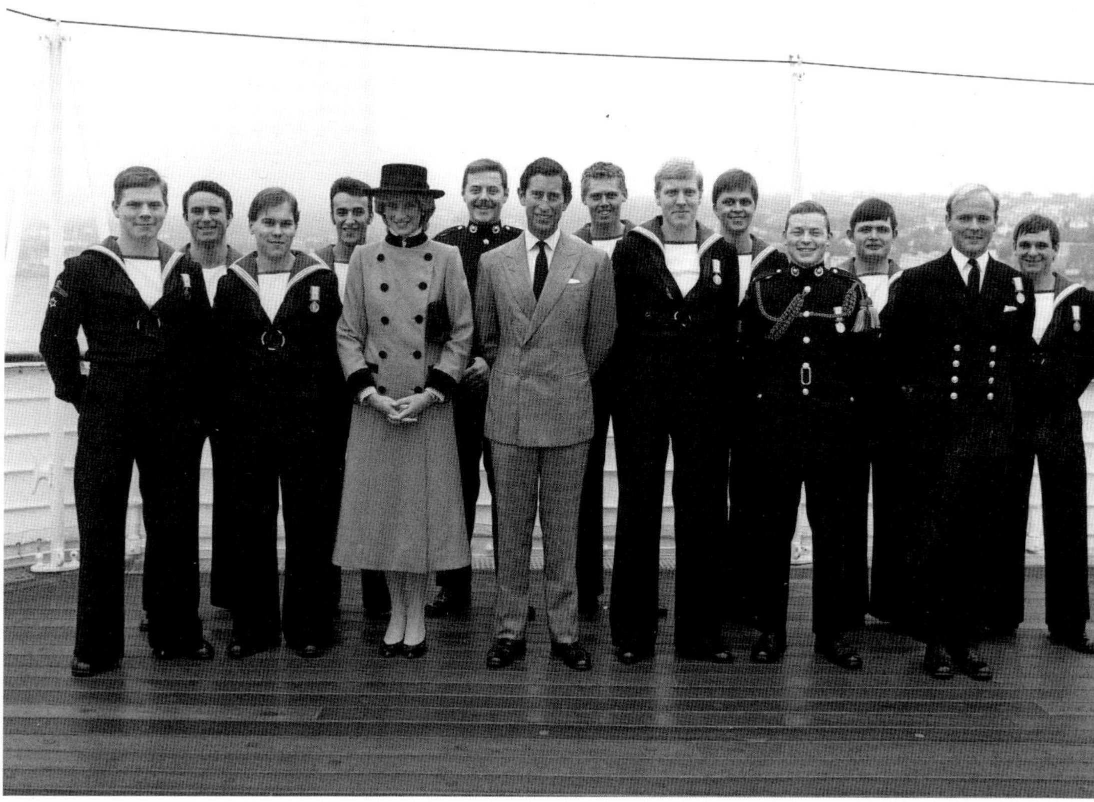

The first of the many thousands of official ceremonies she would attend in future both with Charles and alone. This time the Royal couple are surrounded by the Heroes of the Falklands War.

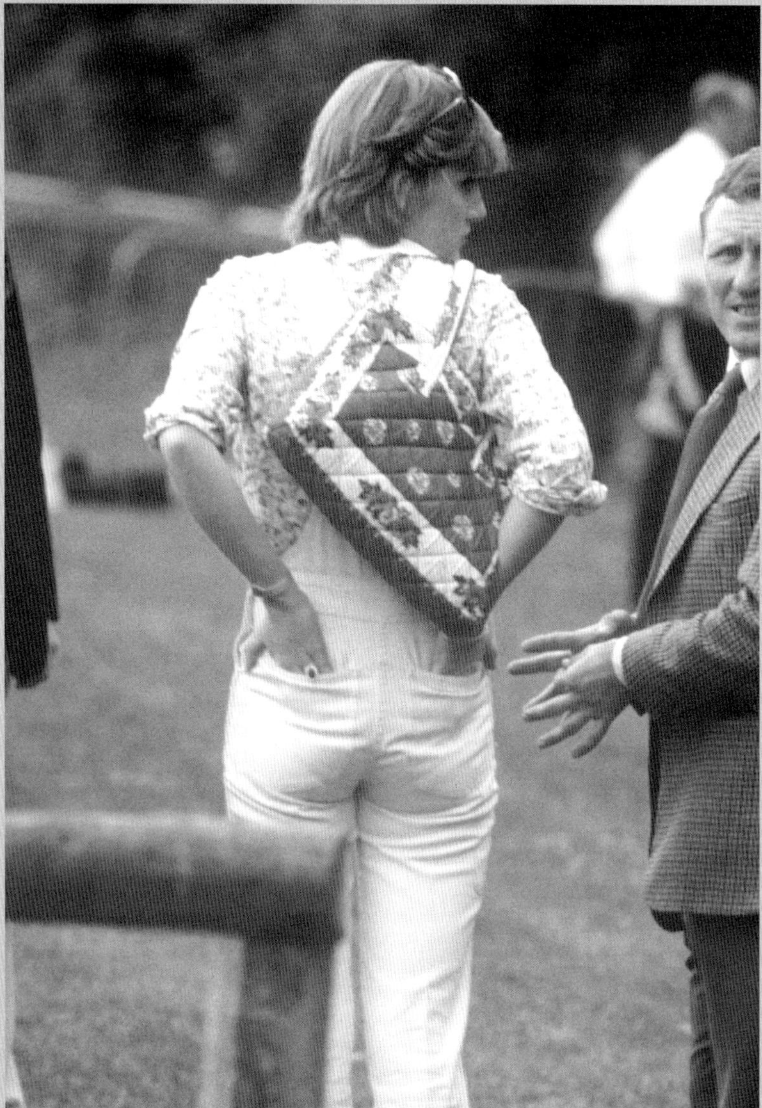

This pair of yellow dungarees, worn by Lady Diana Spencer at a polo match before her marriage, became must have fashion accessories for countless teenage girls.

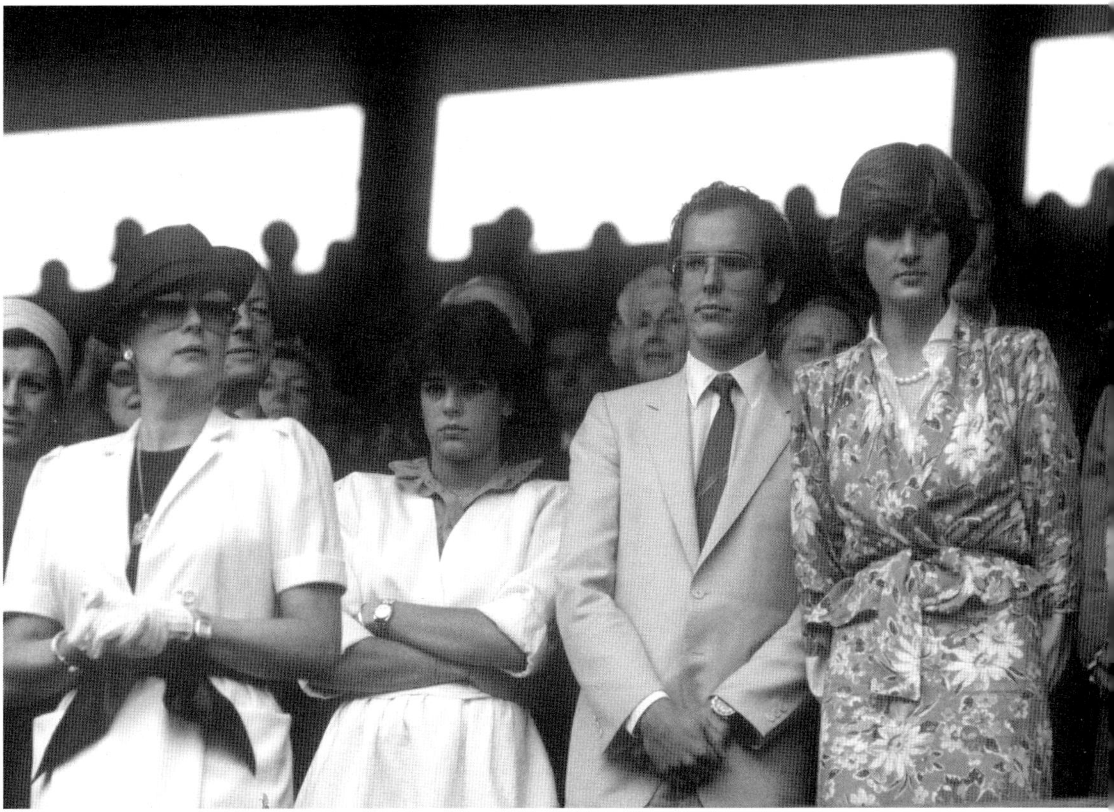

In the box at Wimbledon with former film star Grace Kelly who ironically died in a mysterious car accident. Also there Princess Stephanie and Prince Albert.

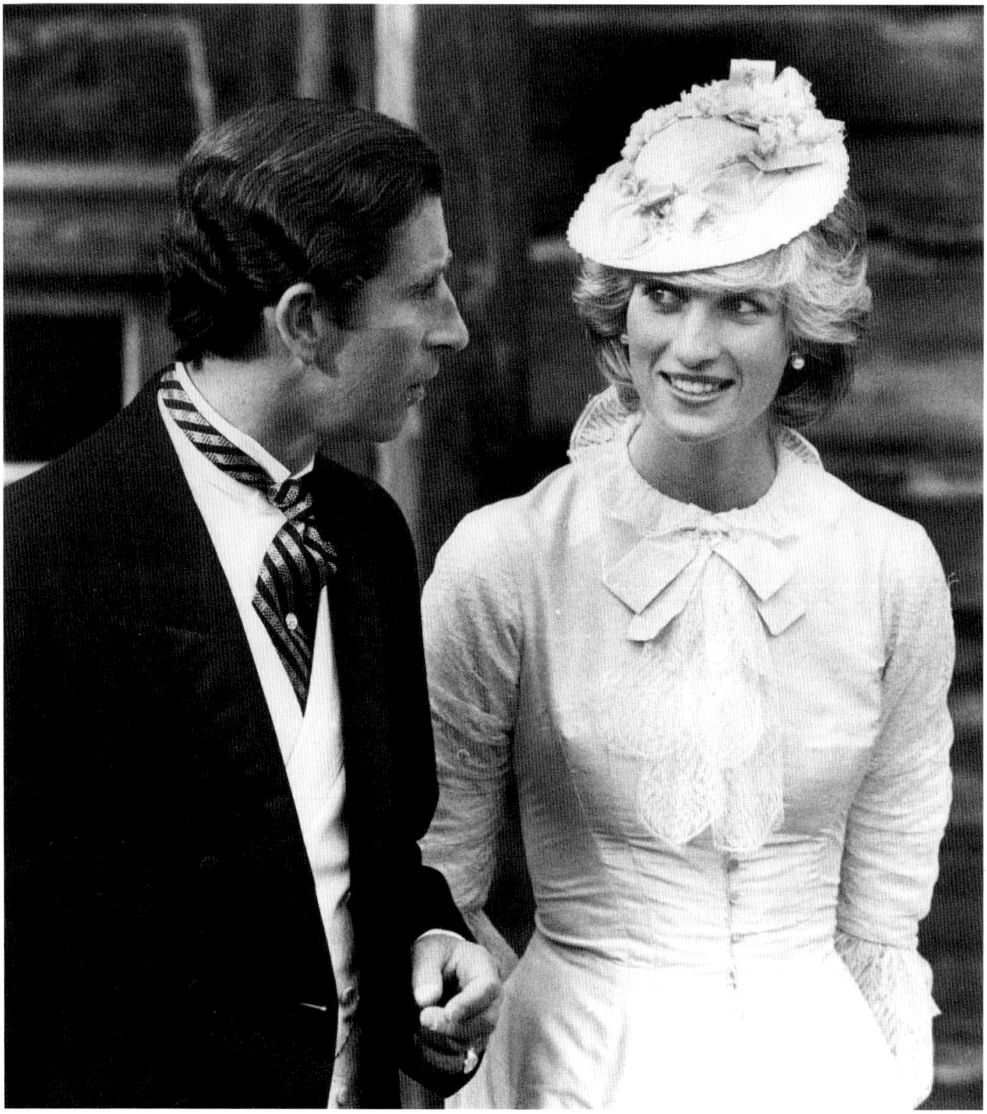

One of the first of the many Commonwealth tours. The couple are in Canada dressed in period costume for a charity event. Diana was nicknamed 'The Klondike Queen'.

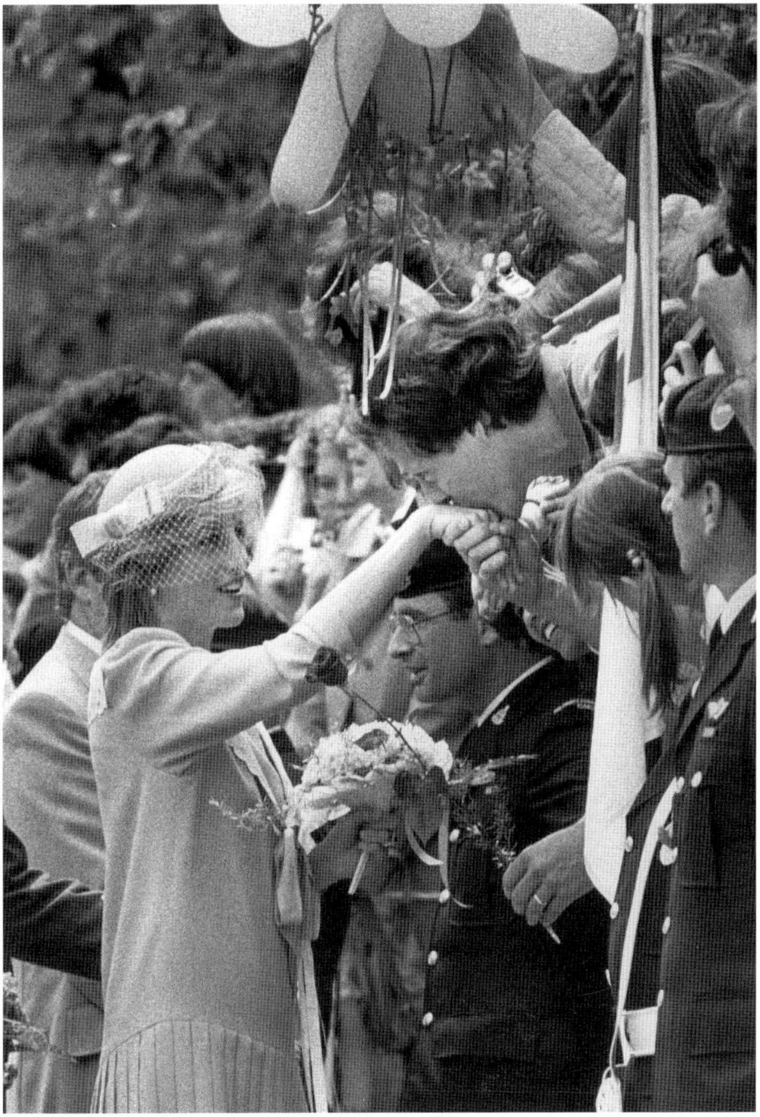

The People's Princess and a very public kiss on the hand from a handsome 'Prince'.

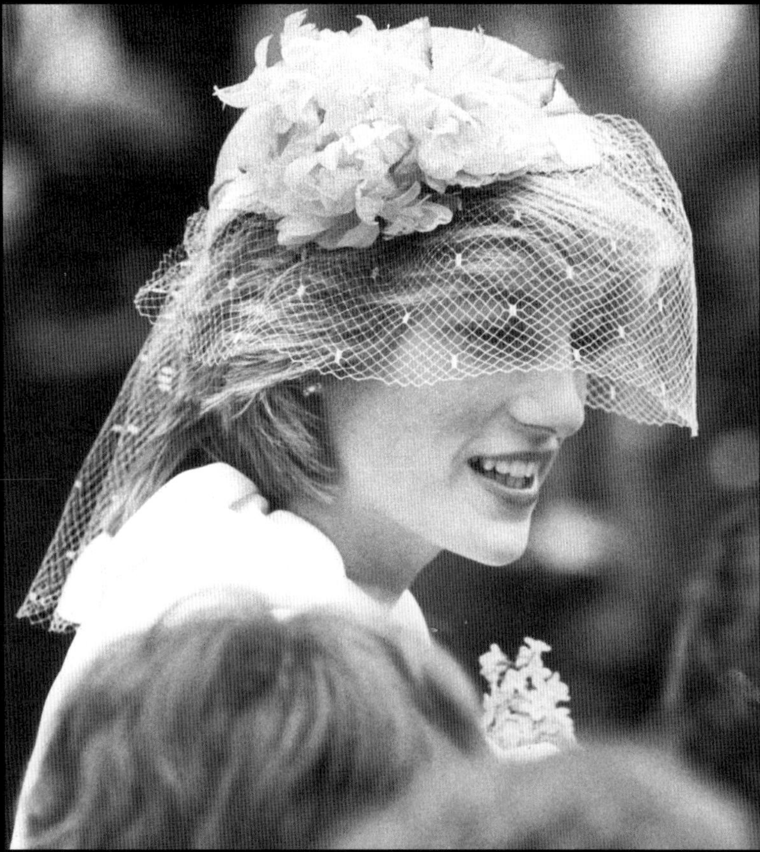

A church service in Canada where she was a huge media star from coast to coast.

RIGHT: A close up in Canada, the look loved by her millions of fans. Diana was becoming a beautiful and confident Princess.

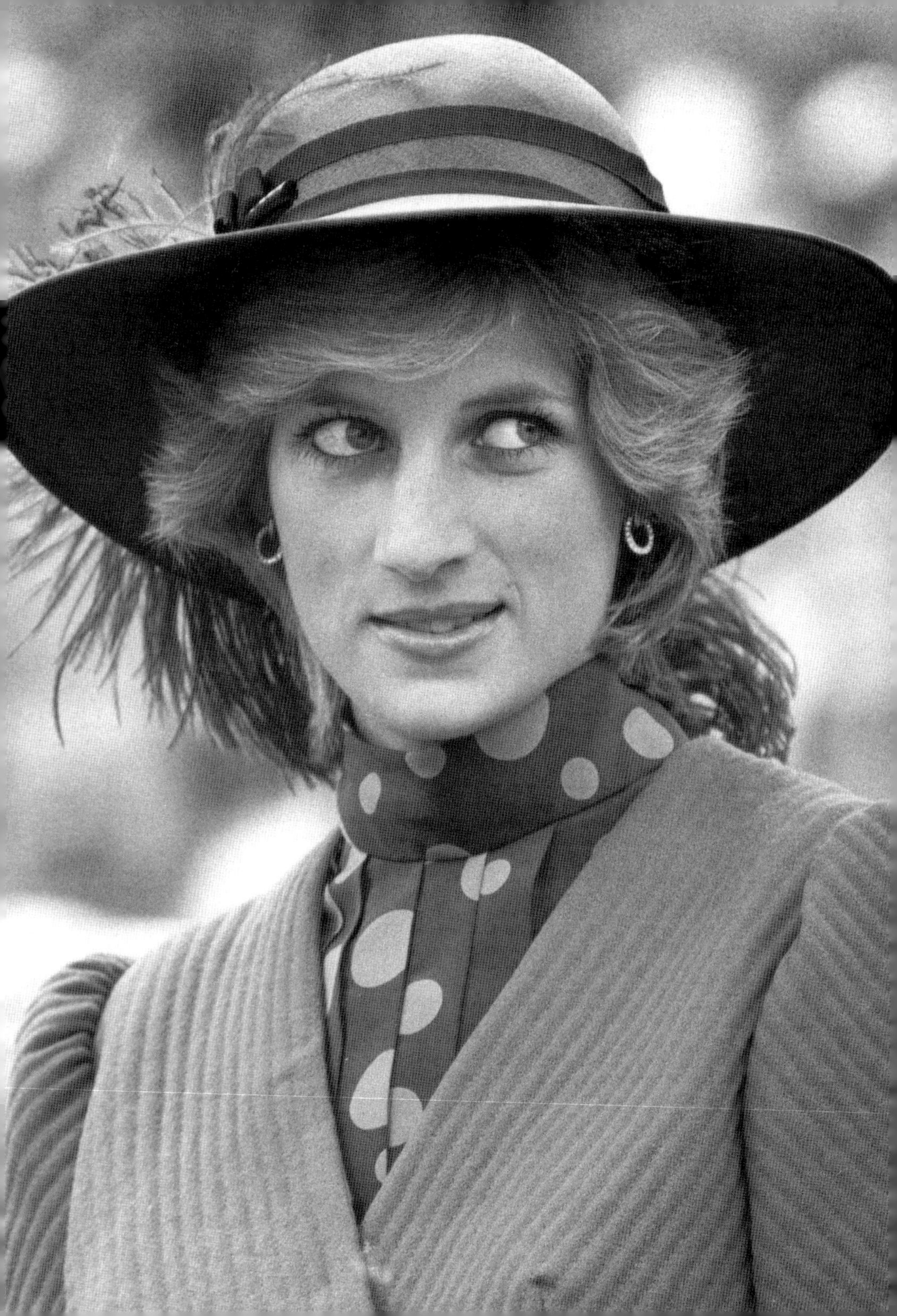

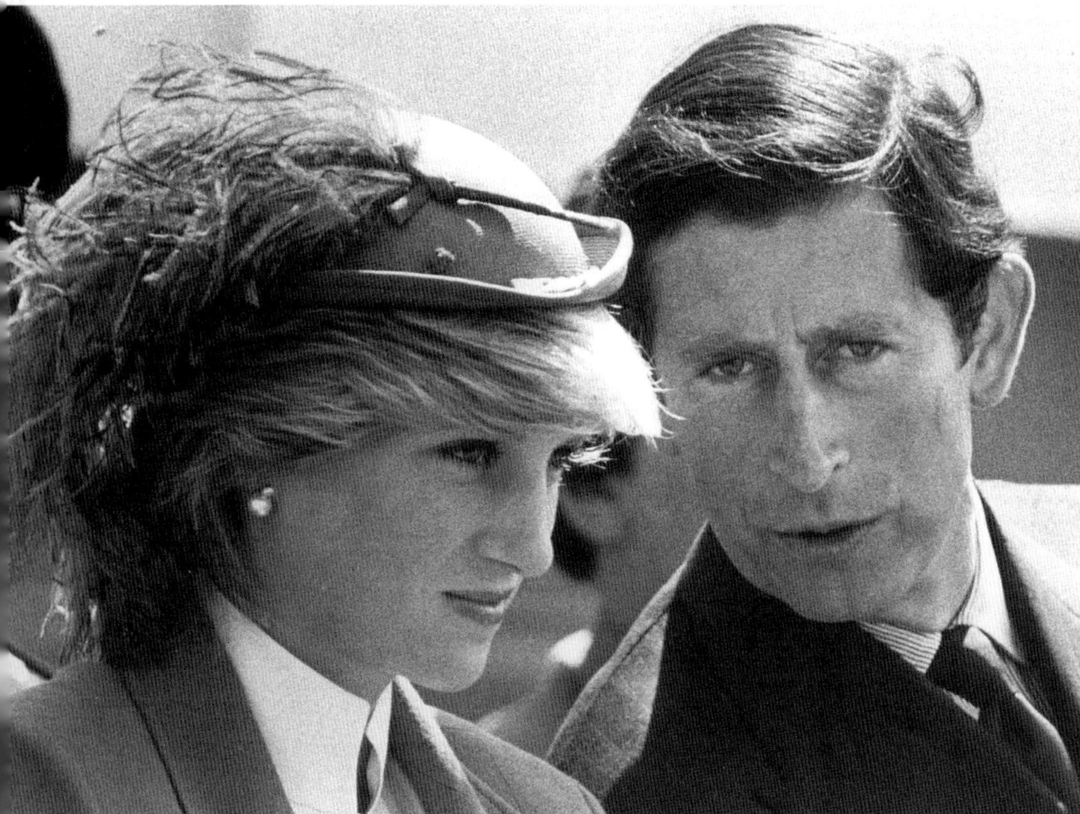

The Way We Were! This is why reporters wrote about a real Royal romance as the Prince whispers tenderly in her ear.

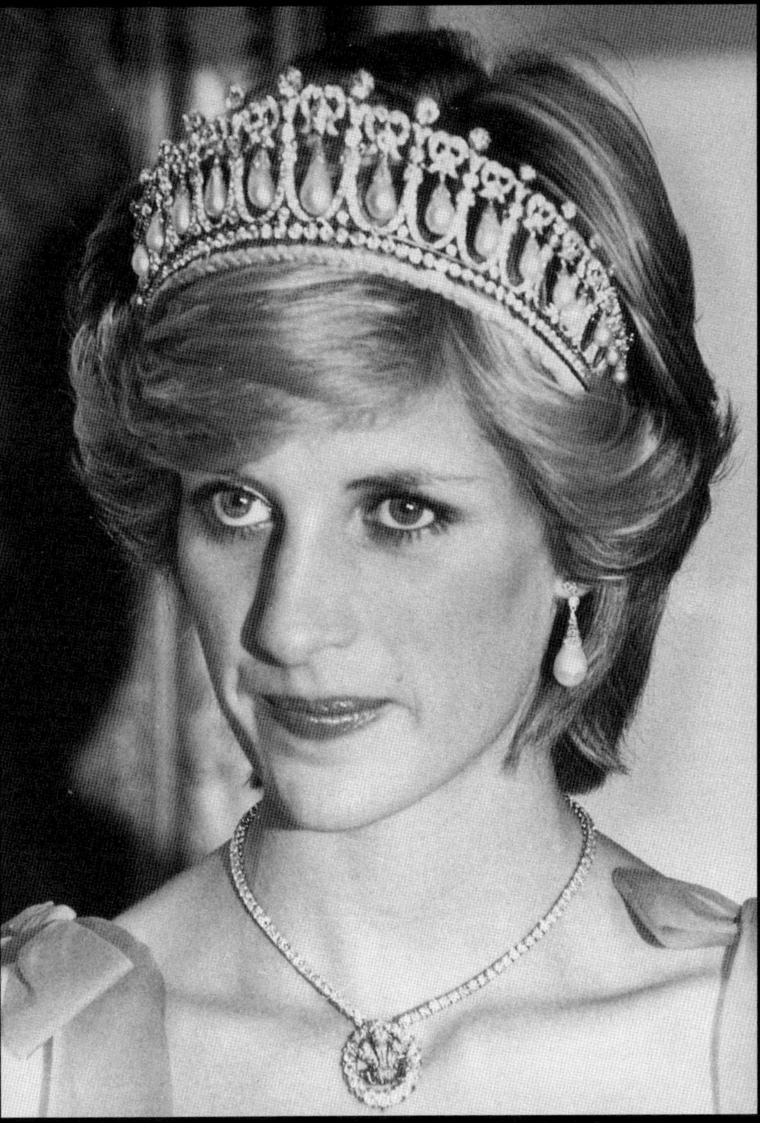

The weight of Royal responsibilities. This is one of the first times Diana wore a tiara, this one diamond studded with huge pearls and matching pearl earings, worth a fortune.

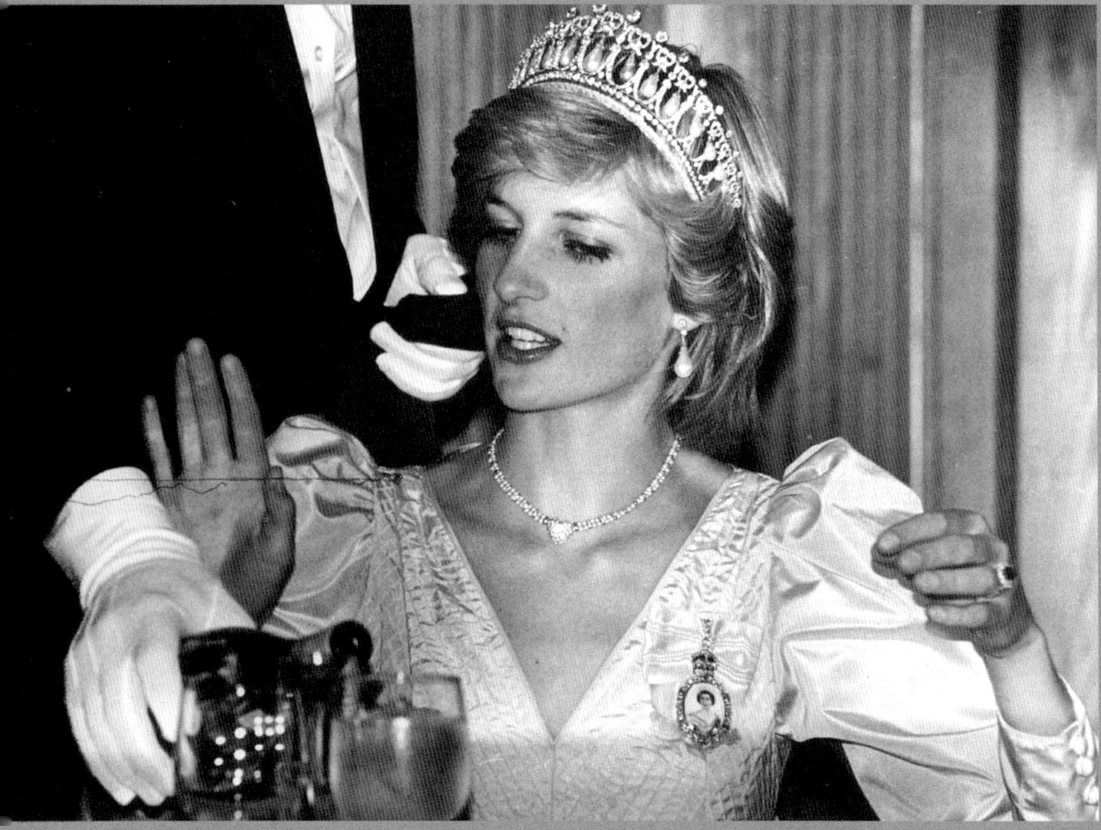

No more for me! The princess was virtually teetotal but stopping an eager waiter from overfilling her toast glass.

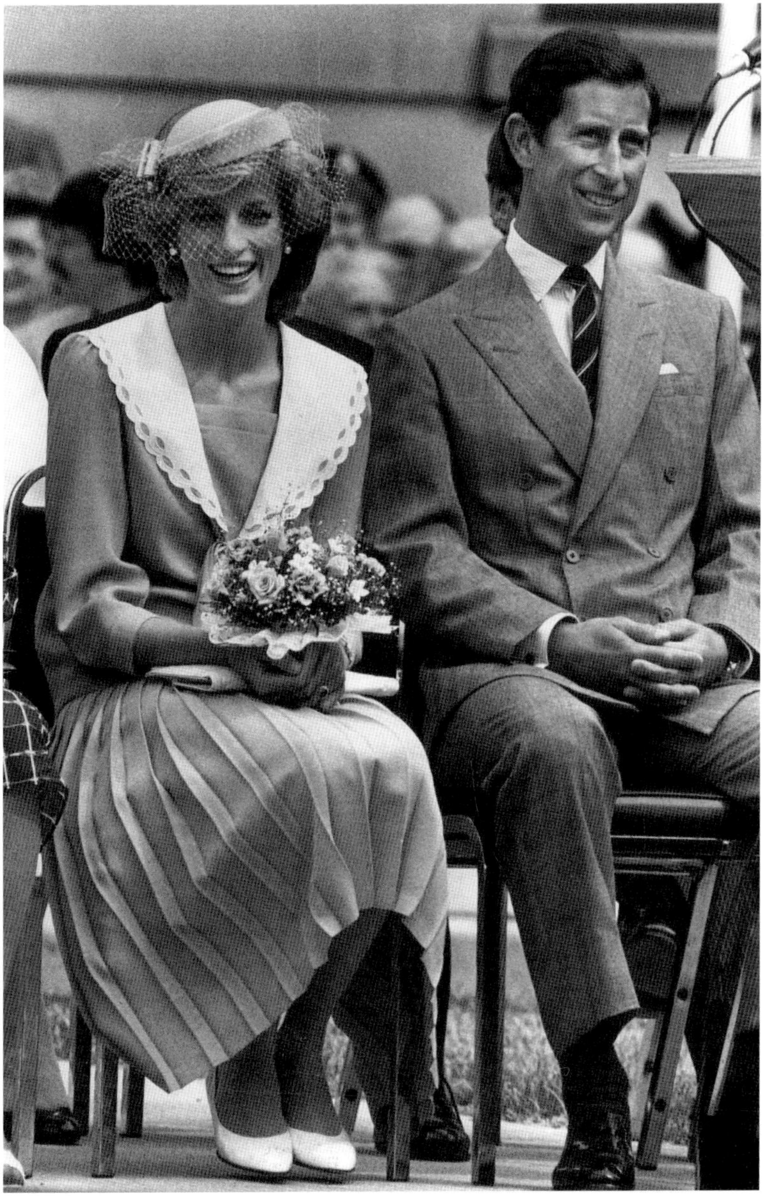

Gaining in even more confidence, laughing with Charles but still managing to look straight into the camera. The lady knows exactly the look that will get her on to page one.

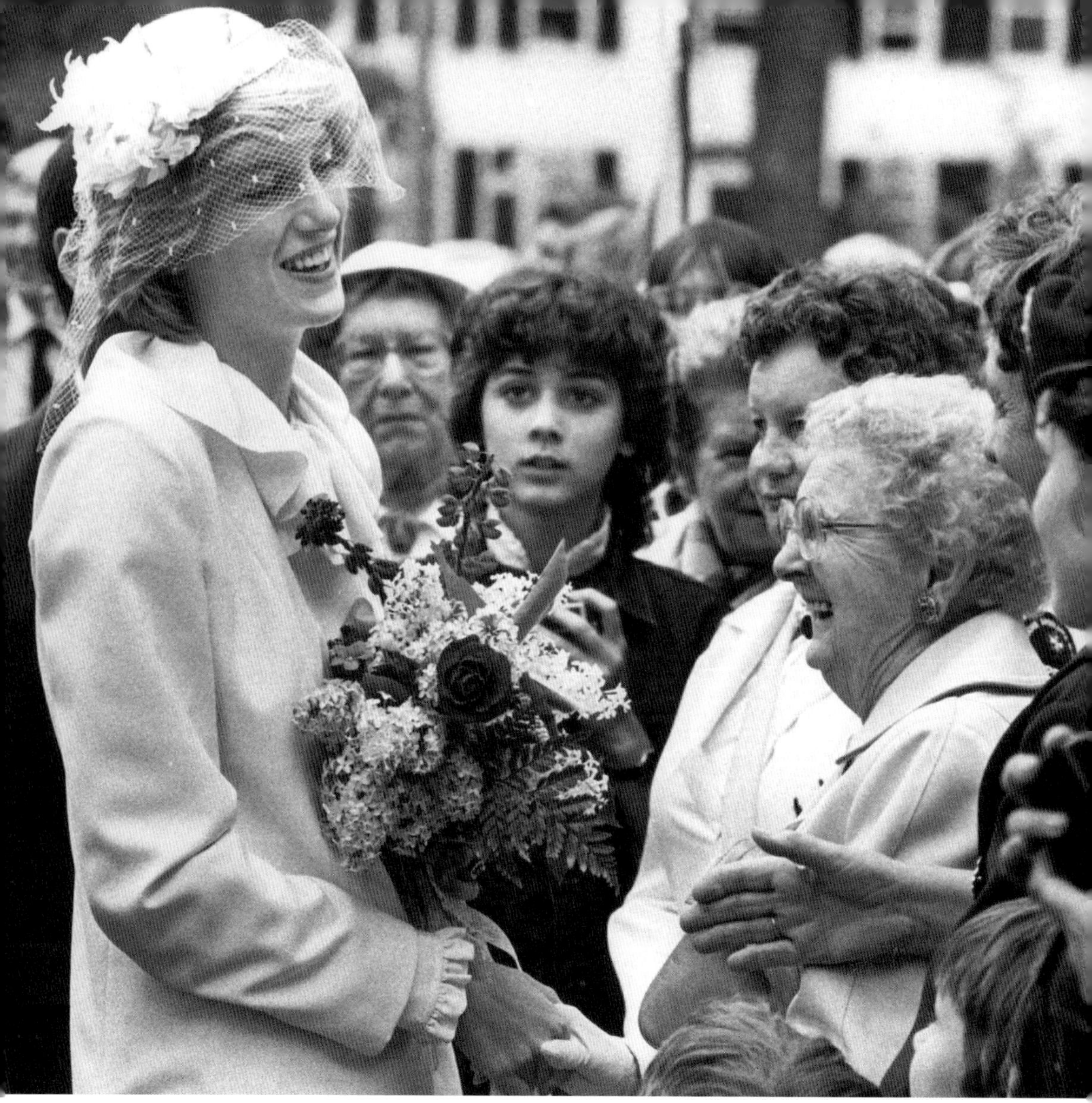

Back in the crowd and learning fast how to endure and even love a walkabout with a public desperate to get close to her.

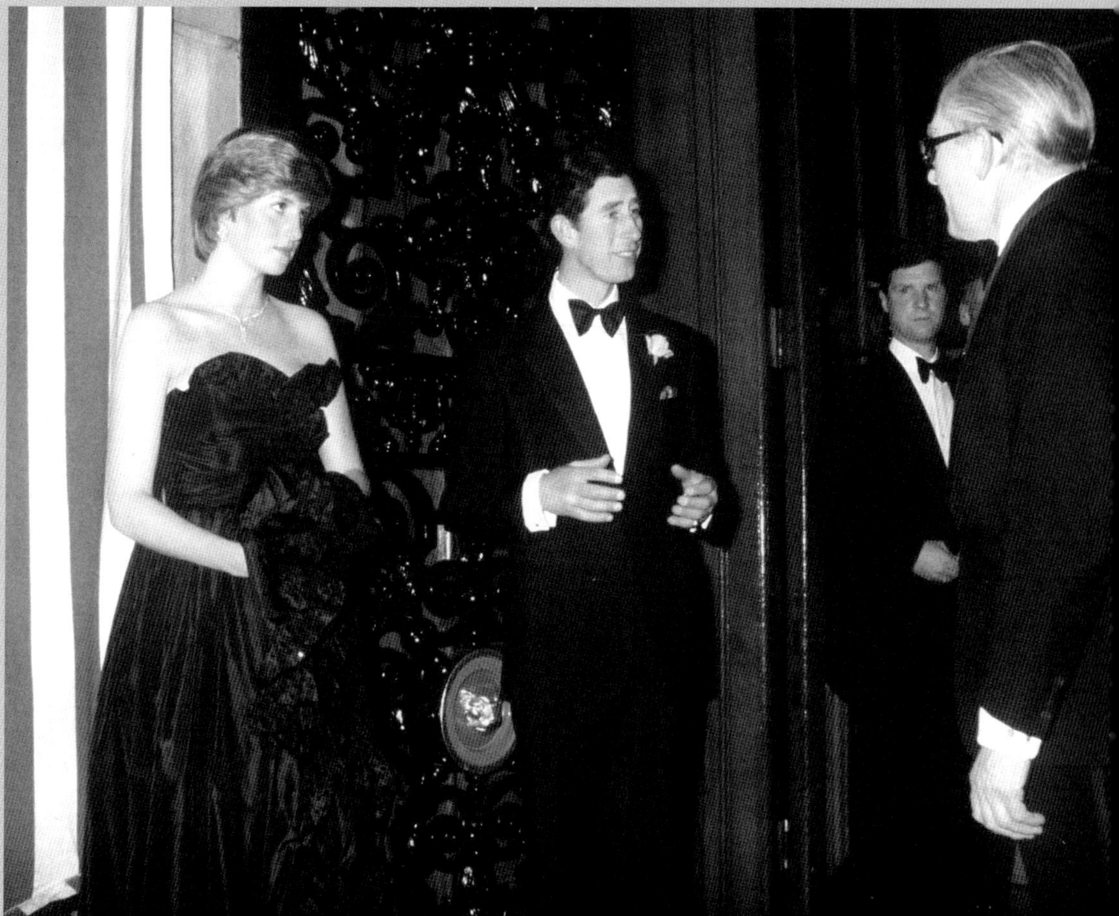

Very nervous about her low plunging neckline at her first official evening out with Prince Charles before their marriage. It was a daring move which made front pages all over the world.

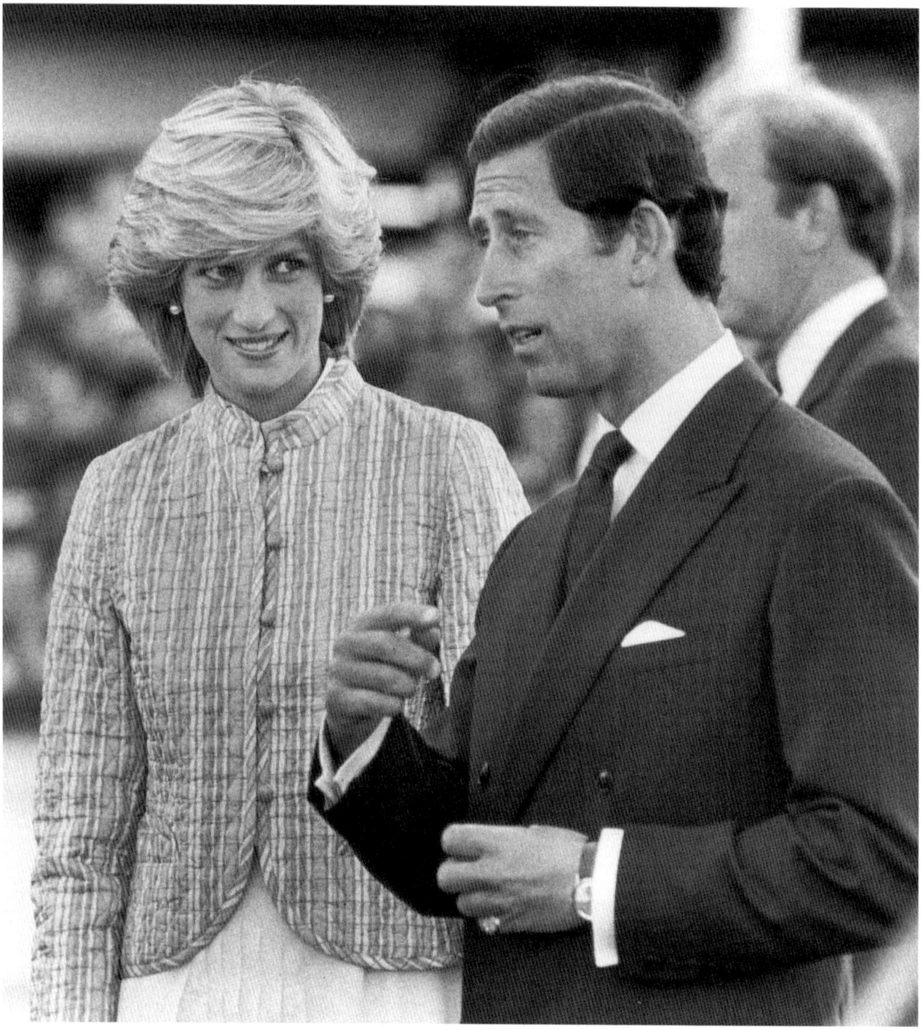

More laughs with Charles in relaxed times. These magic moments would become so much rarer in the future

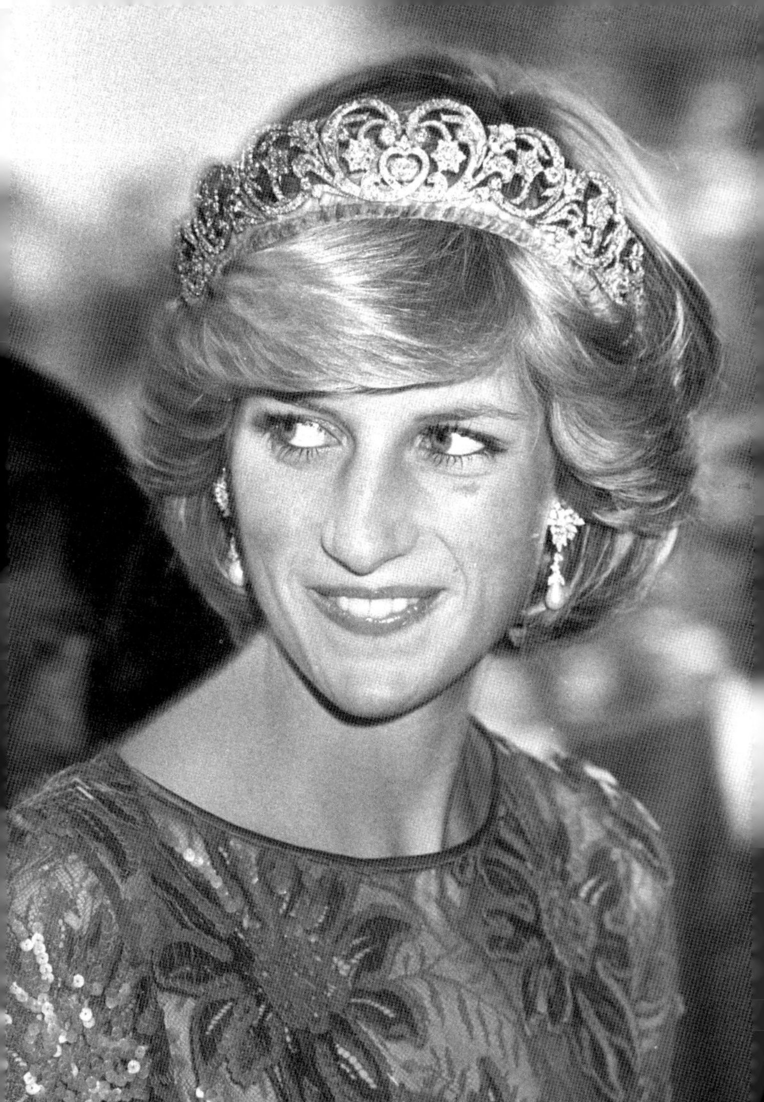

In yet another weighty, and hugely valuable tiara on a birthday date in London. People were already beginning to talk about her immense

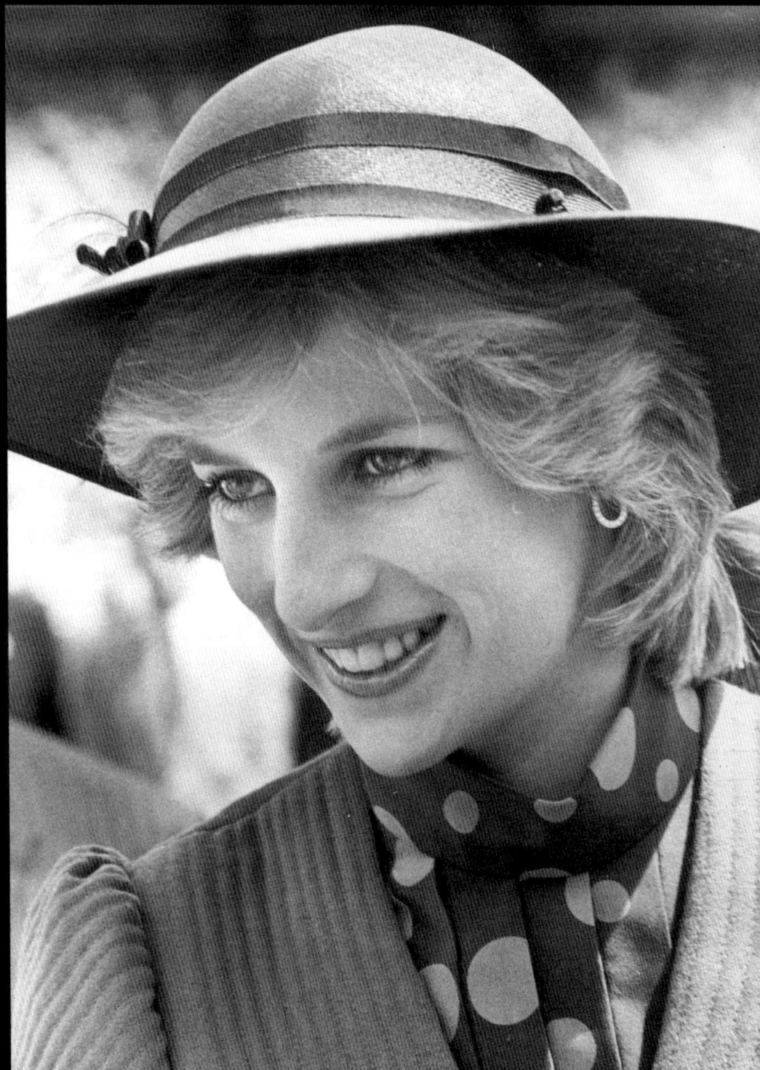

Diana steals the show at the World University Games in Alberta, Canada. The crowd rose to applaud her the moment she entered the stadium.

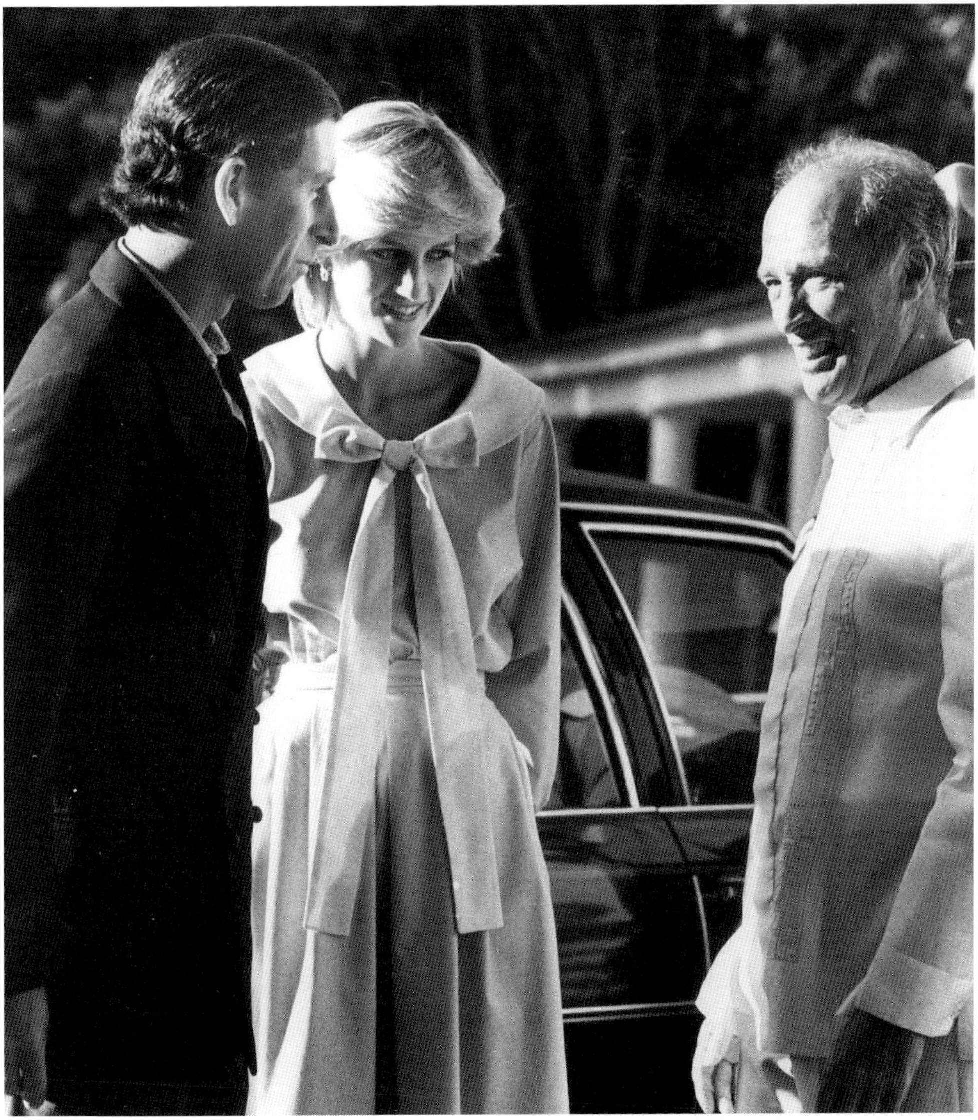

With former Canadian Premier Pierre Trudeau who was wearing an embarrassing see through shirt. Charles kept his eyes firmly on Trudeau's face but Diana couldn't hide her amusement.

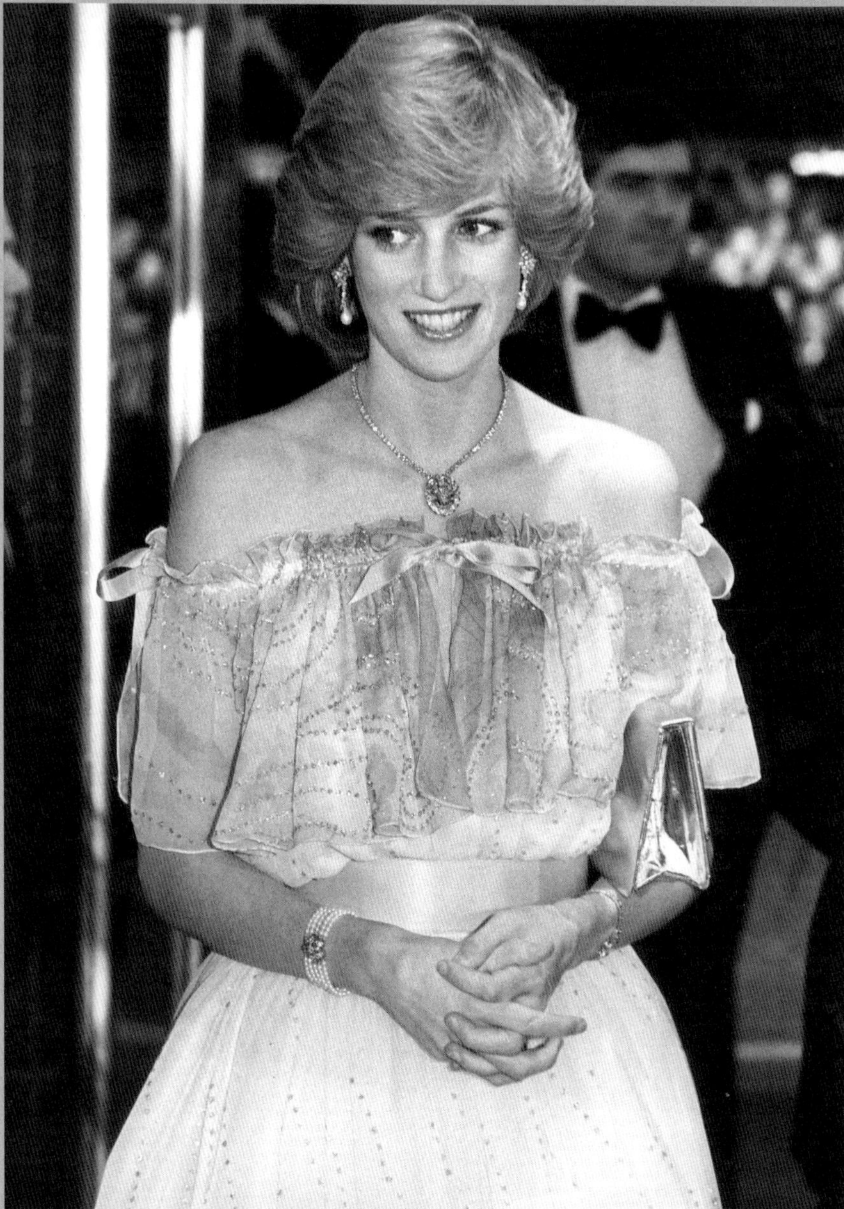

A London West End Premiere where the crowds loved the elegantly dressed Diana more than the film stars.

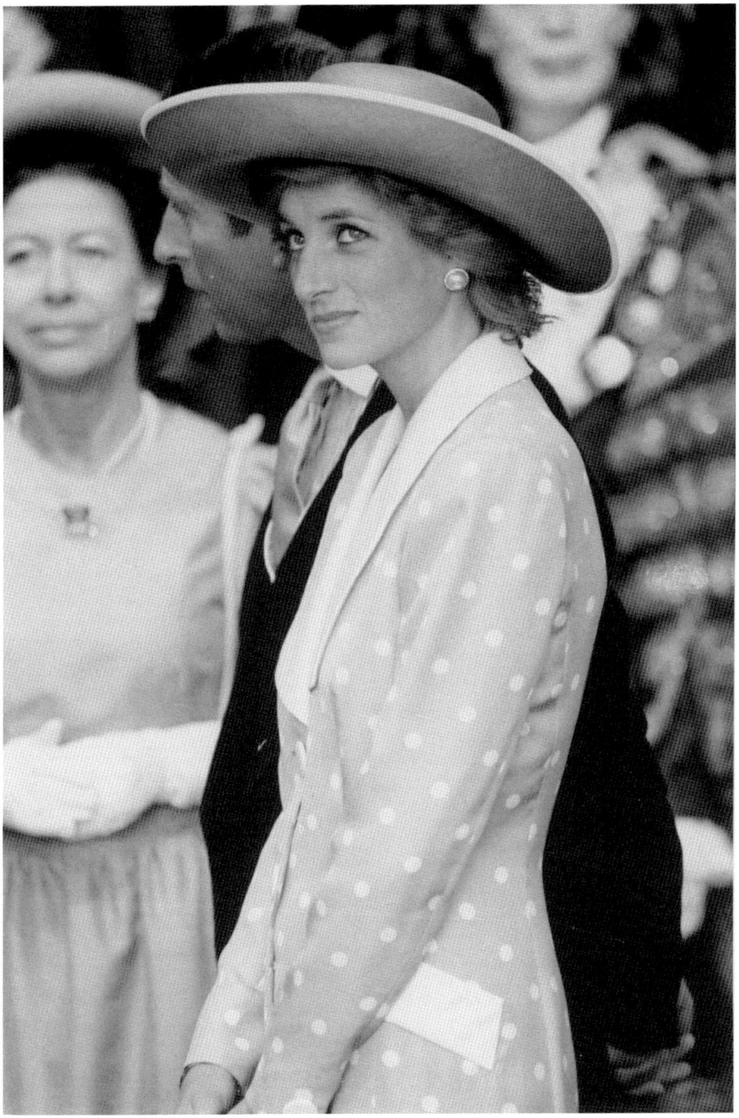

A ceremonial welcome at Victoria Station. Diana was still the star, standing alongside Princess Margaret as they waited to greet their official visitors.

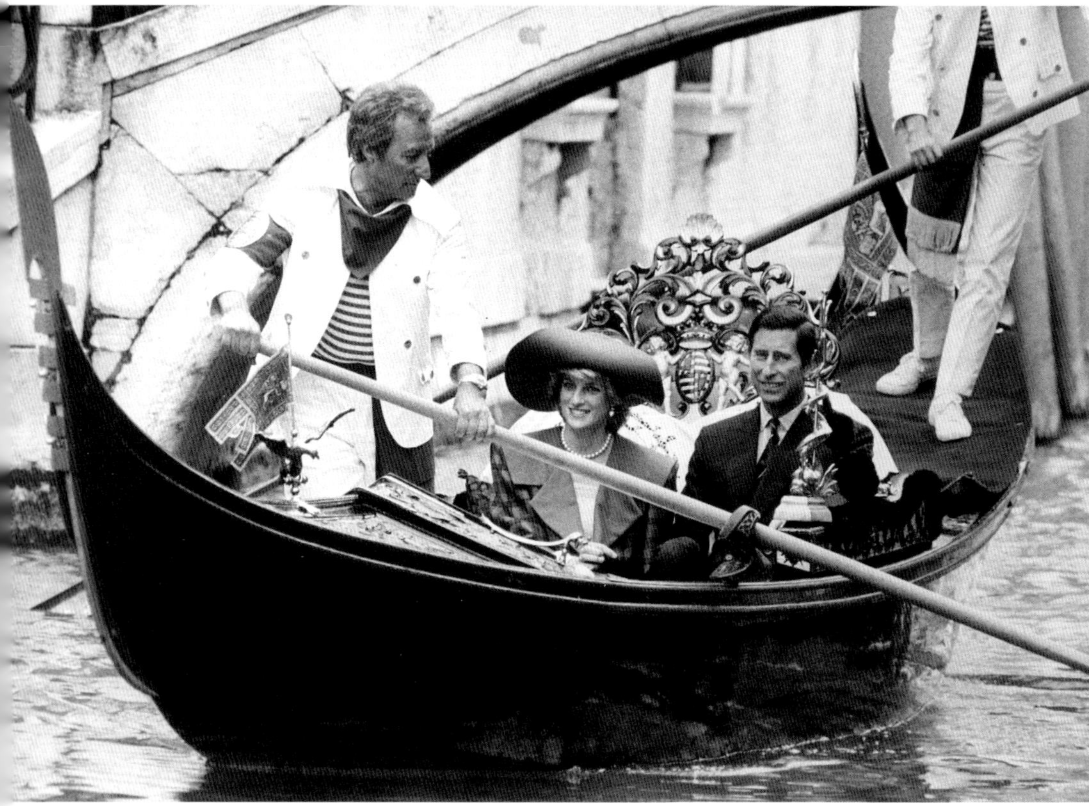

The Royal couple's tour of Italy was a fantastic success. Diana's incredibly good taste in clothes delighted millions of fashion conscious Italians. Their short trip in a black gondola in a Venice canal was one of the highlights.

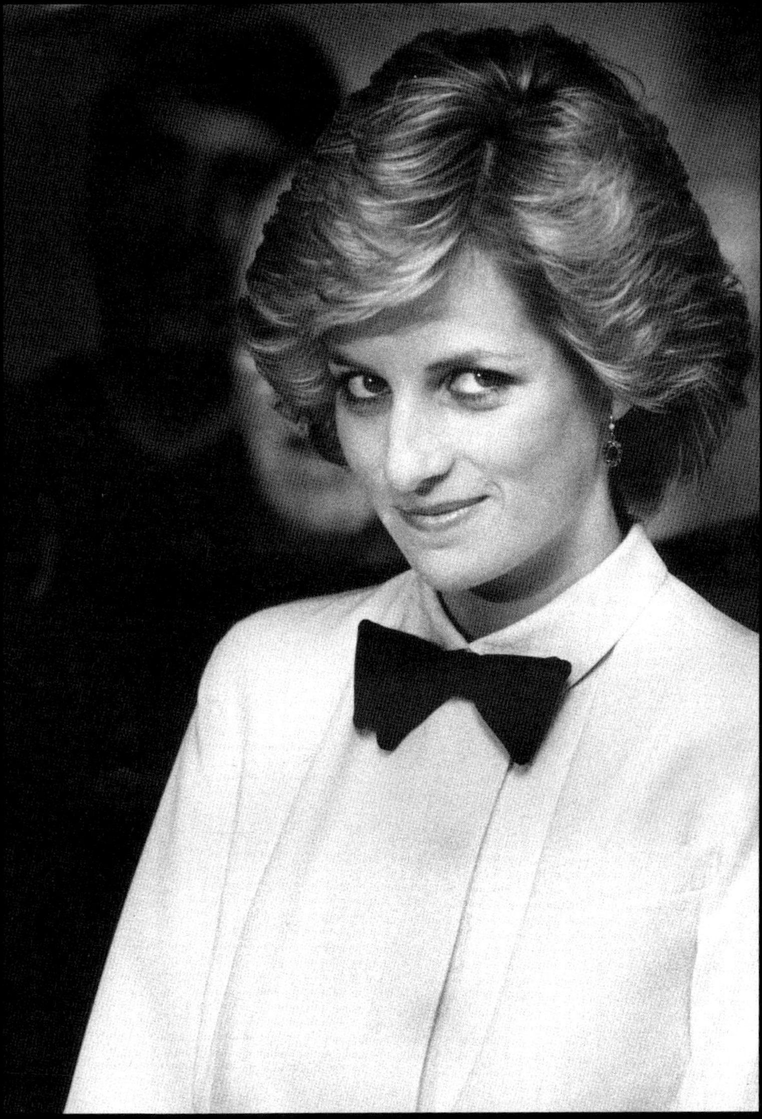

A fashion spectacular in Italy. Diana wore a version of an Italian waiter's uniform , complete with black bow tie. Only she could have got away with such an outrageous outfit but she carried it off with huge style.

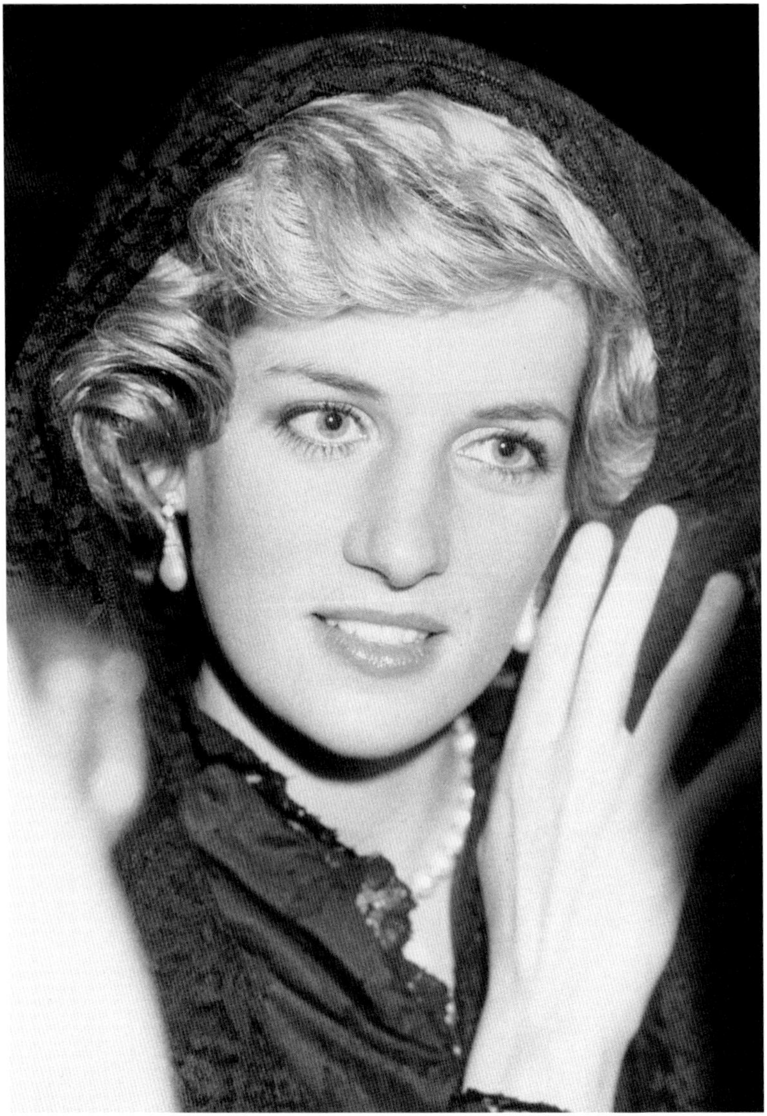

Sombre but beautiful in black, her hair hidden in a lace shawl to meet the Pope in the Vatican. Diana was a walking ambassador for British fashion.

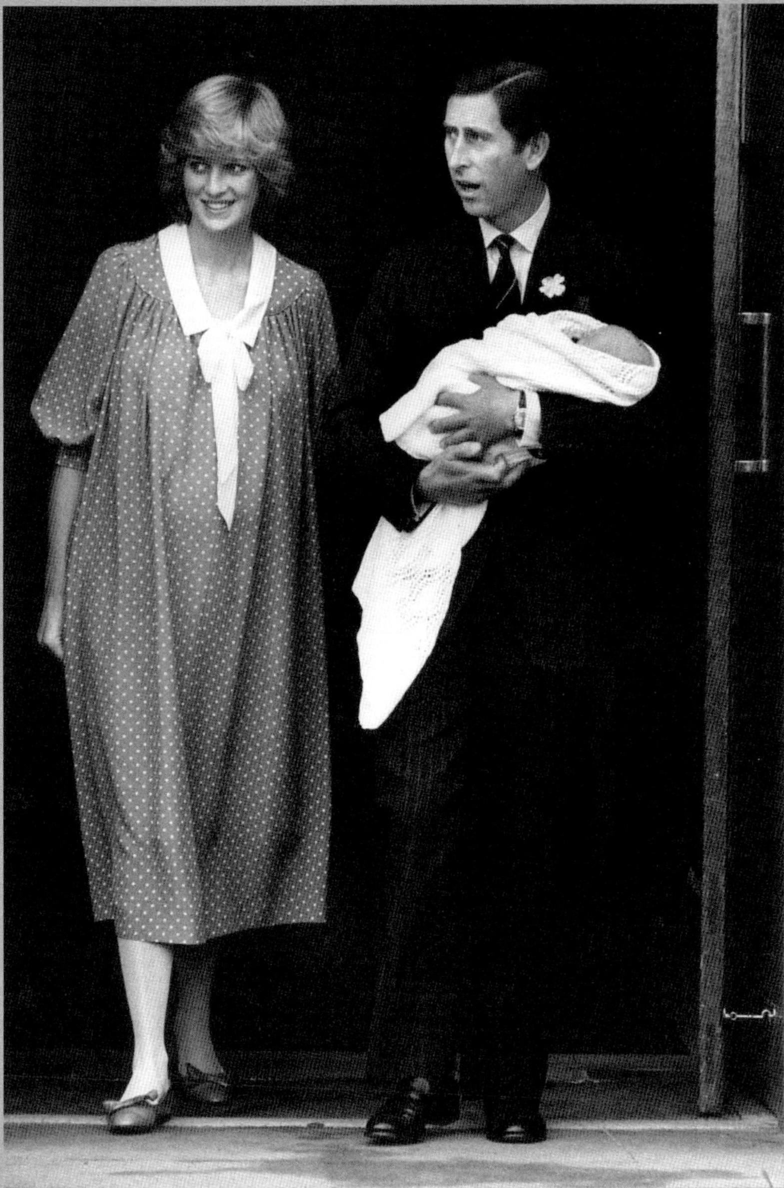

Leaving St Mary's Hospital in London's Paddington with newly born Prince William carried tenderly in Prince Charles' arms . Diana still looked terrific in a red polka dot dress but didn't realise that her pair of comfortable pop socks were on public display.

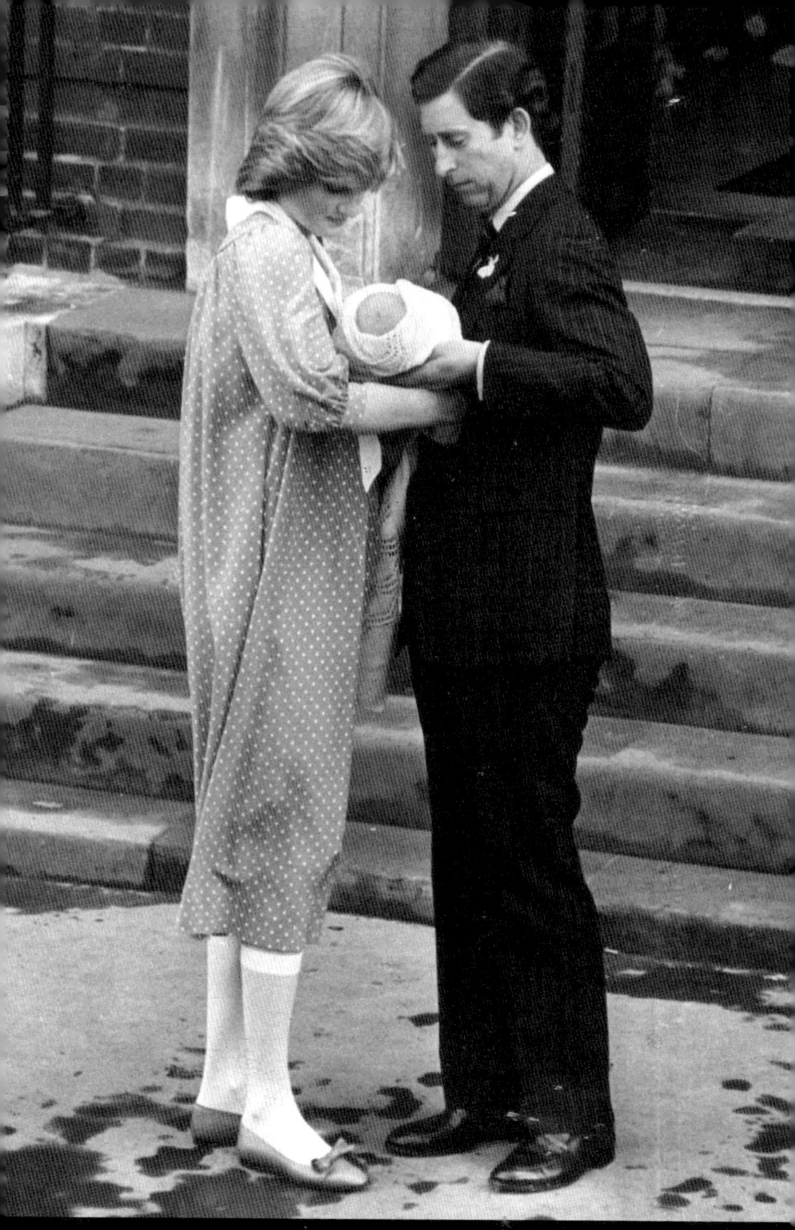

A tender moment that flashed round the world as Charles hands the baby to Diana. You can still see those pop socks.

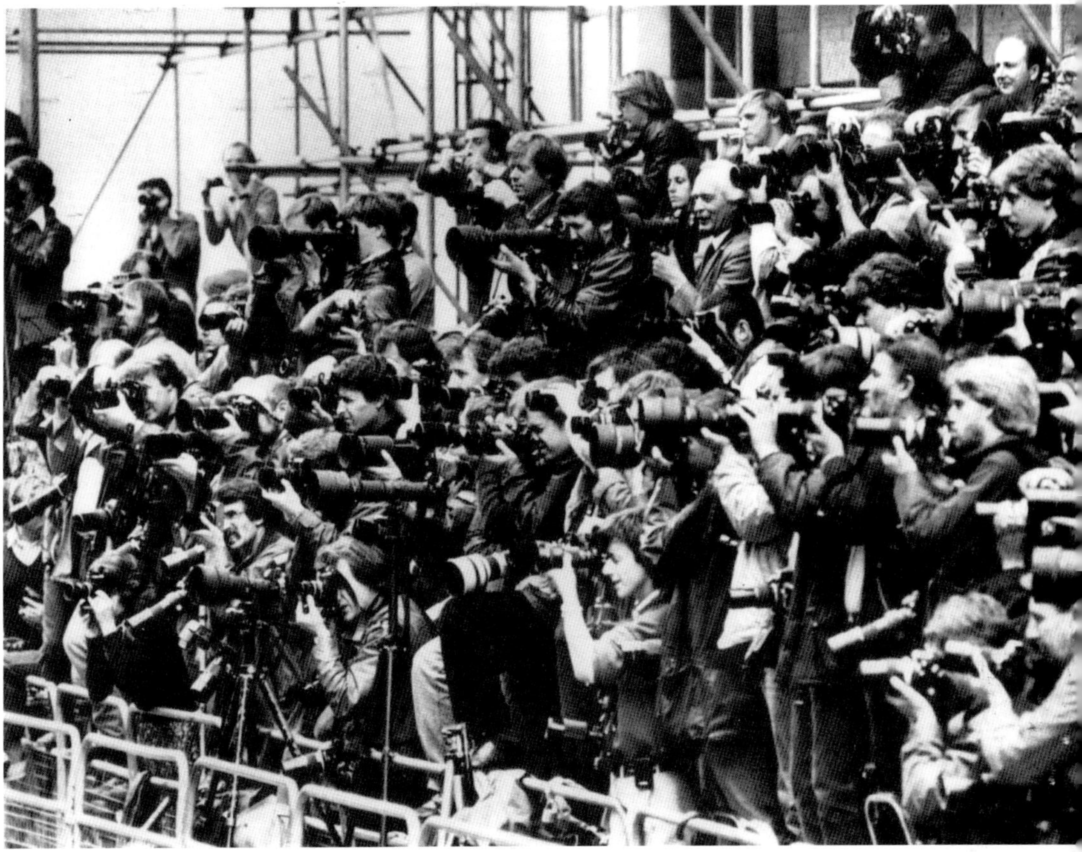

This is the wall of photographers who faced the Prince and Princess. Steve is somewhere in those ranks. The whirling motor drives sounded like a forest full of angry bees.

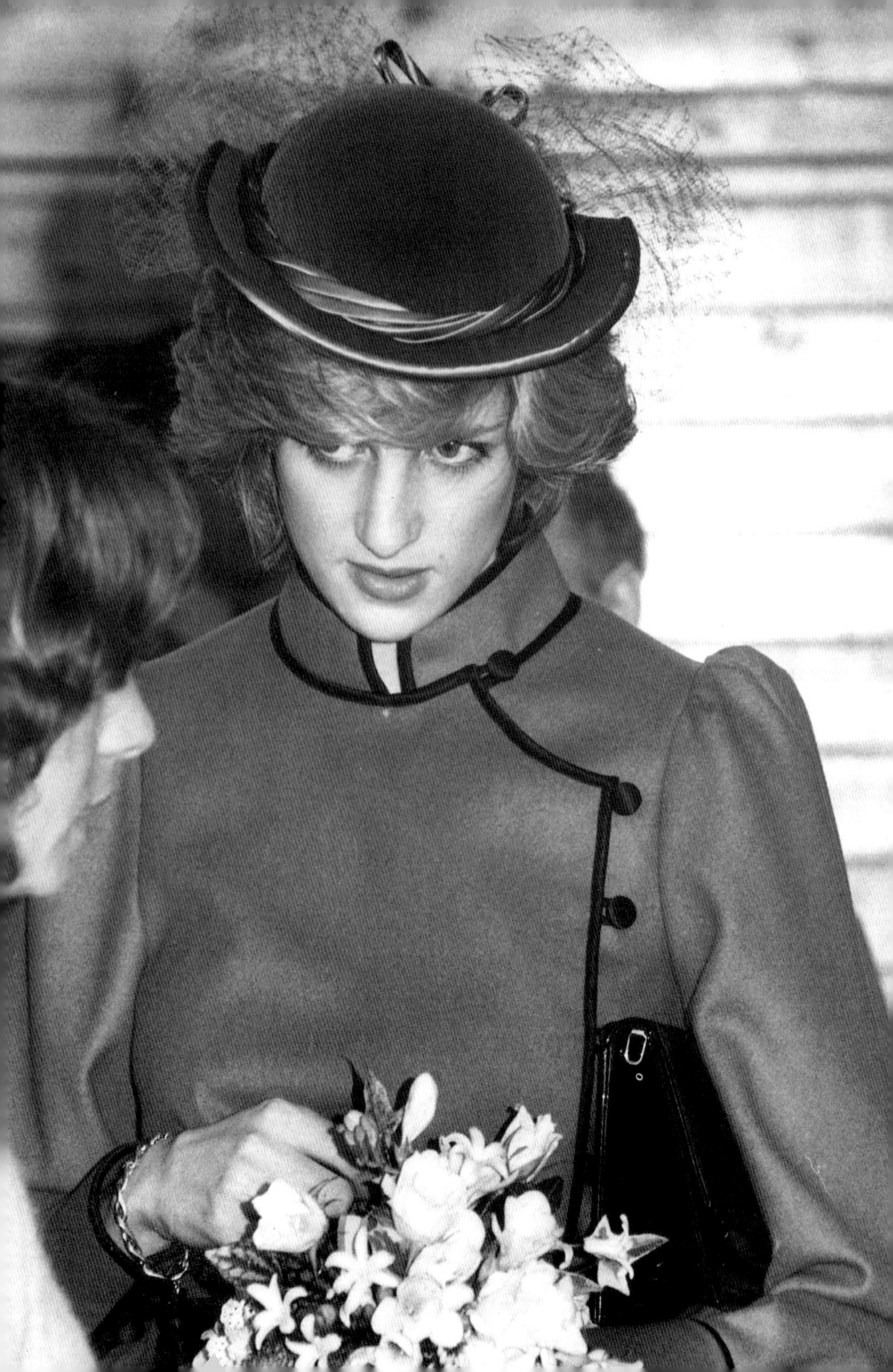

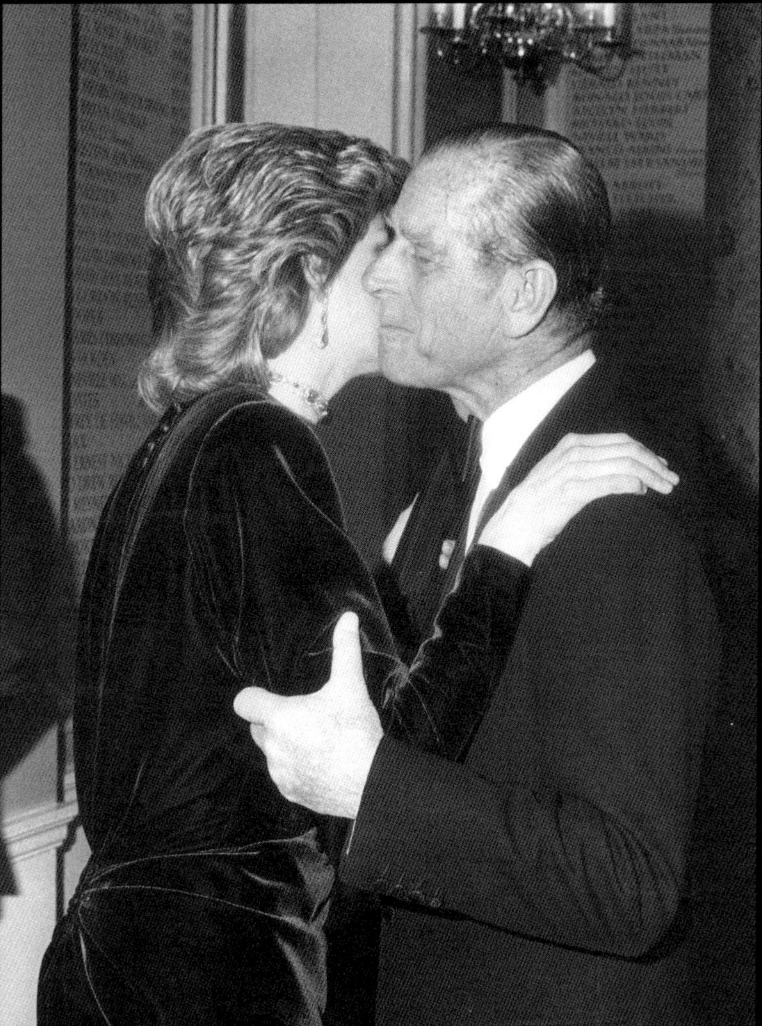

An affectionate kiss from her father in law Prince Philip at an official engagement. At the beginning of the marriage the two genuinely liked each other, but relations became tense towards the end.

LEFT: Back to work as usual after the birth. Royal engagements are planned months in advance, her diary was incredibly tiring because Diana was so much in demand.

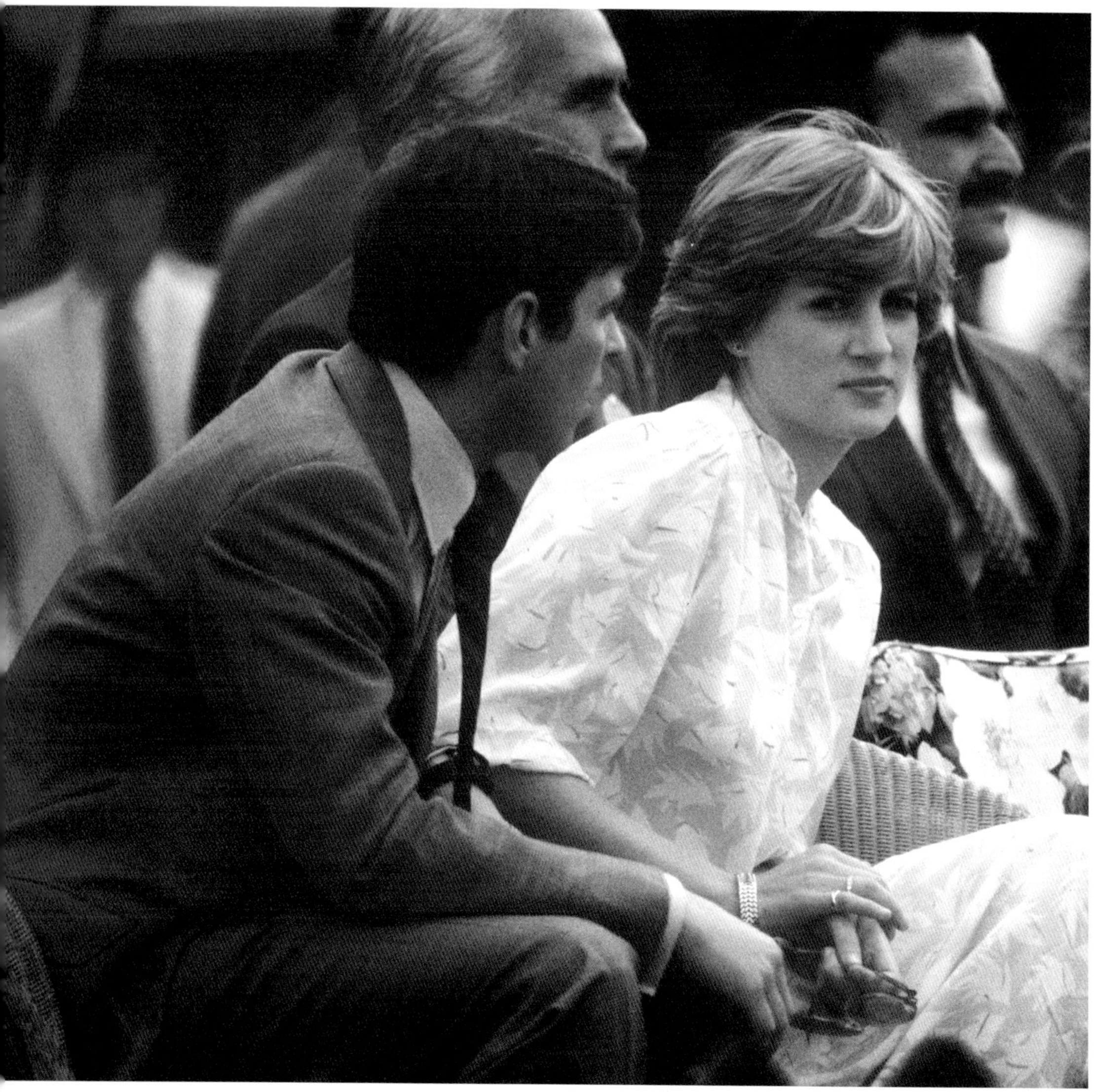

Lady Diana Spencer with Prince Andrew at a polo match at Windsor before her marriage to Charles.

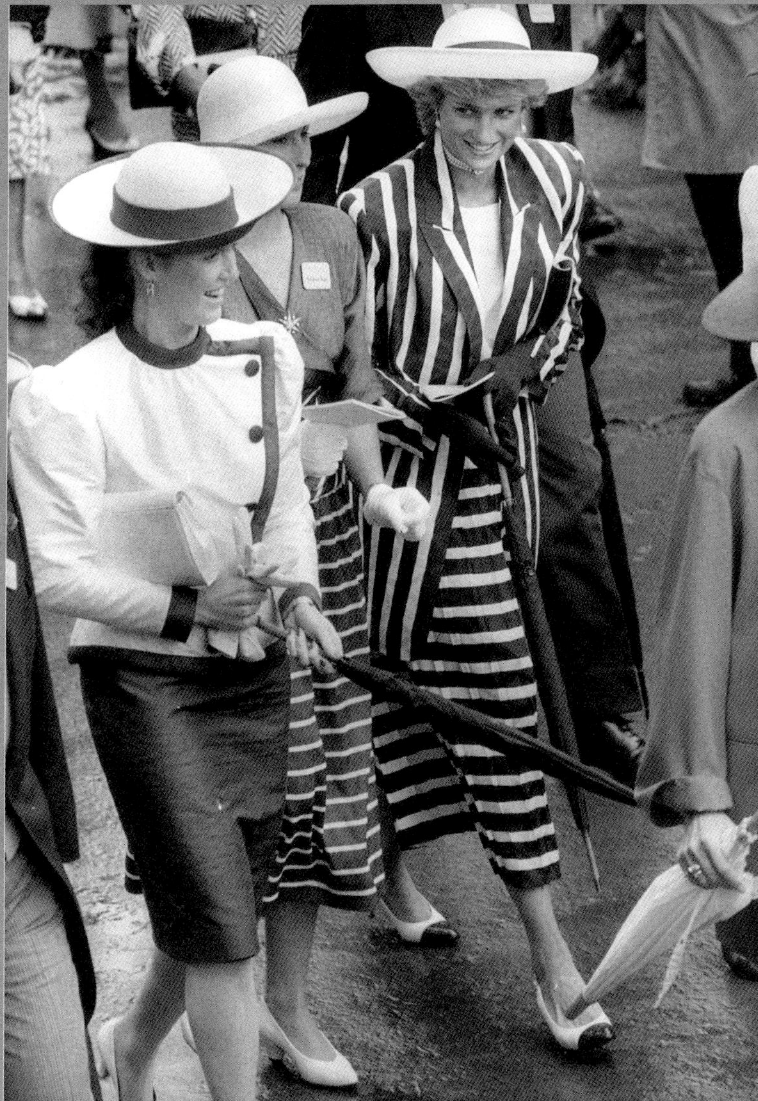

When Fergie entered the Royal Family as Duchess of York, Diana gained a friend of her own age. But they got carried away at Royal Ascot, prodding people they knew with rolled up umbrellas and giggling in the hallowed Royal Enclosure. The Queen was said to be not amused.

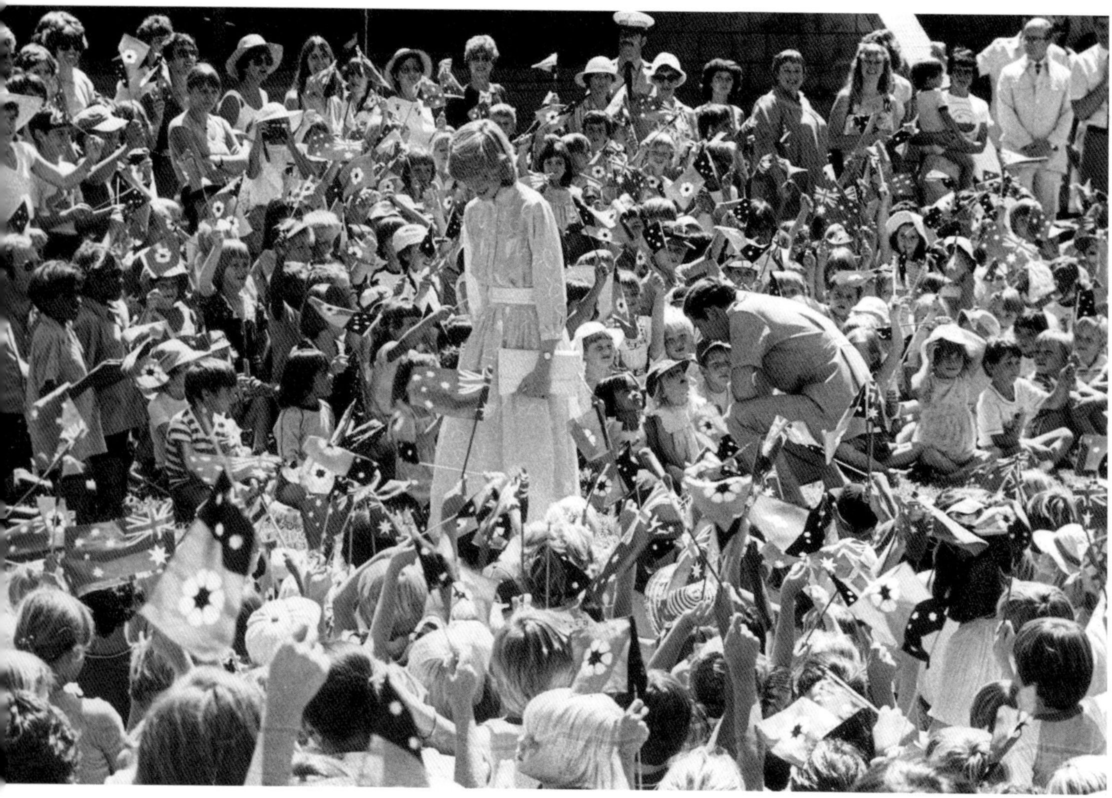

Massed crowds greeted Diana wherever she went in Australia. No one seemed to notice Charles.

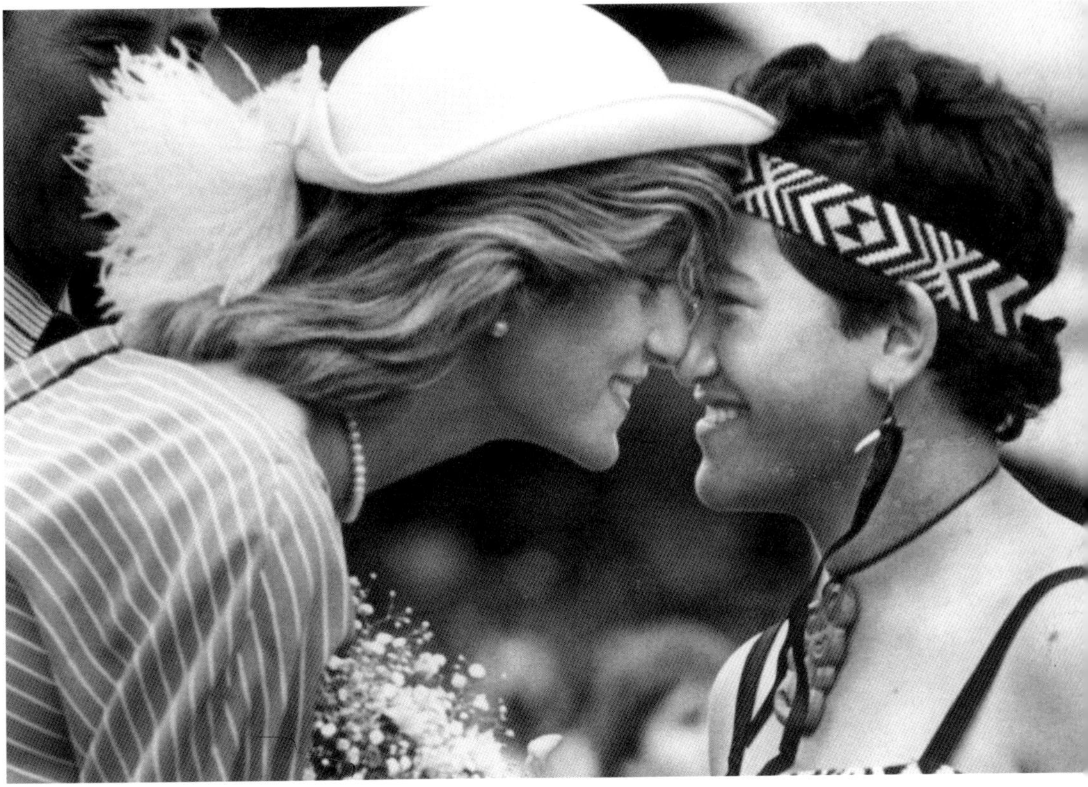

'You rub noses' rather than shake hands in New Zealand and Diana did it perfectly with the Maoris

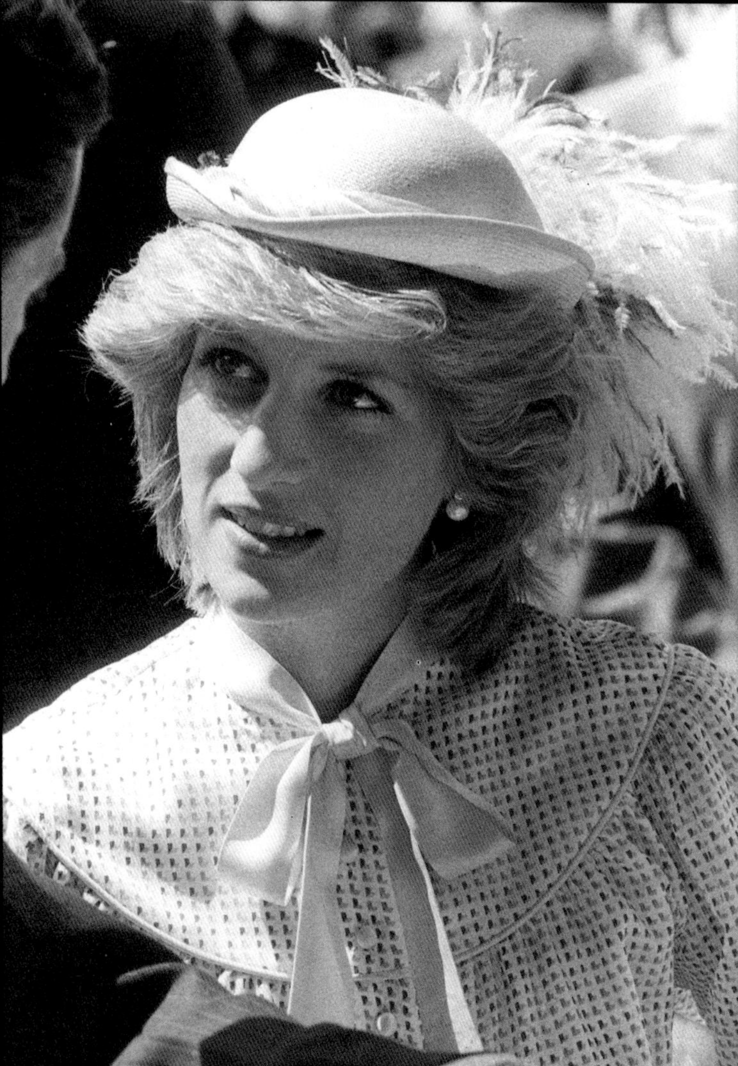

In the crowds in Sydney Diana where Diana let her guard down telling a mother in the crowd who said she was going home to look after her own baby: "I'd swap places with you any day." Diana really did just want to be with William but Royal duties came first.

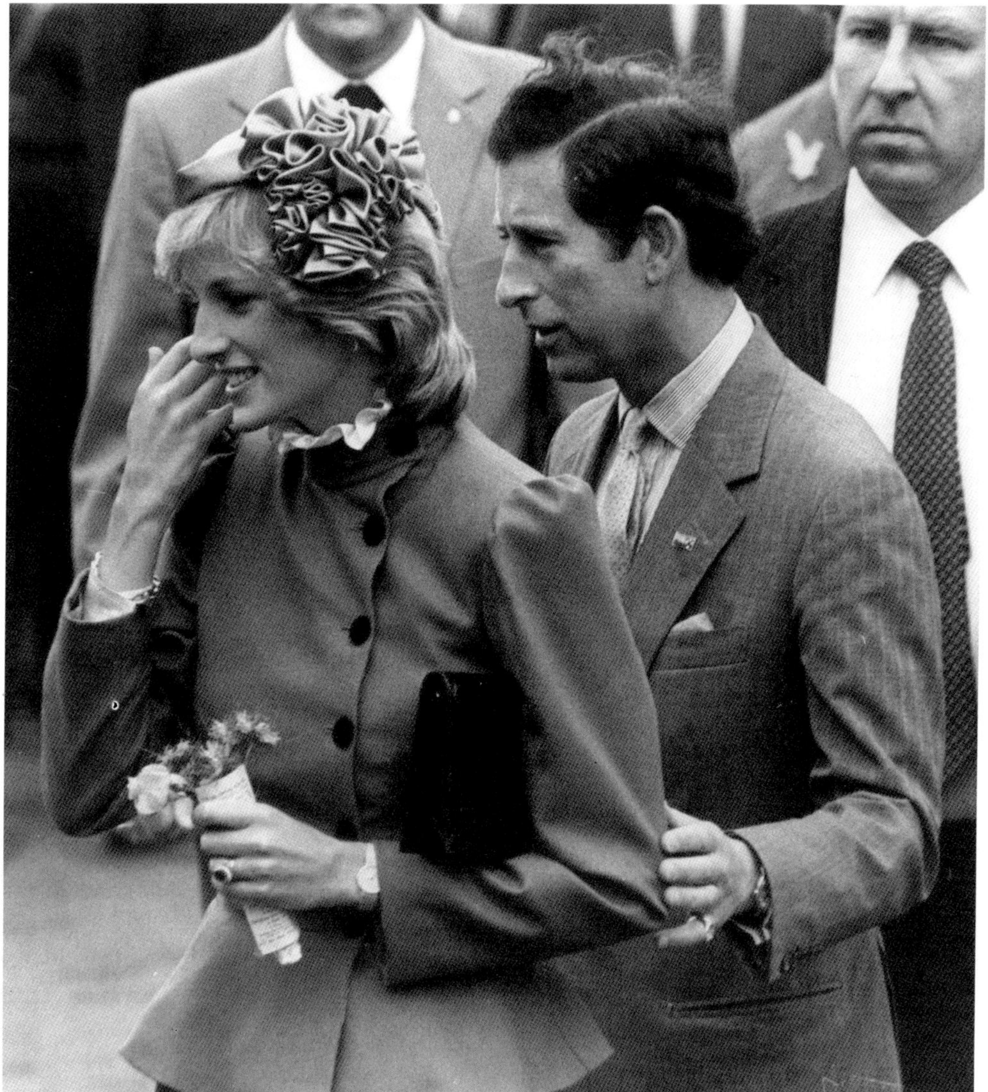

Charles looks worried in a densely packed crowd in Brisbane where he told people "I'm the man who came with Princess Diana." He was feeling sidelined, beginning to know the reality of marriage to a superstar.

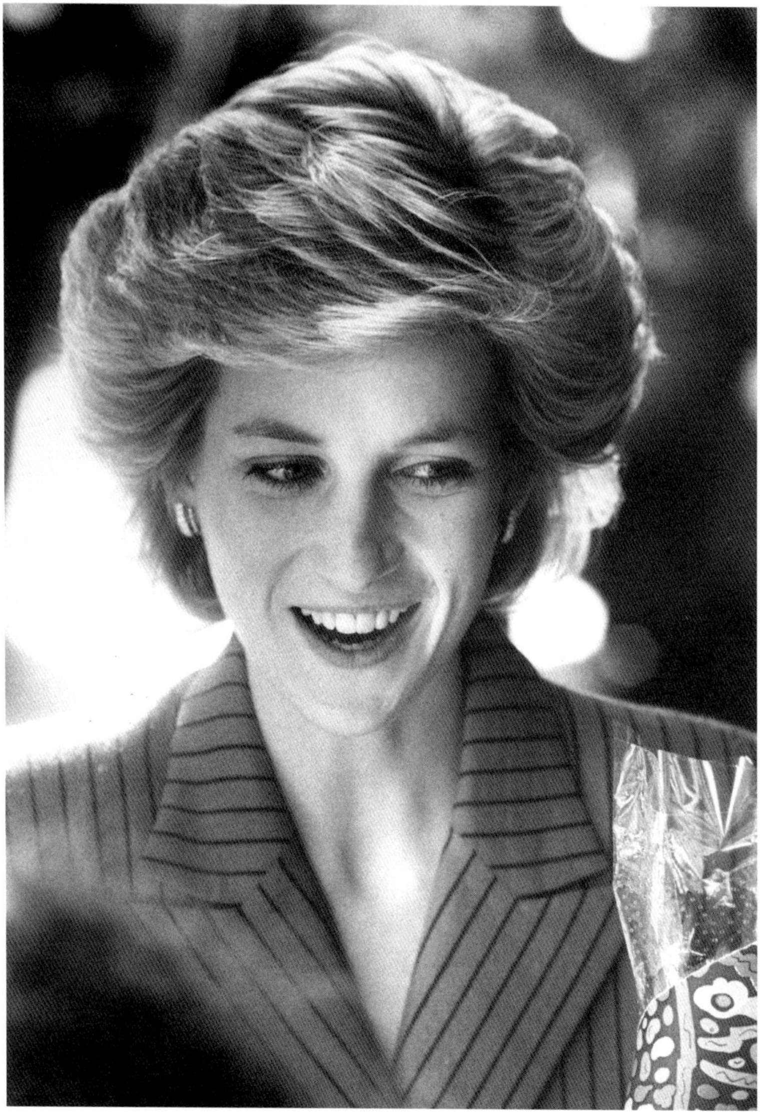

Another Royal engagement and another new look from Diana who had learned that whenever she changed her hairstyle or even her make up it would guarantee a front page photo.

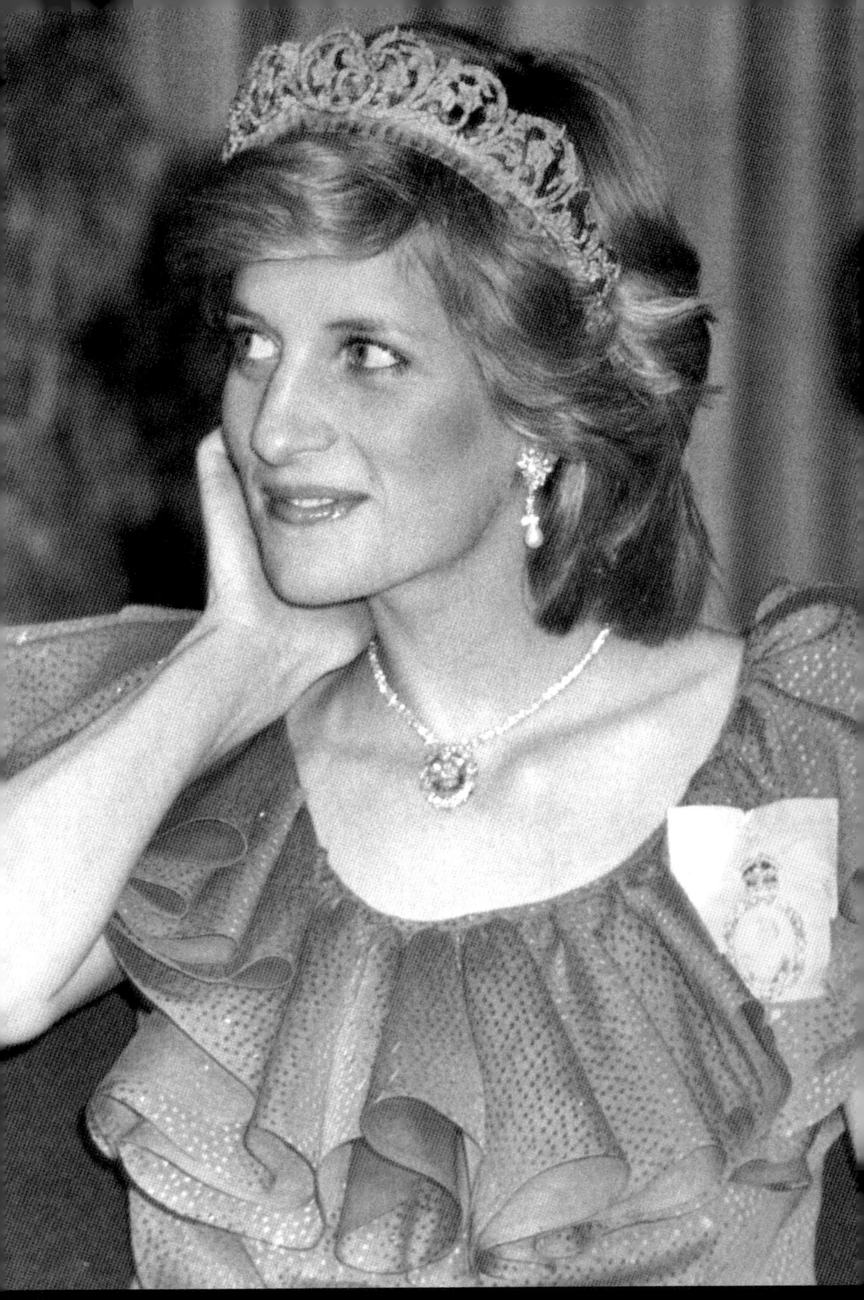

Diana smiles as Charles gives her a public compliment in Hobart, Tasmania

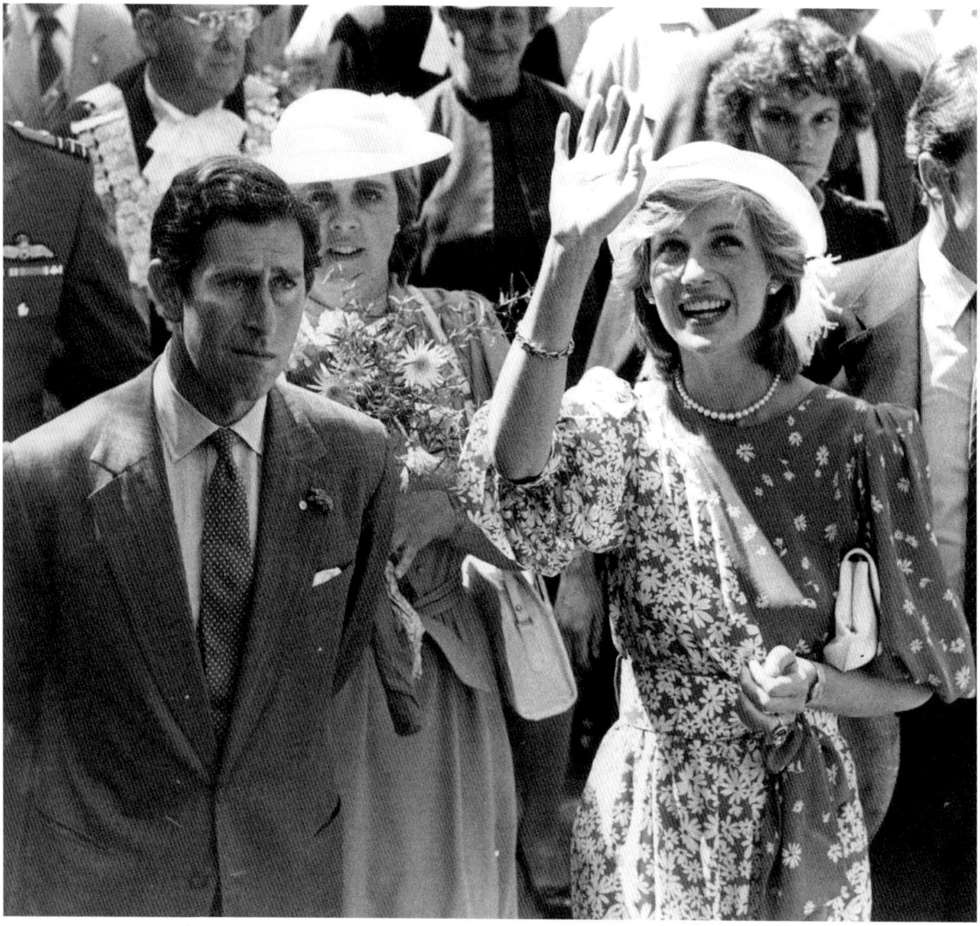

The effects of Di-mania. Charles looks concerned as the crowd threatens to get out of hand in their rush to see the object of their affections. Her not him.

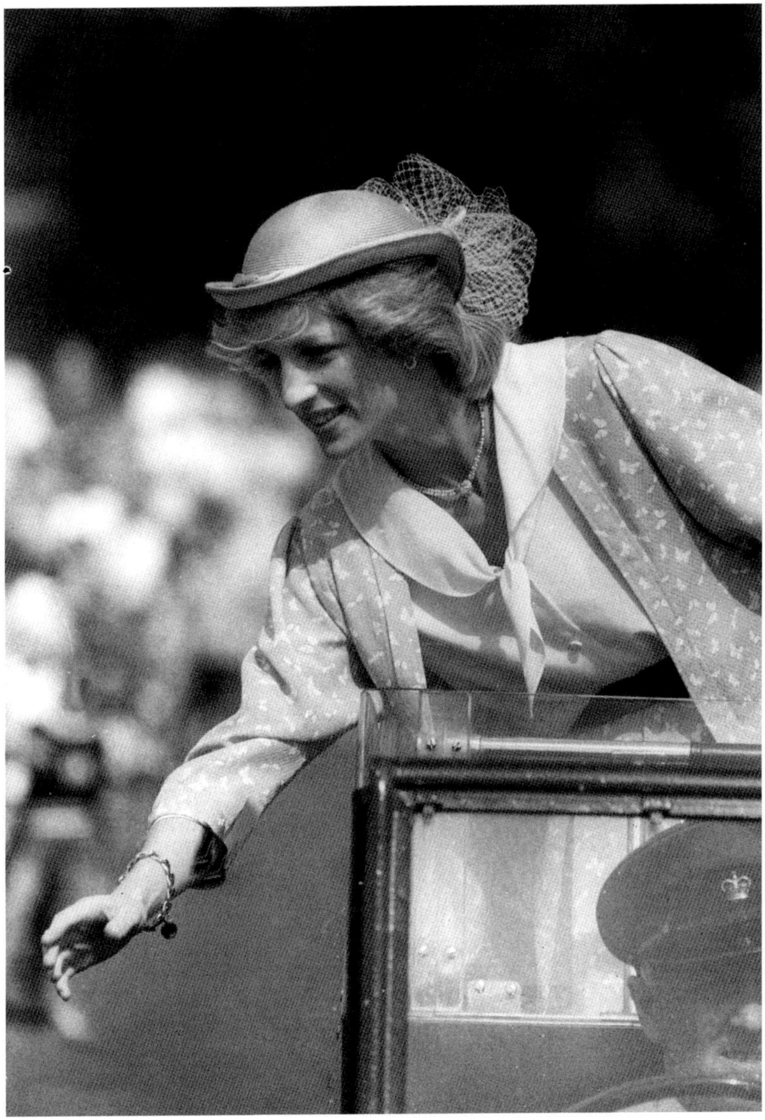

Diana reaches out from the back of the open official car for the offer of a bunch of flowers in the outstretched hands of a Royal admirer.

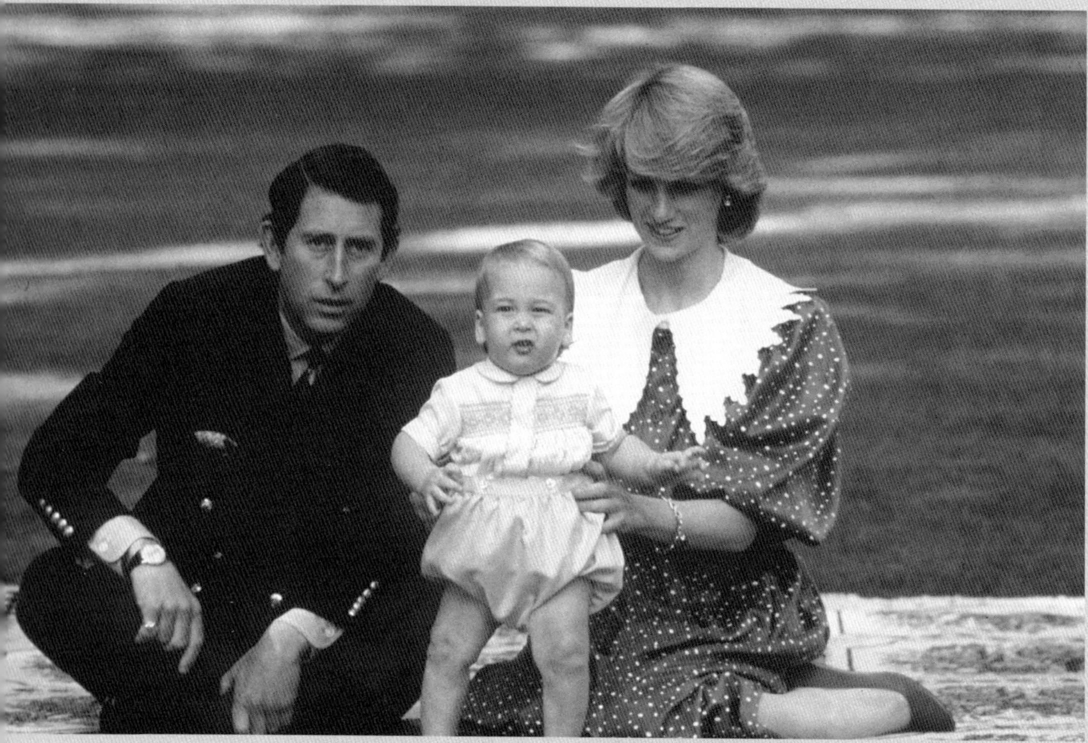

Proud parents show off Prince William to the world's press in the grounds of the British High Commission in Auckland. The couple spread a tartan rug on the grass and simply played with their child. It was a wonderful and heartfelt simple moment.

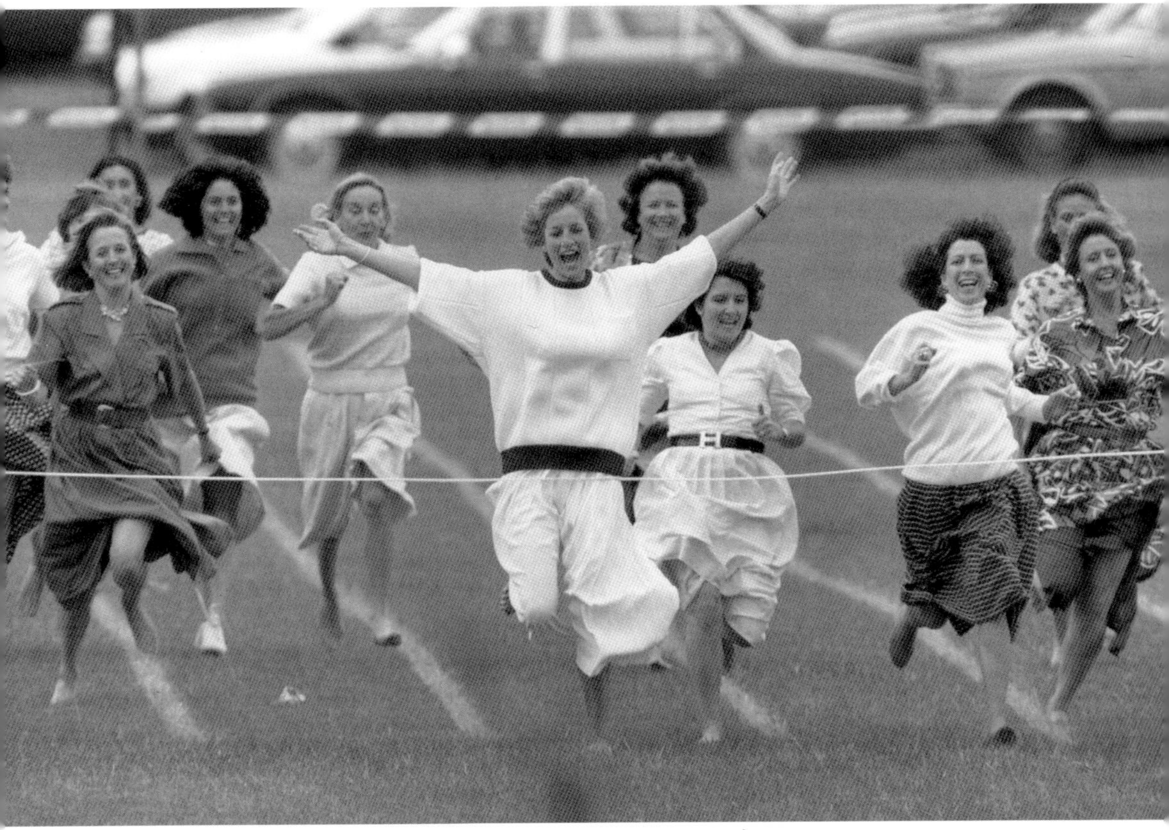

Diana was always a winner! She tossed away her shoes to sprint the 100 yards mothers race at William's prep school. She won by a short head and she knew that the cameramen, including Steve of course, were in position at the finishing line.

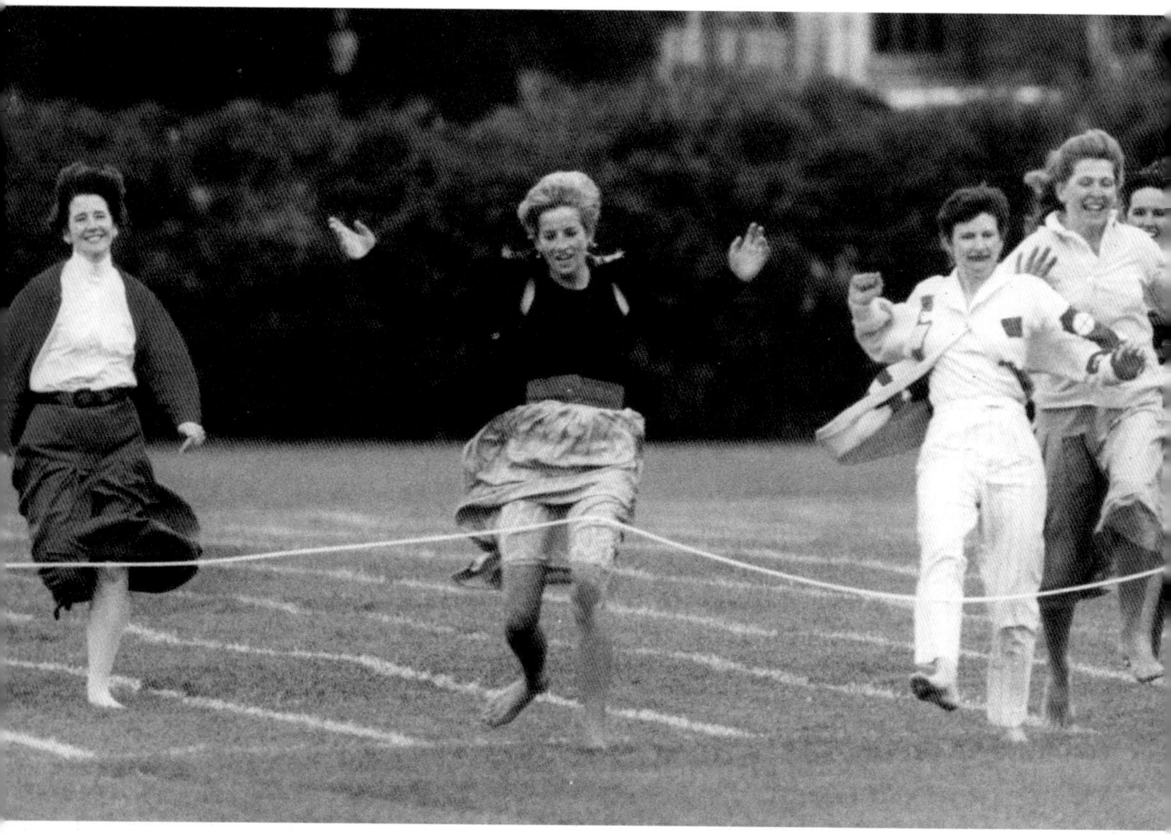

Diana wins for the second year. She was very competitive and a lot of other young mothers had tried desperately to beat her. Did she go into serious training just for the race?

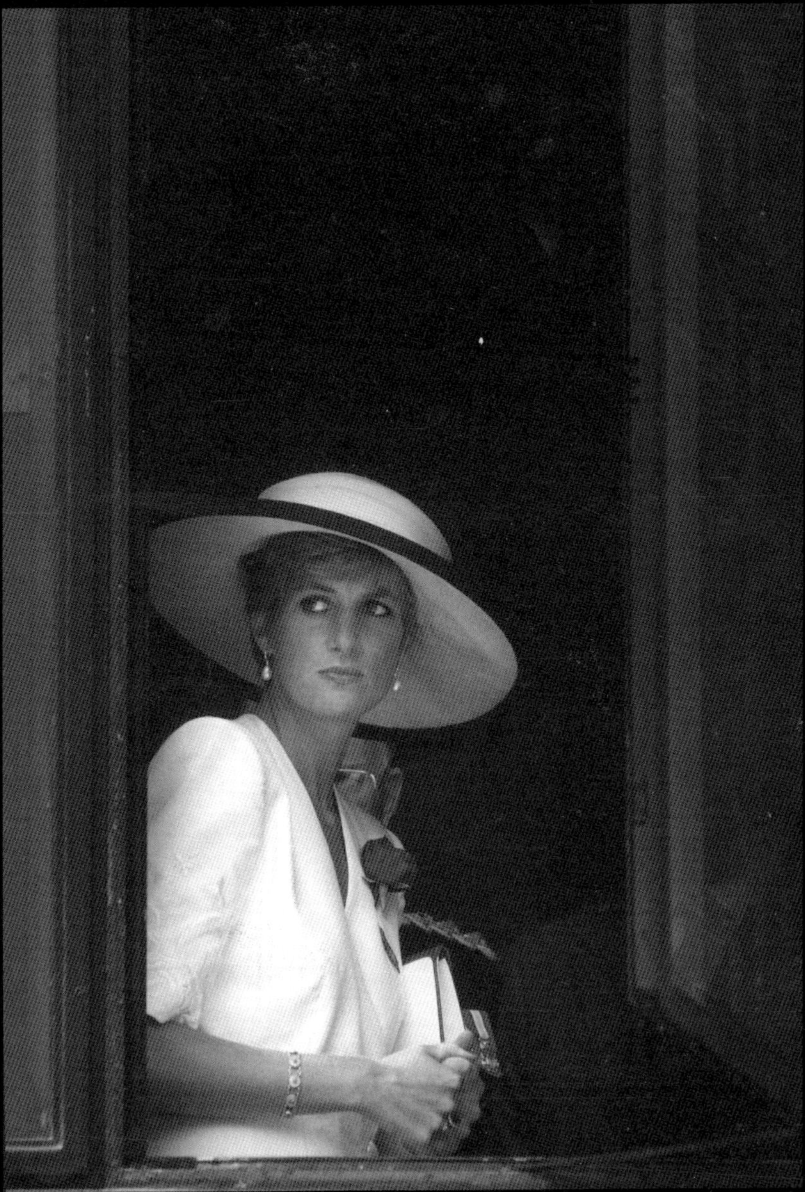

Another day, another foreign tour and a camera conscious Princess who instantly understood that a window would perfectly frame her beauty.

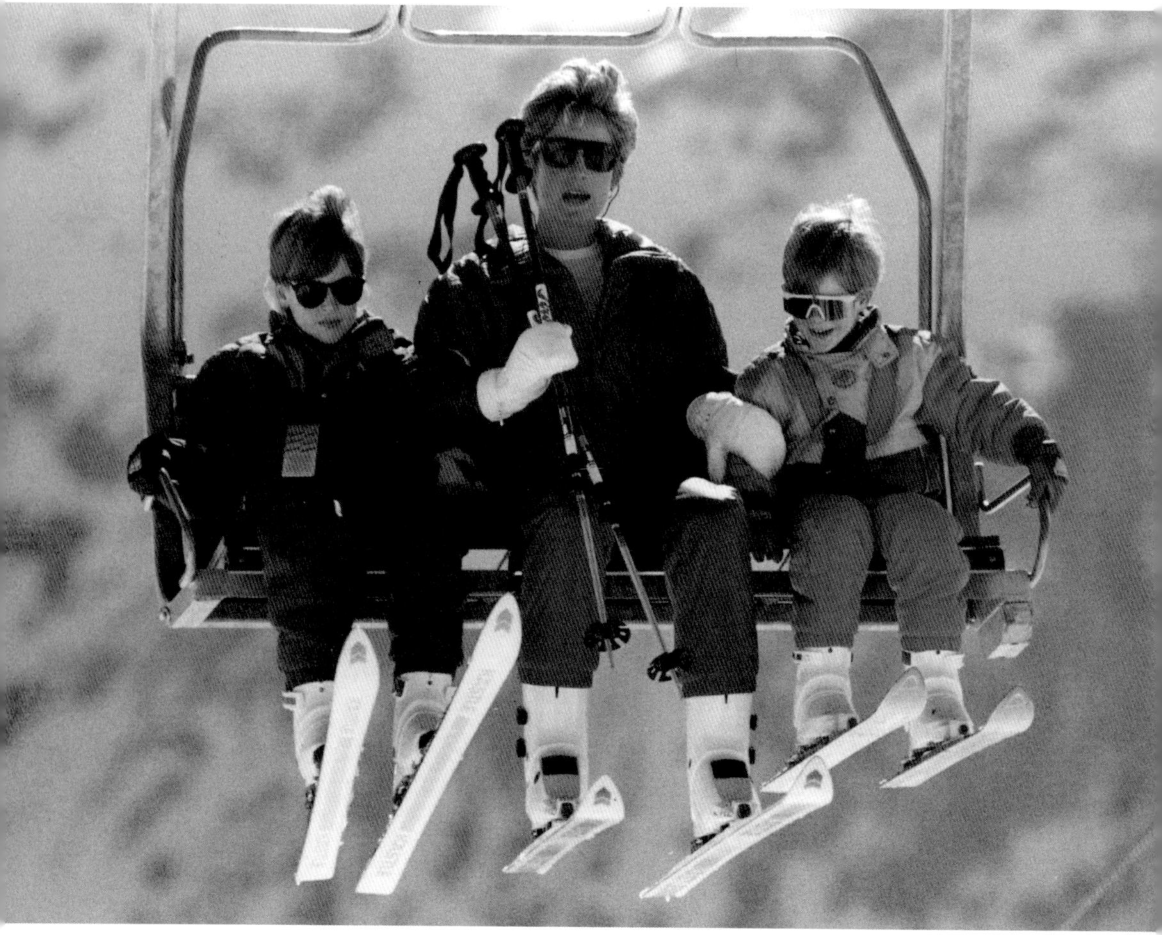

Getting the boys used to a ski lift and the ever present cameras during a family skiing holiday in Lech, Austria.

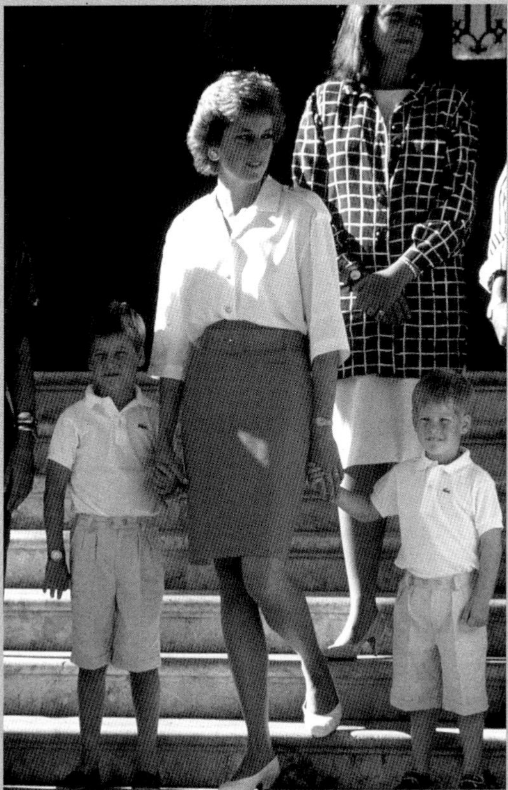

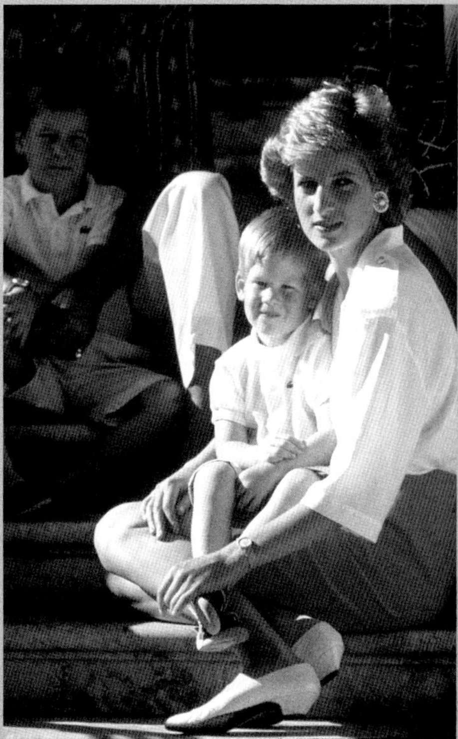

Steve was twice invited into the summer palace of Spain's King Juan Carlos for these very relaxed informal family portraits. These are taken on two consecutive years.

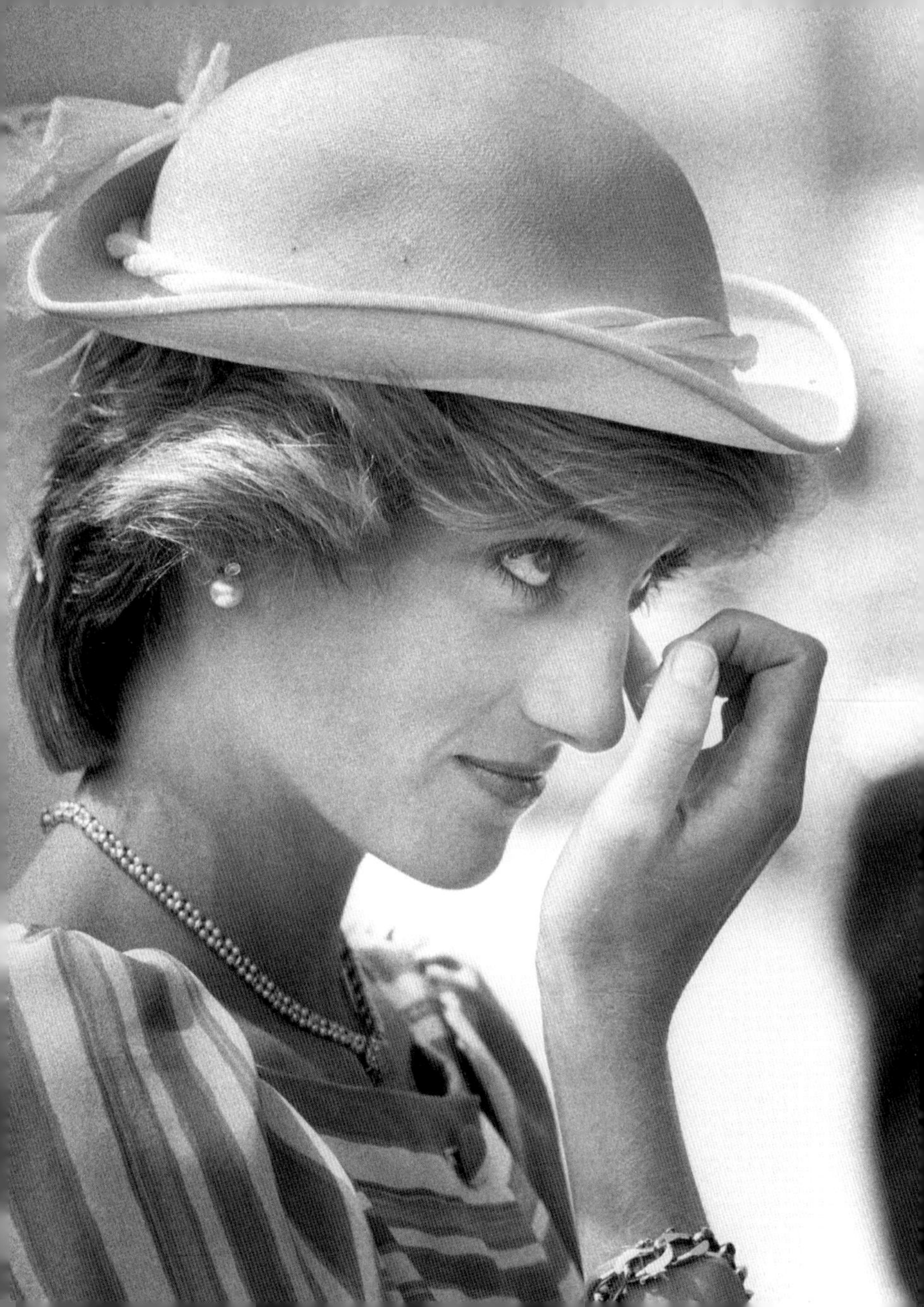

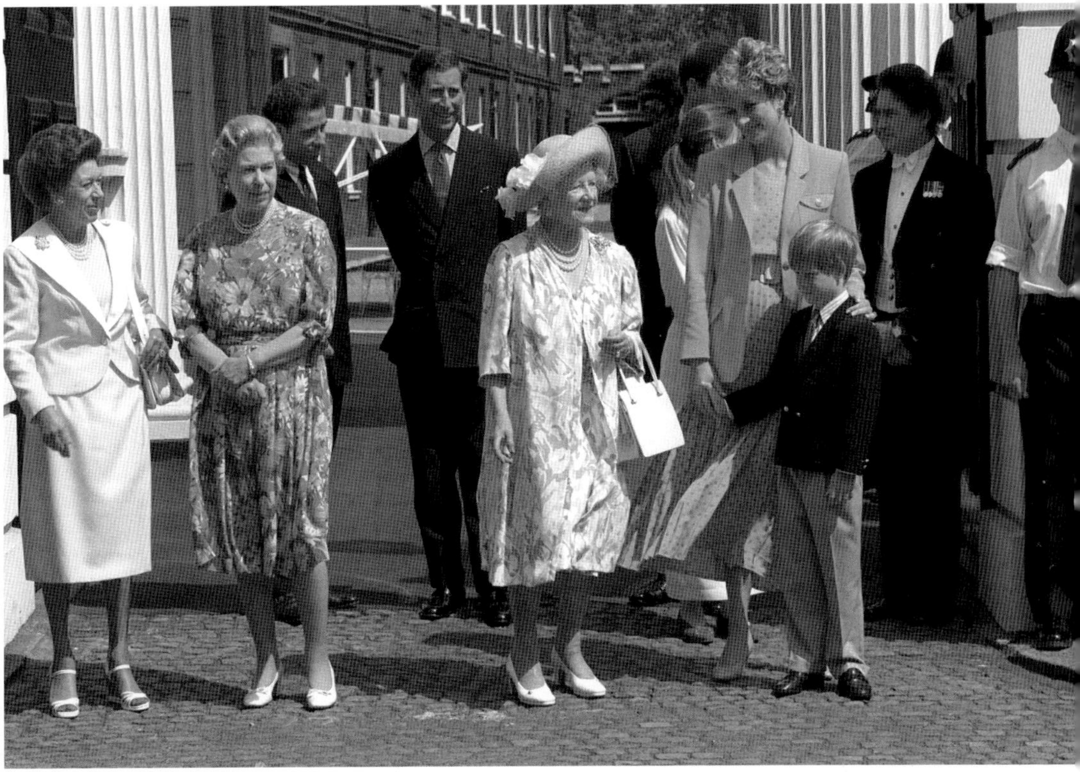

Outside the gates of Clarence House with the entire Royal Family for the birthday of the Queen Mother. The Queen Mother always came outside on her birthday morning to thank the crowd, many of whom had wait on the pavement all night for the best vantage point.

LEFT: A touch of mascara. Diana knew that every second she was in public, a camera shutter would click but she was still able to look sensational even while adjusting her make up.

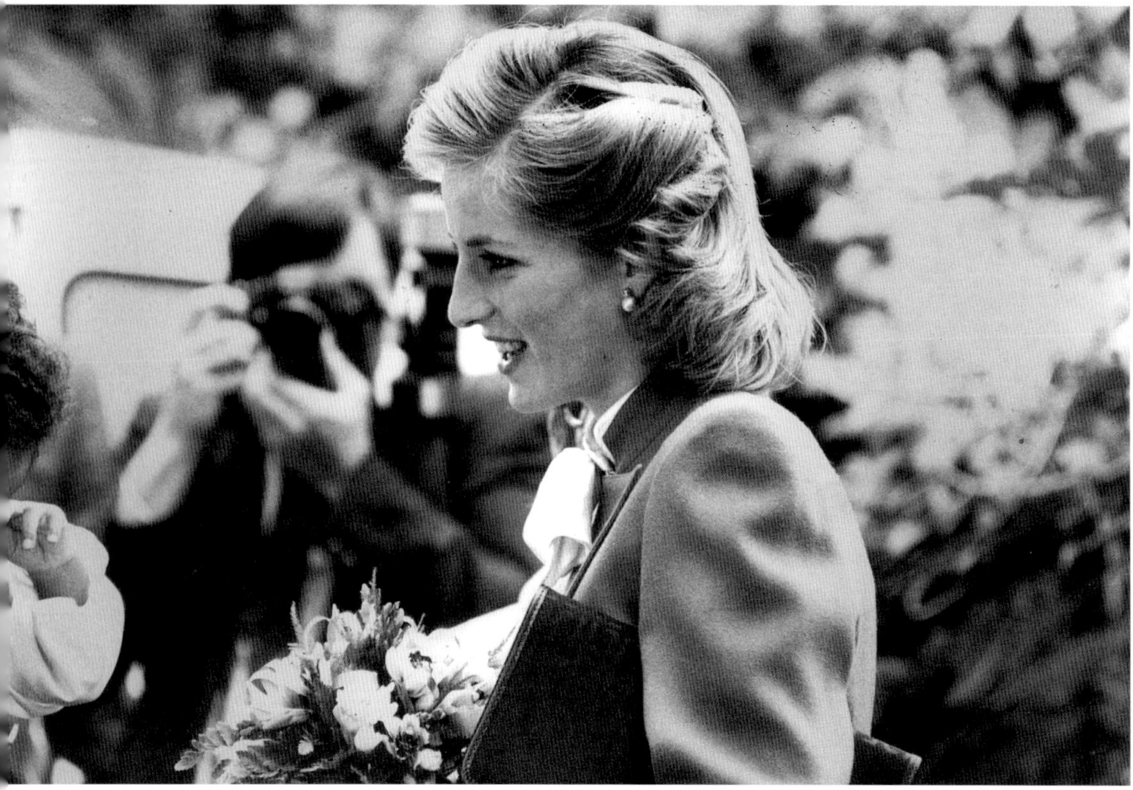

Diana just after the birth of Harry in a hairstyle she quickly abandoned.

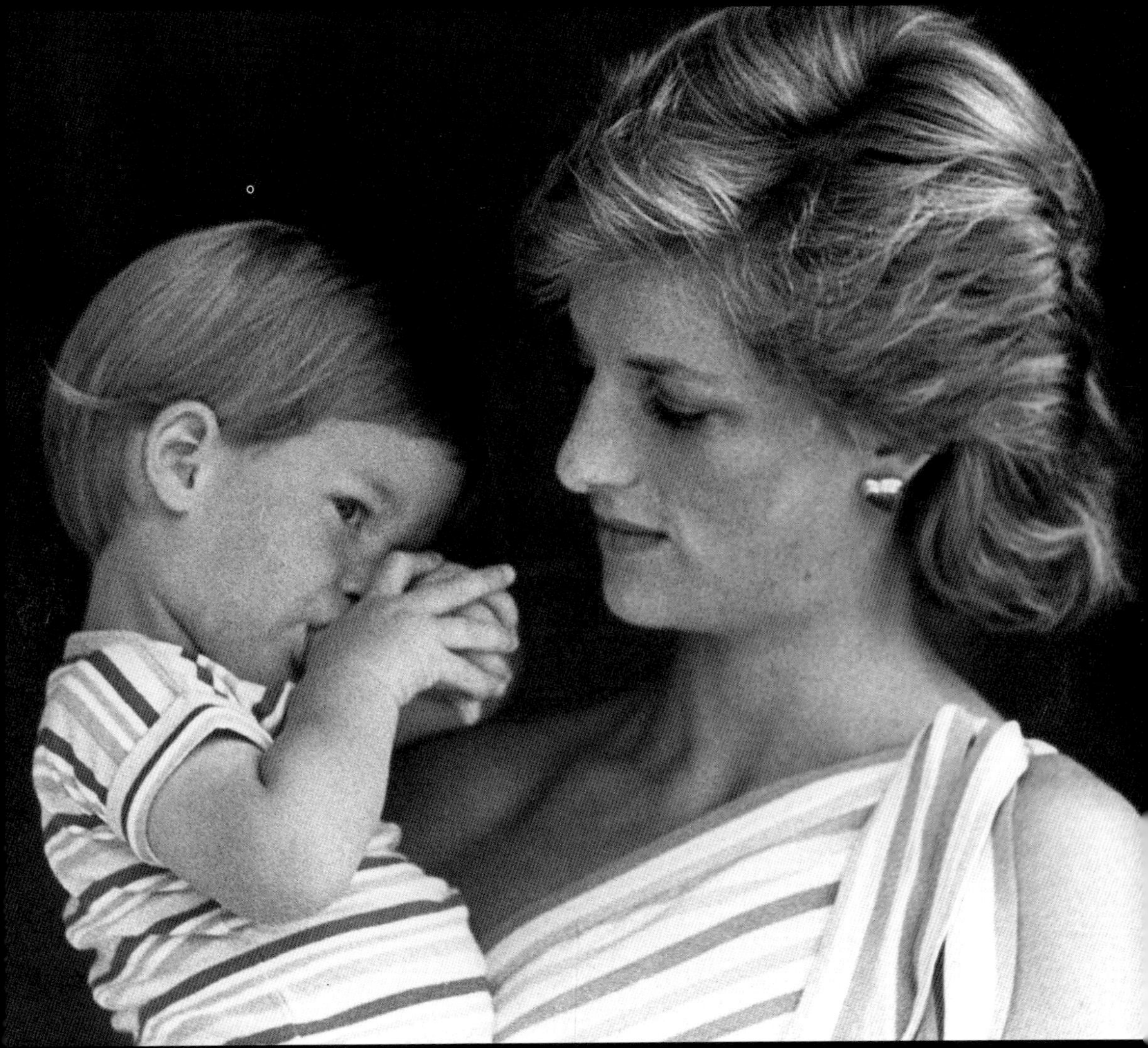

Diana is said to have loved this picture, an intimate moment during a Spanish holiday with young Prince Harry sucking his thumb. Steve was invited into the garden of the Royal holiday home to take this informal portrait.

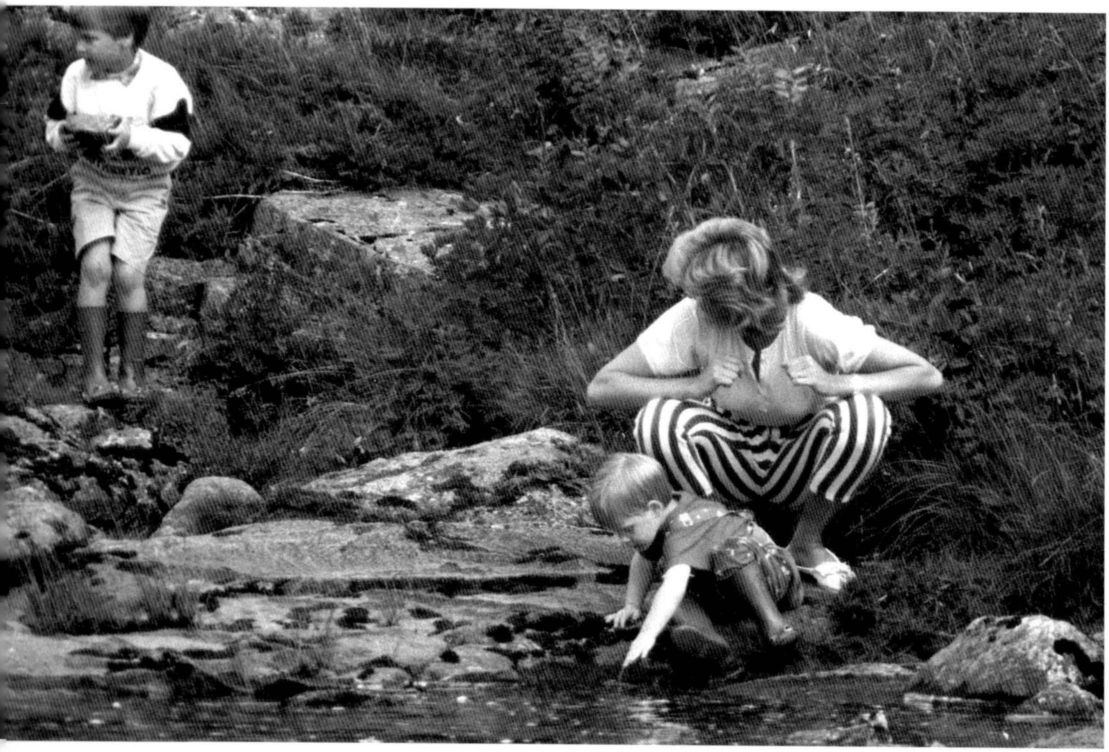

A tender moment by the River Dee in Scotland with William and Harry. This photo was take from the public side without any comment from the Princess.

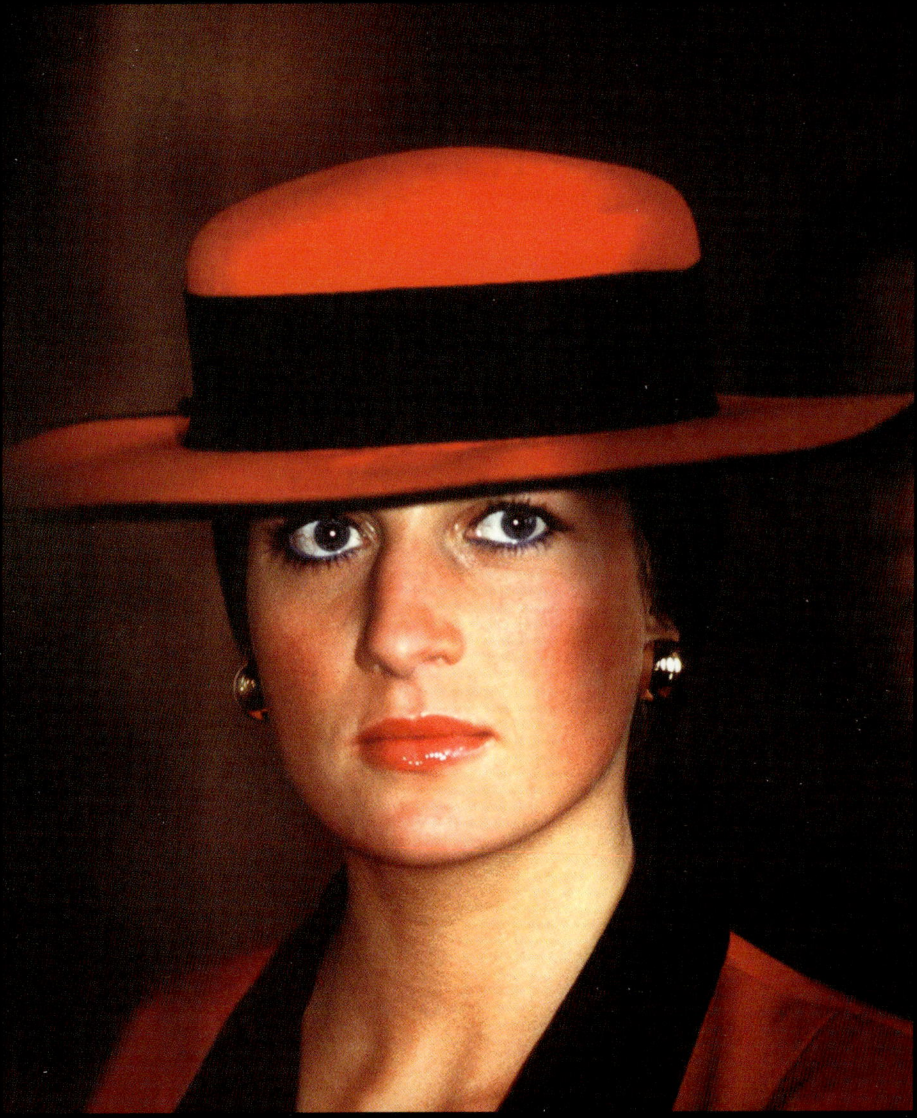

Diana looking absolutely fabulous.

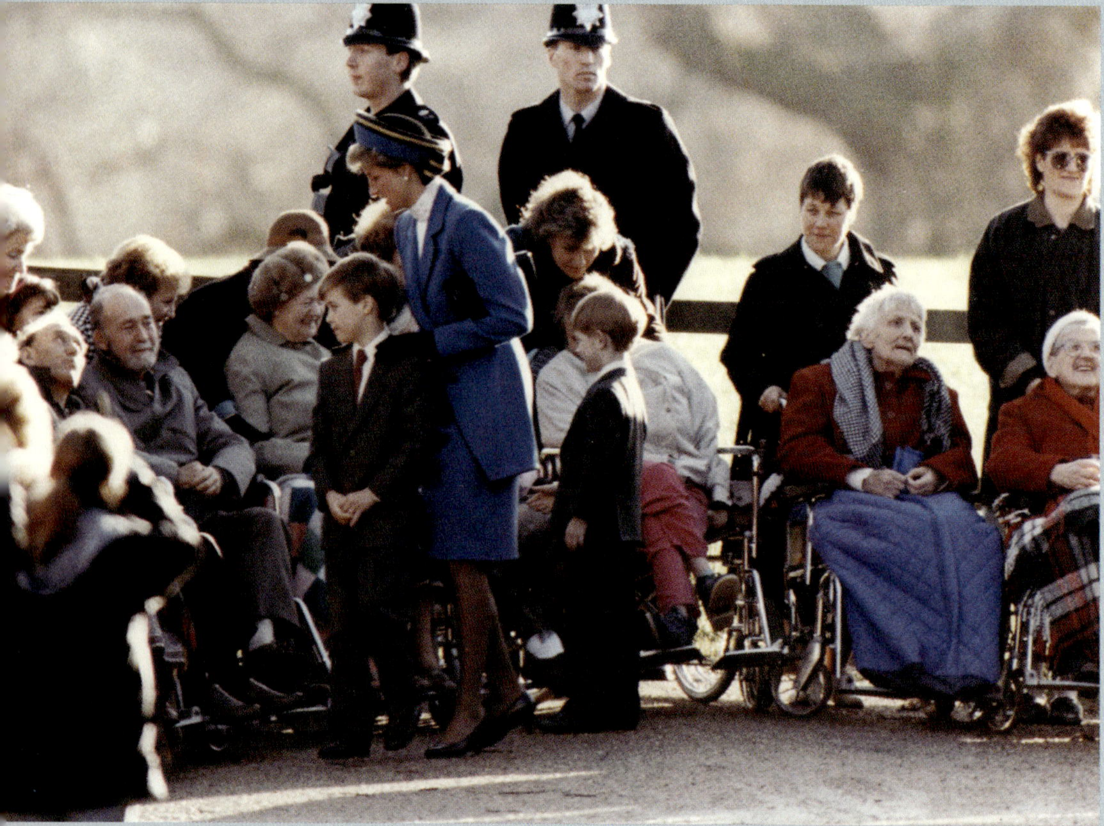

Getting William and Harry used to meeting the great British public. Carefully at first and in well chosen situations, this was a mother who knew her sons needed to learn what it is to be Royal, at a very early age.

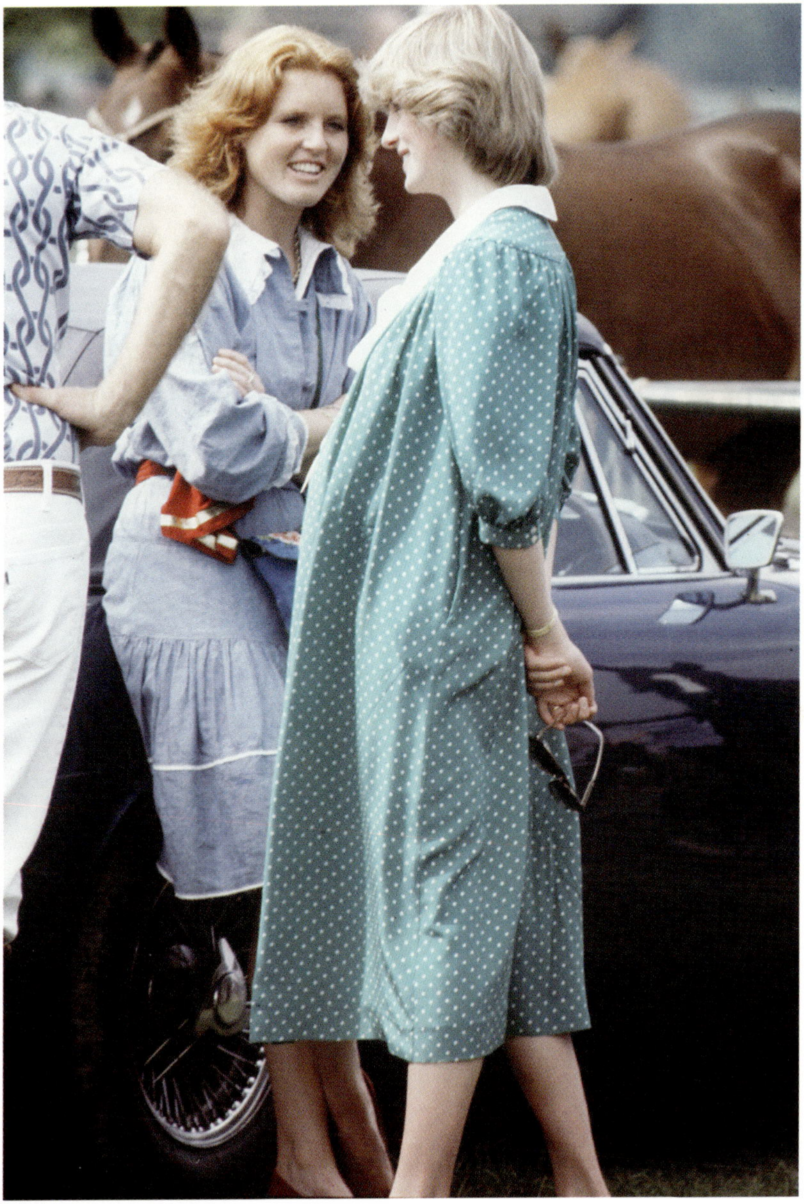

There was a time when a pregnant Princess would never be seen in public. But here's Diana at polo looking radiant.

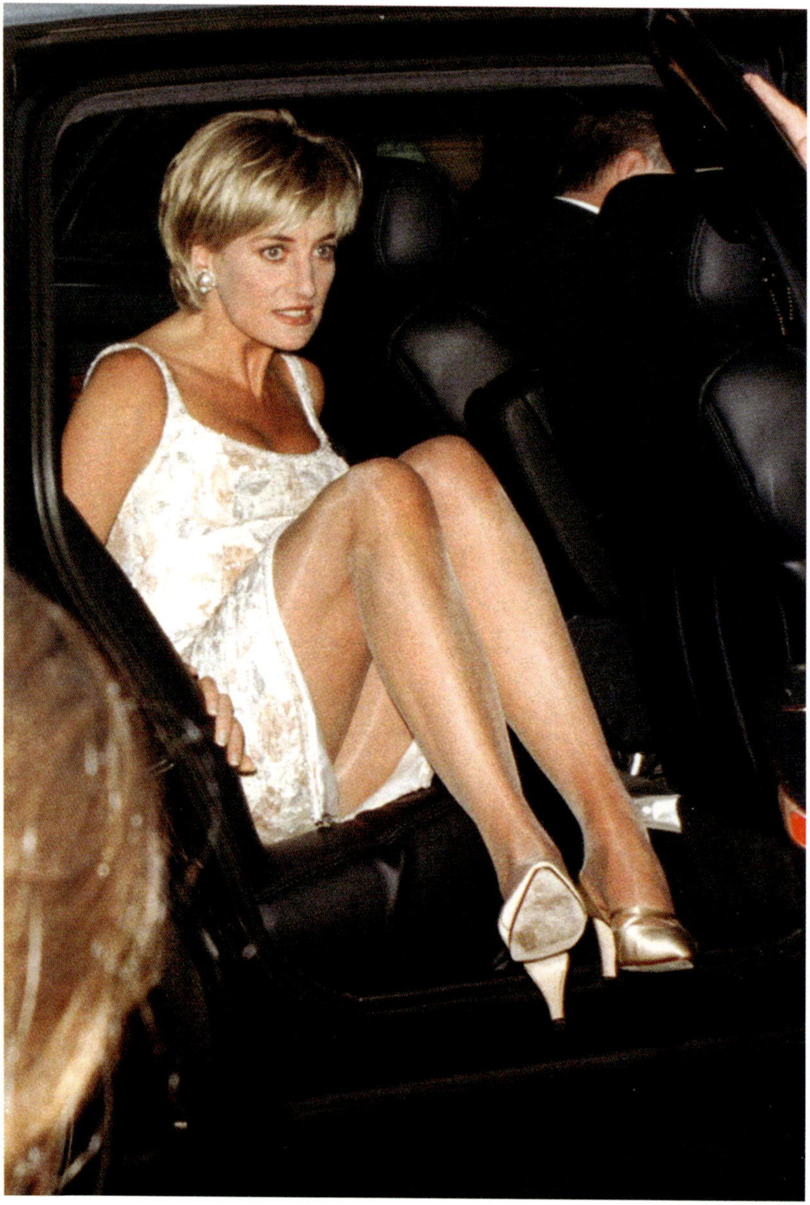

Making a graceful exit.

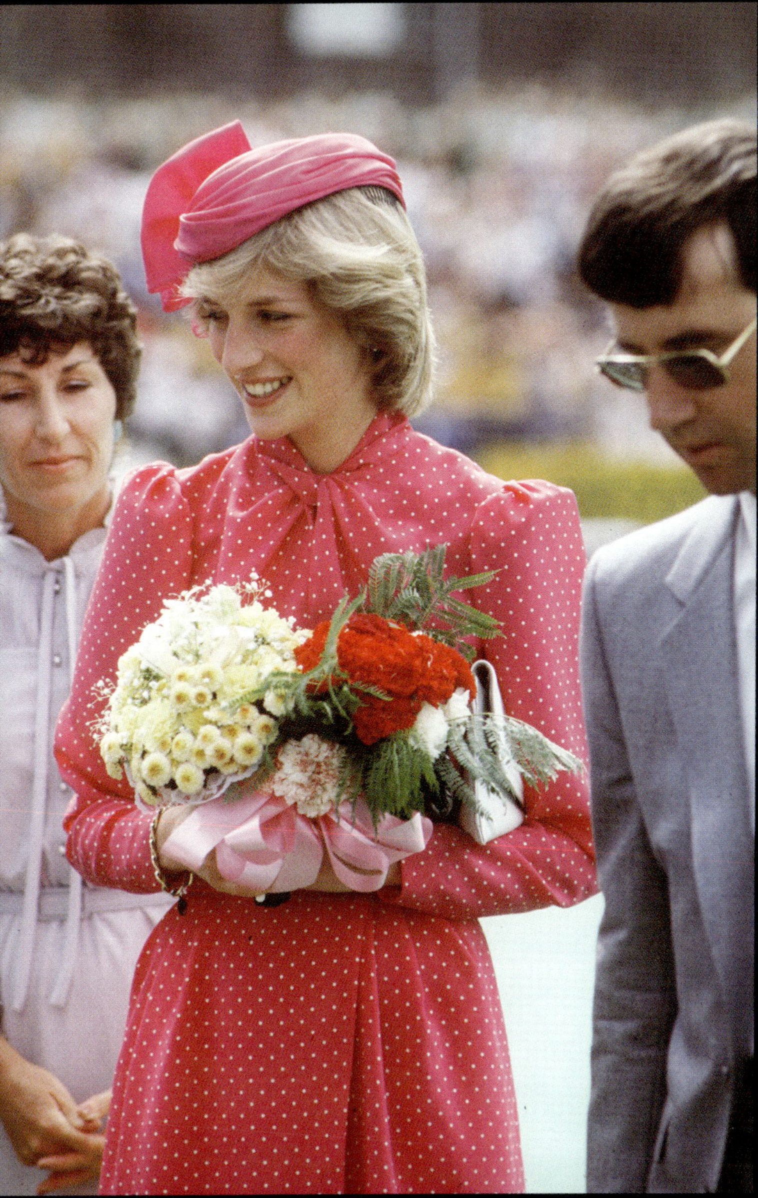

A colourful Diana, perfectly co-ordinated and the camera loved it.

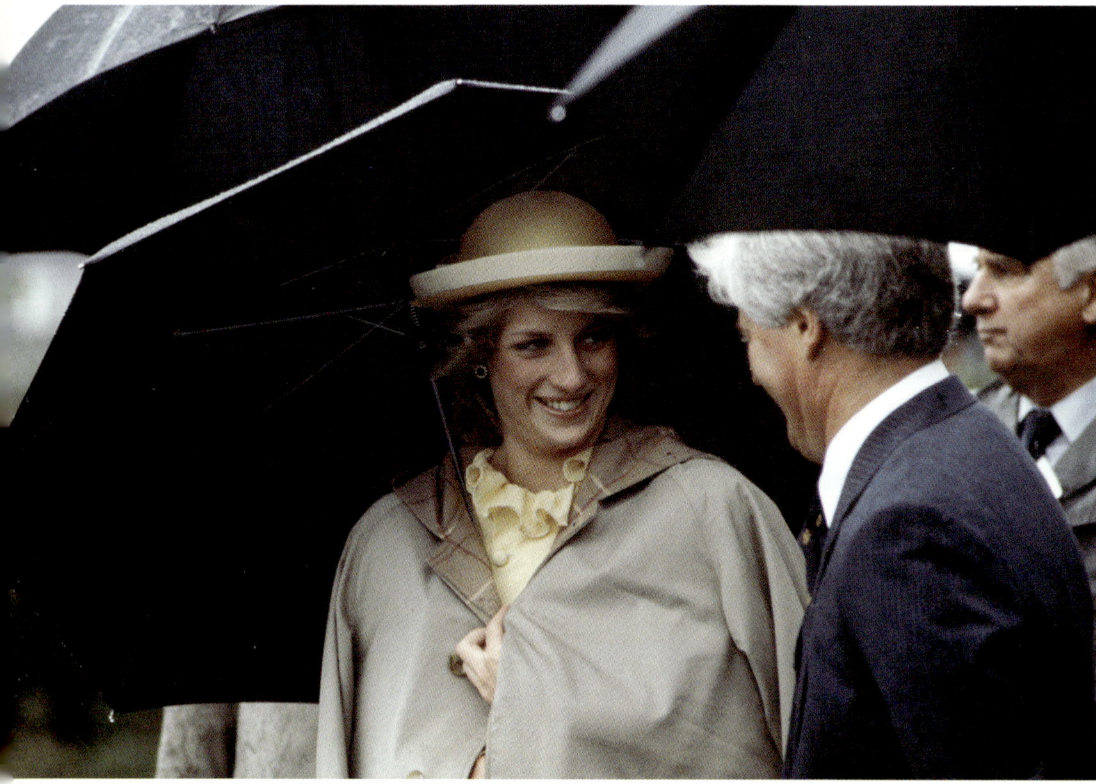

Even under a brolly and leaden skies the Princess brightened a morning.

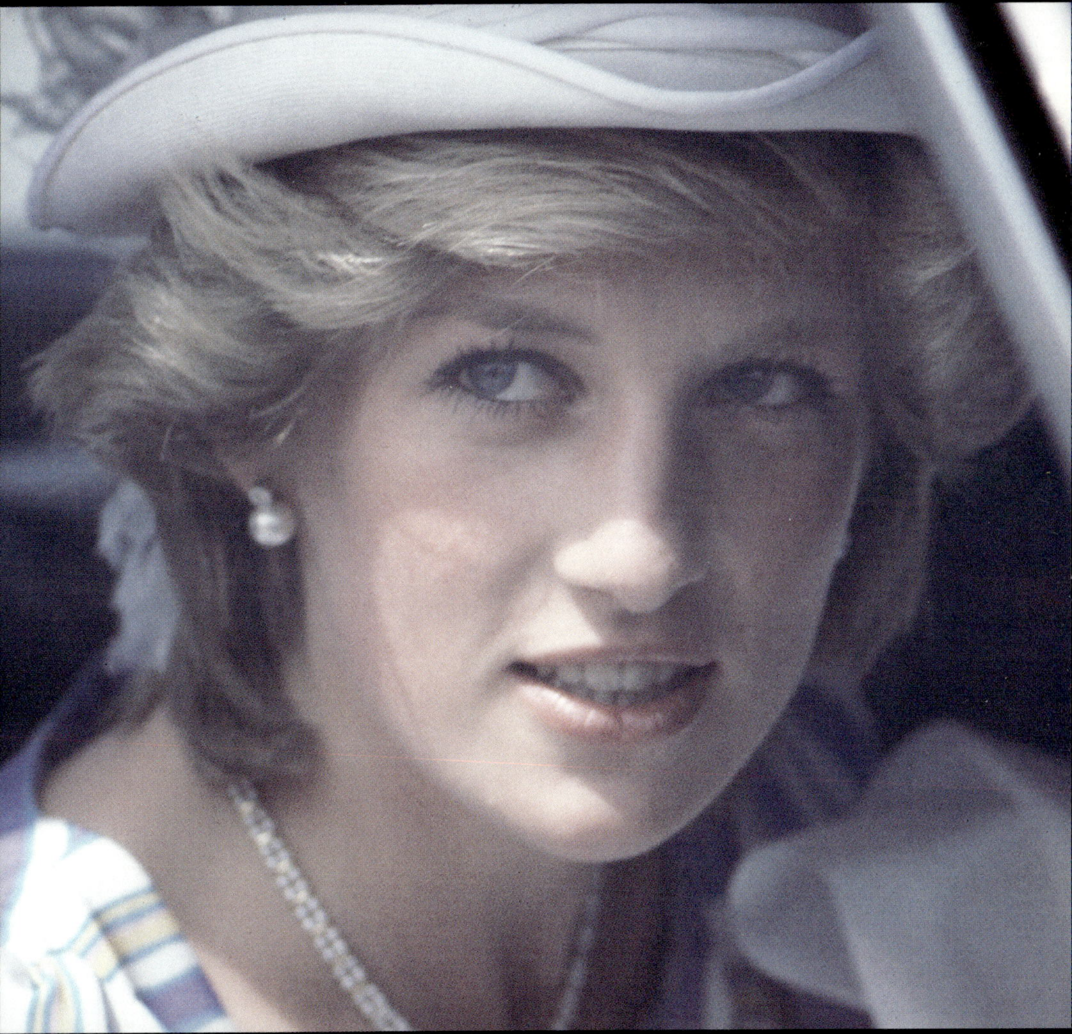

The picture millions of people loved. Diana peering from a car

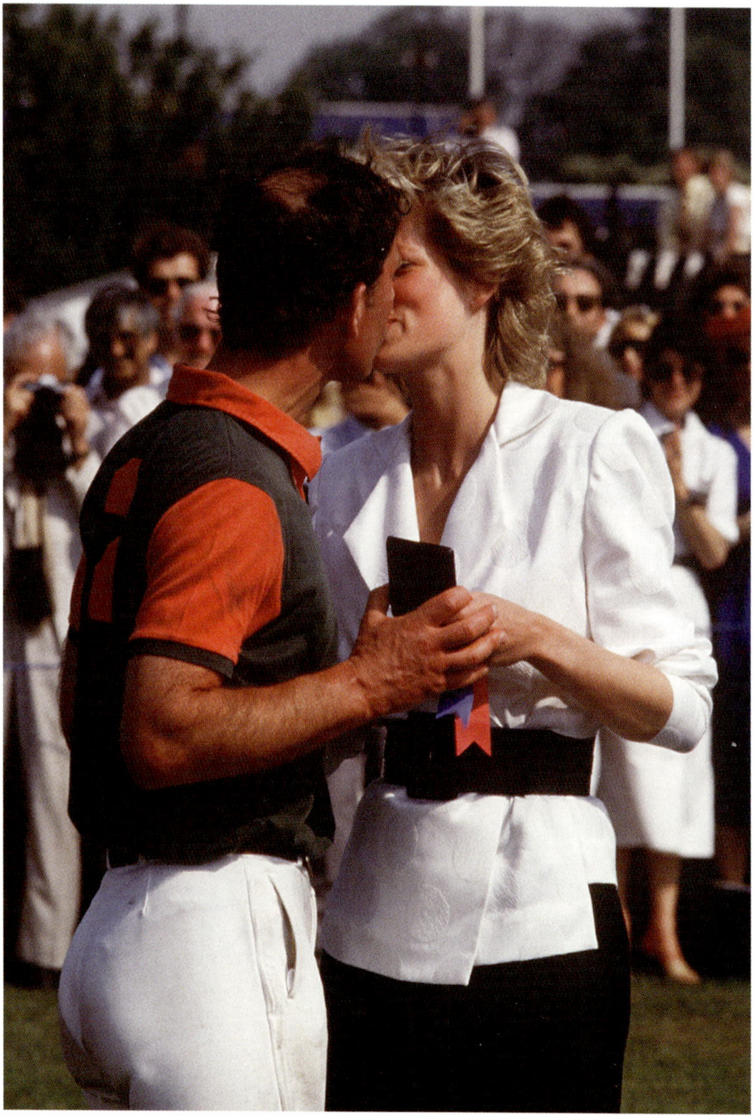

Kissing Charles at a polo match as she presented him with the winning trophy. The affection is clear in total contrast to a photo in later years at the same club where the Princess deliberately averted her head as Charles attempted to kiss her.

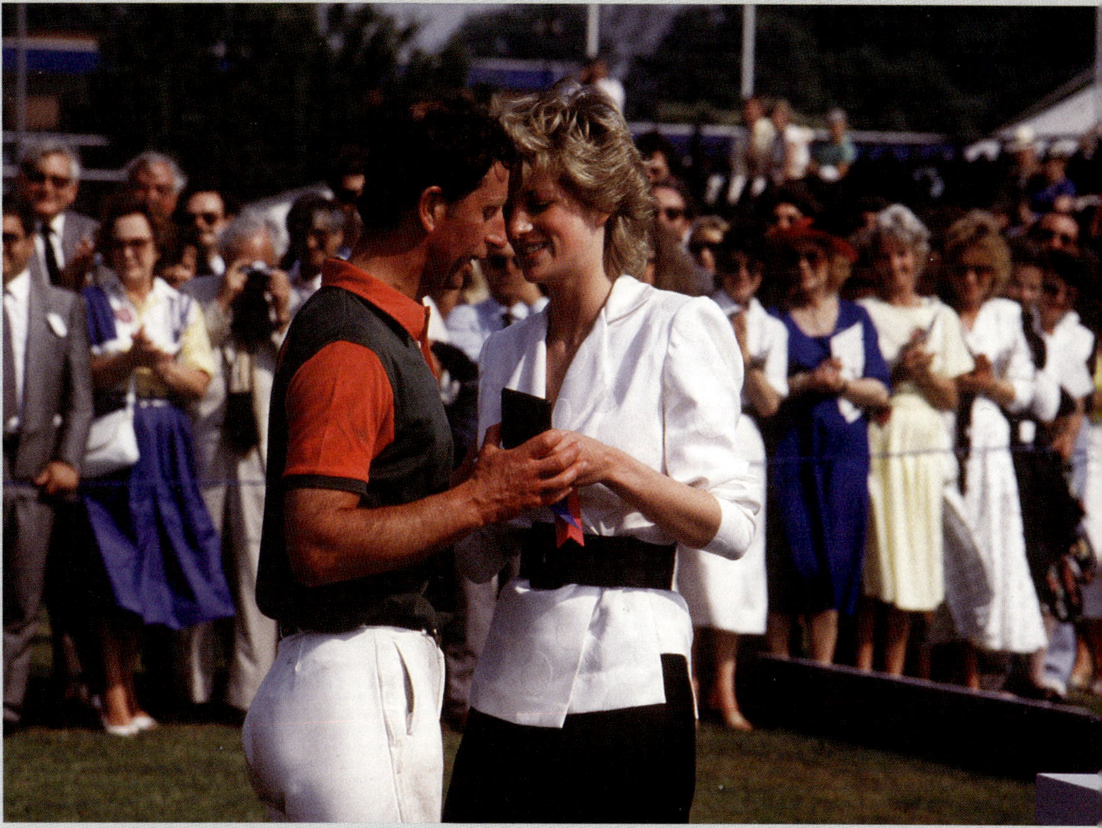

The affection is clear as she nuzzles into Charles after the cup presentation.

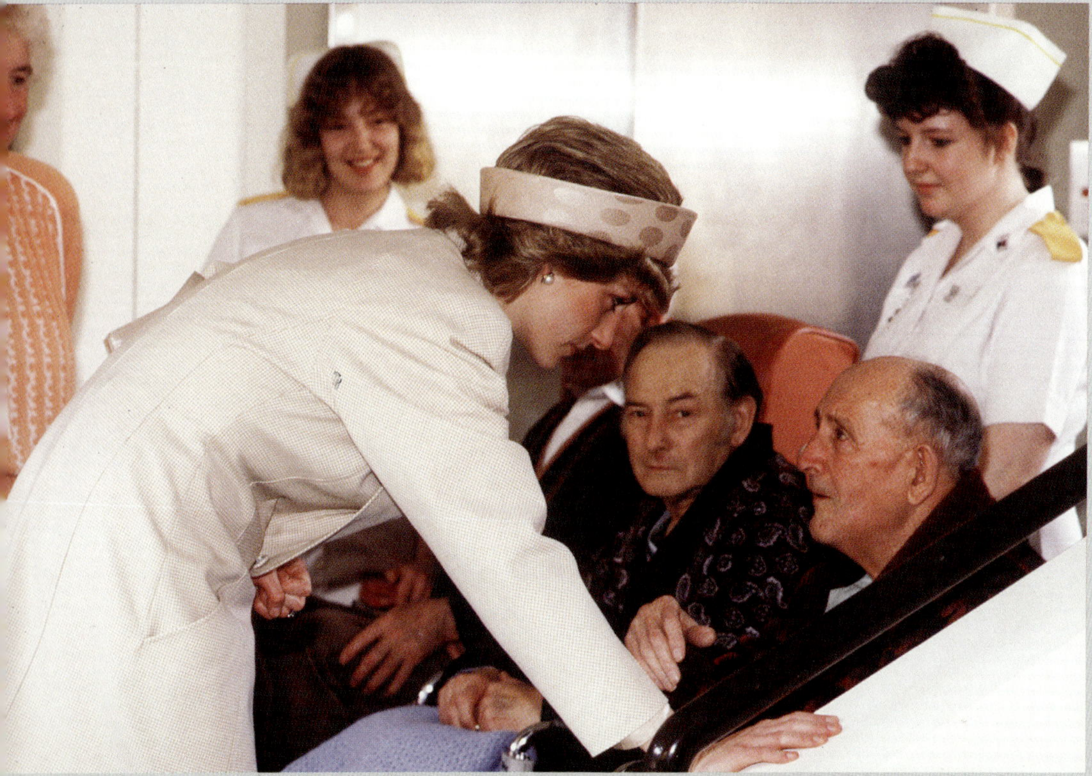

At a home for the elderly in Wales. She was always interested in everyone and anyone who she spoke to was made to feel special.

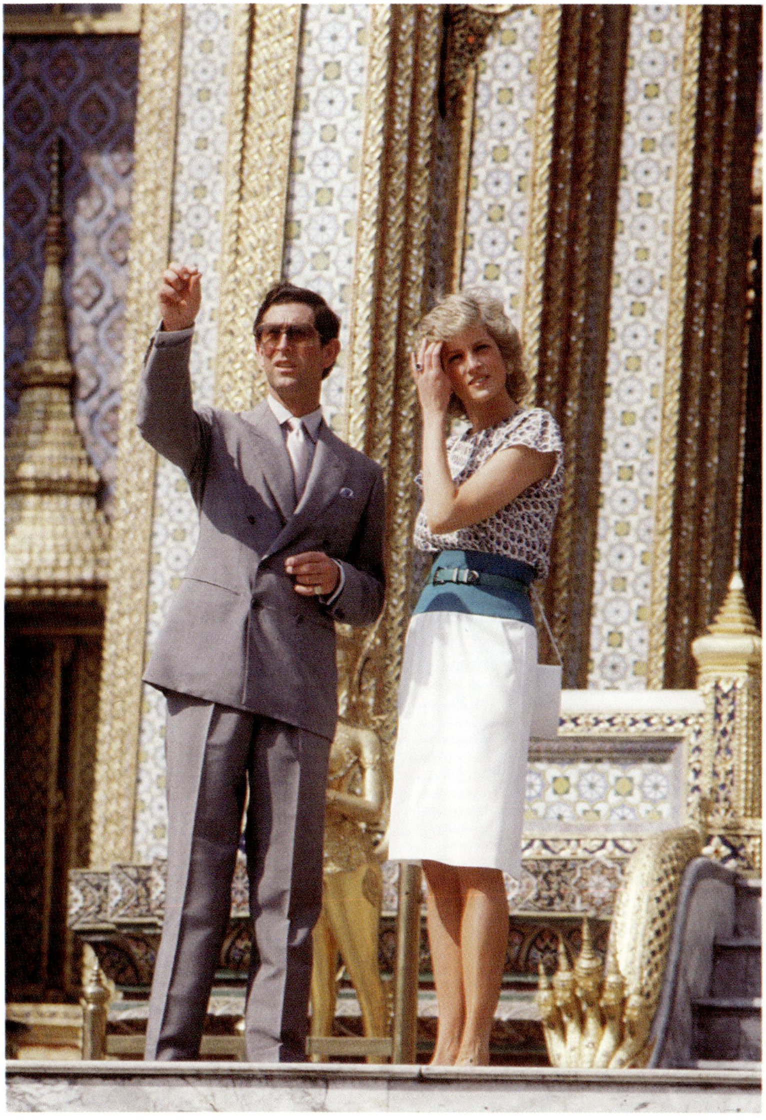

Charles and Diana looking like a couple of rather special tourists in Thailand.

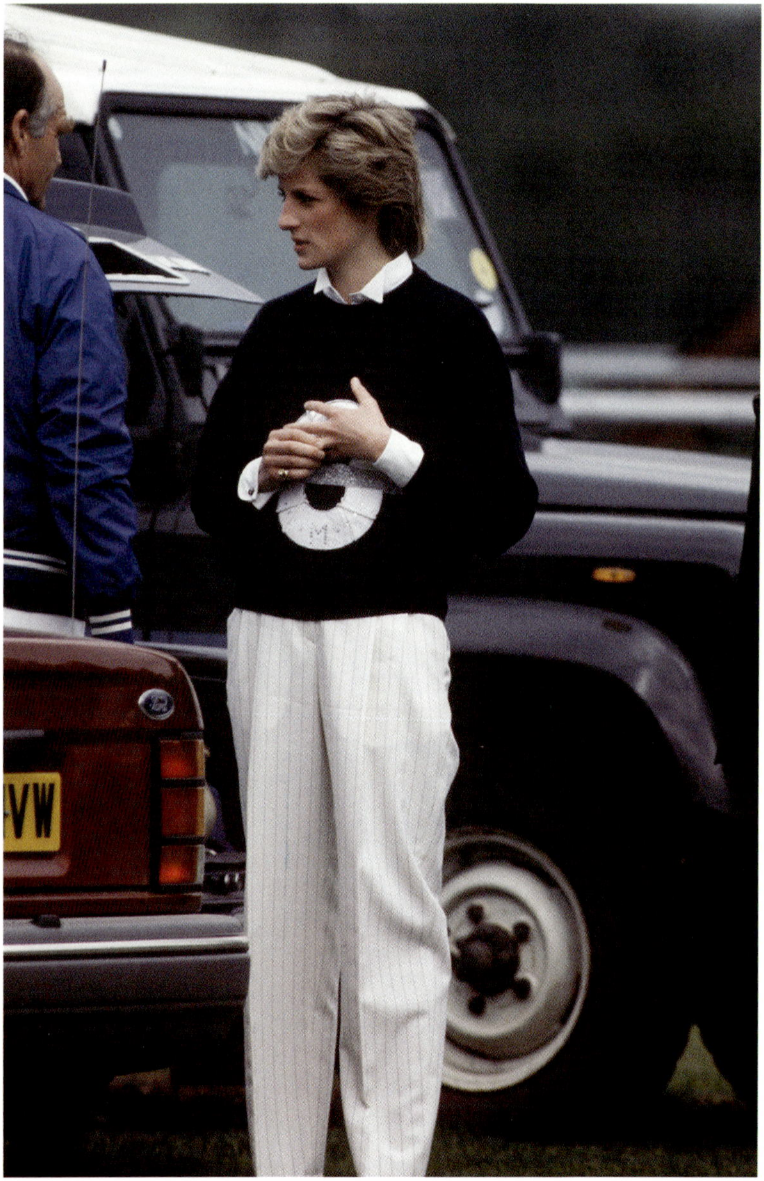

Diana at polo on yet another Sunday afternoon.

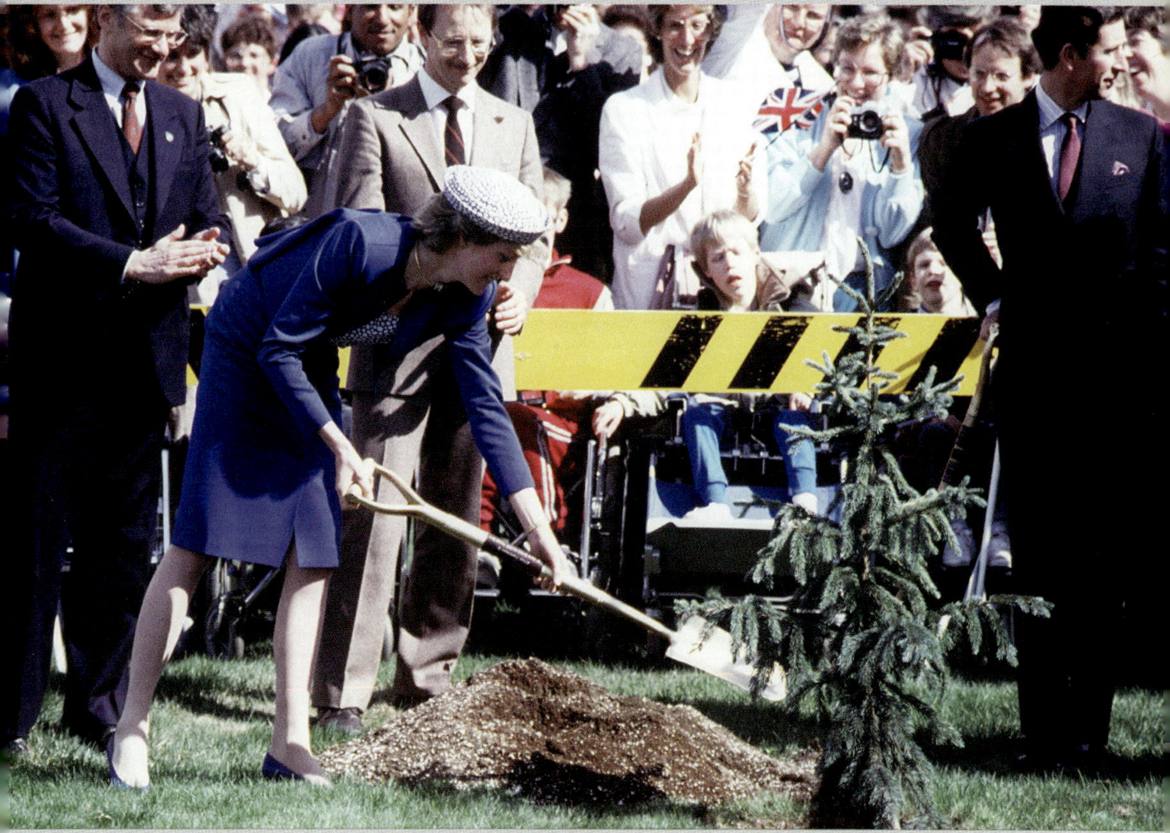

Planting a tree and managing to get a laugh at the same time.

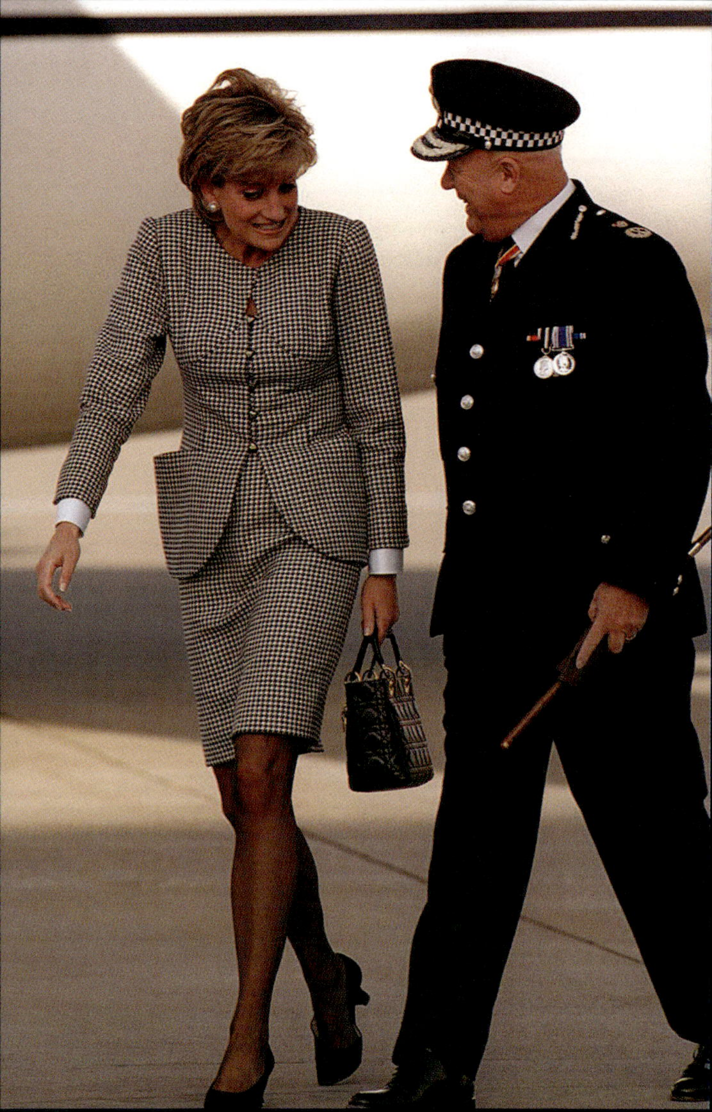

Diana with the Commodore of the Queen's Flight before take off to yet another public engagement somewhere in Britain.

Right: In Canada Diana could even carry off a rather functional pill box hat with style.

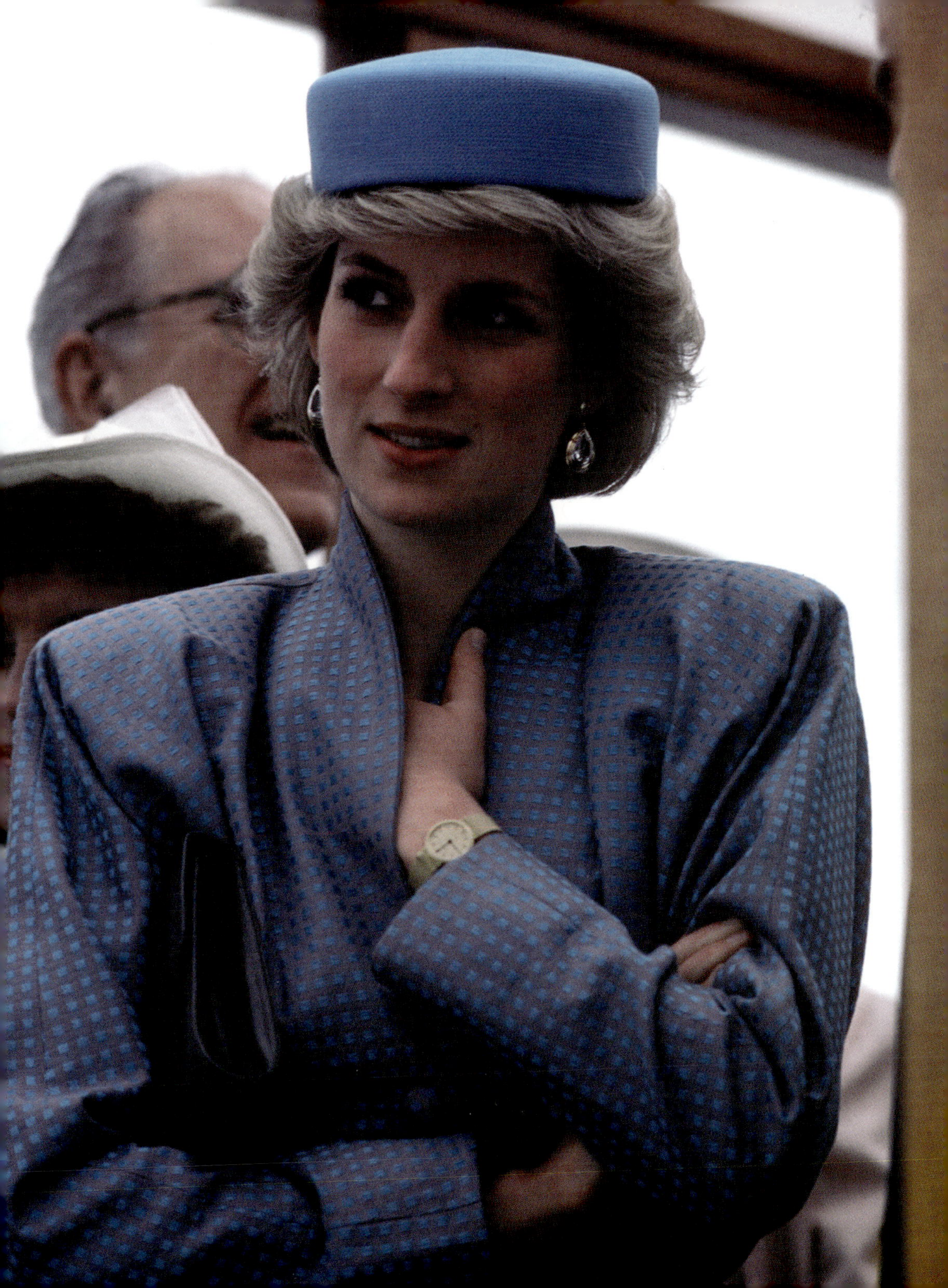

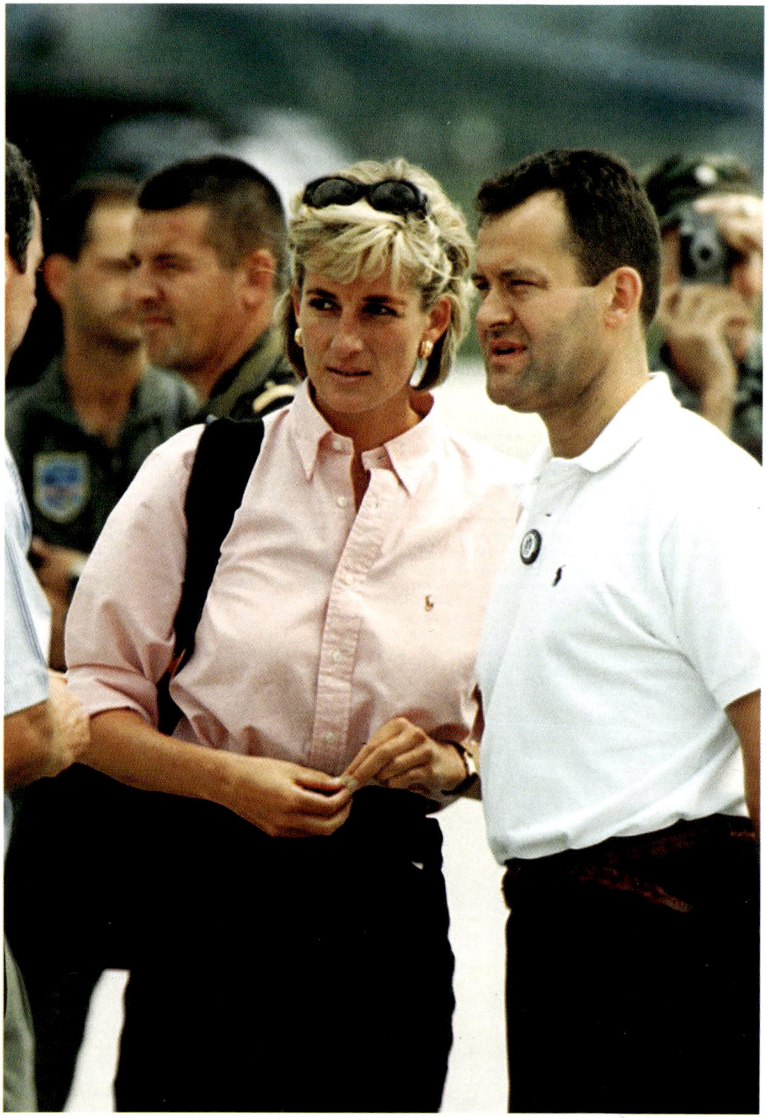

The Princess chats to Paul Burrell. He was her butler at Kensington Palace. She came to rely on him and called Paul "my rock".

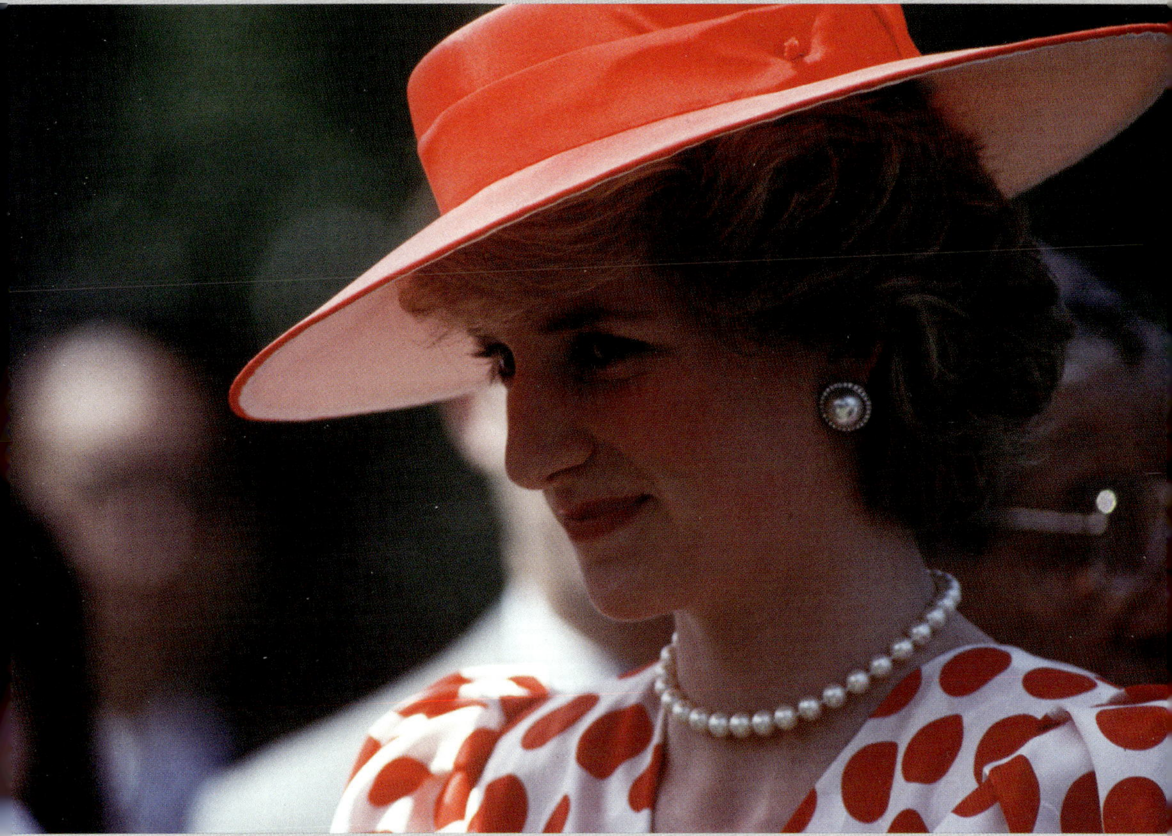

In Japan and looking lovely, managing to hide the exhaustion of a world tour. Just 24 hours earlier she had collapsed in Western Canada before a long flight across the Pacific.

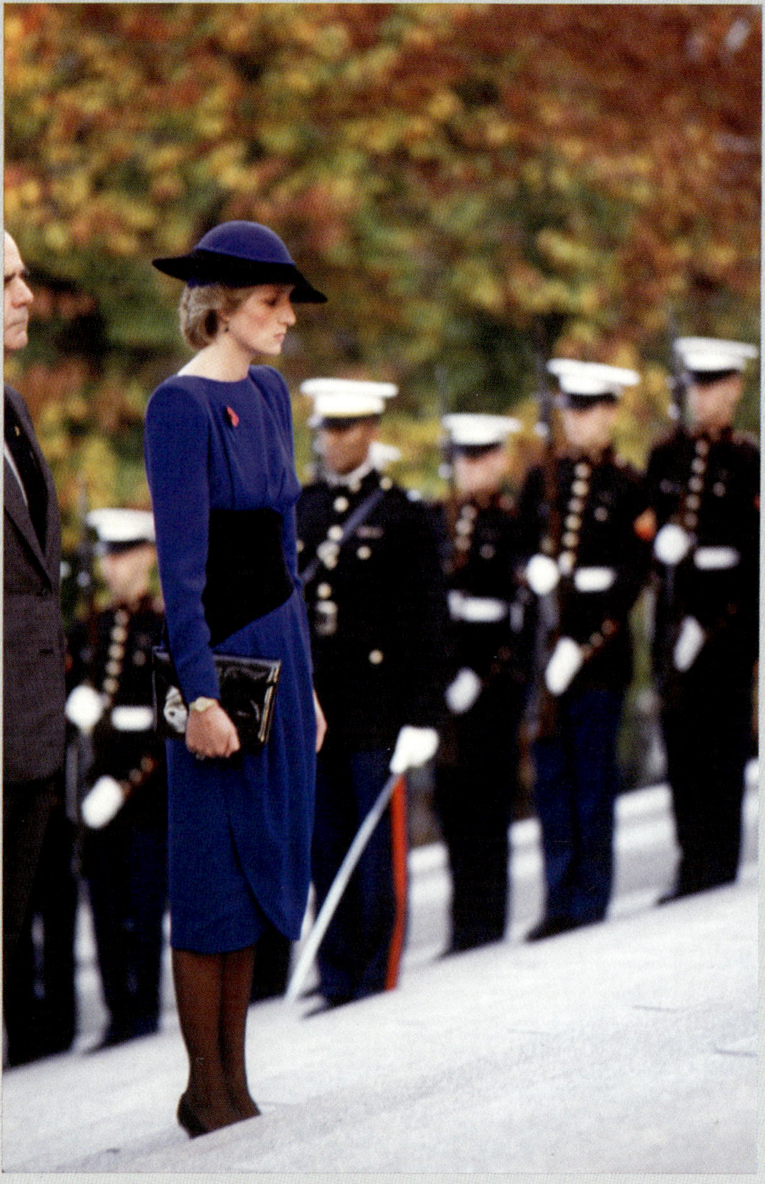

A sombre moment at a military ceremony in the United States where she was feted as a global superstar.

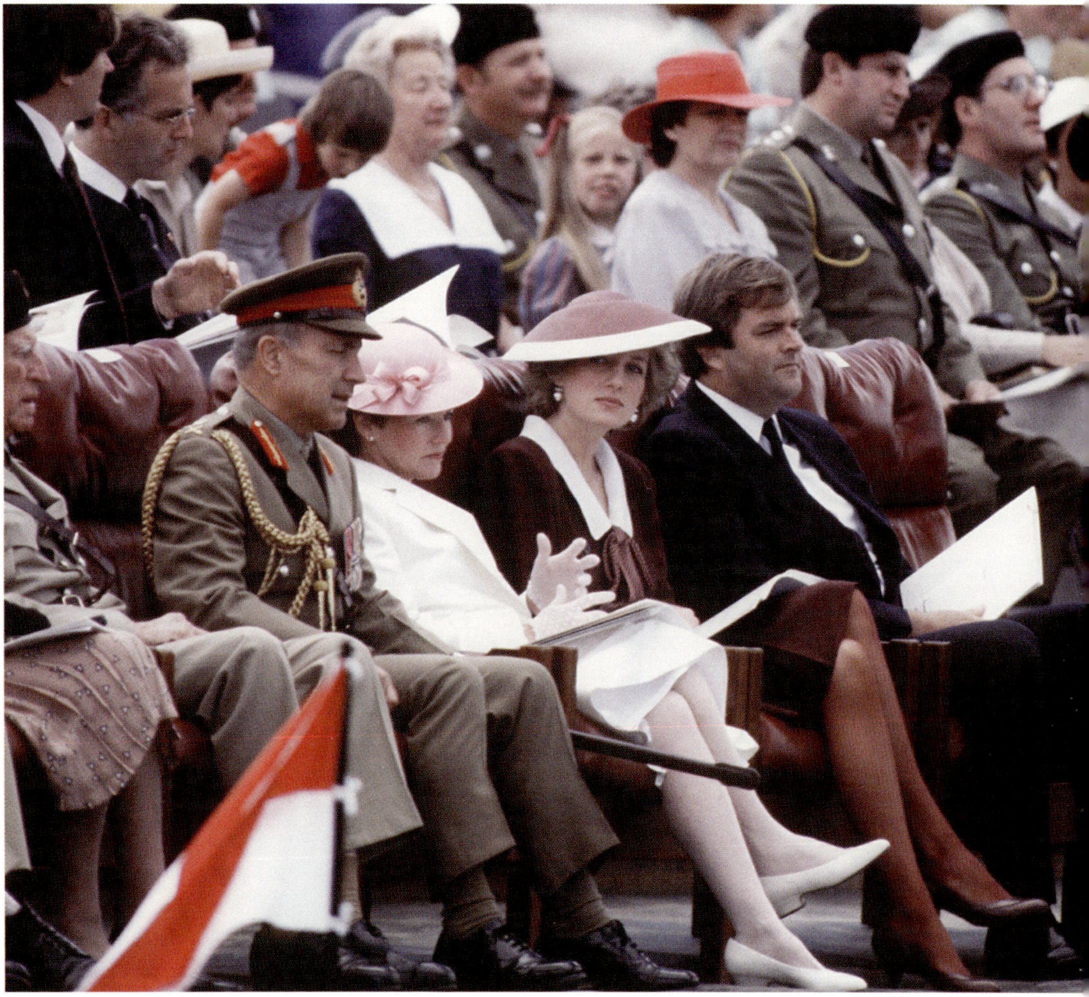

She loved the camera. There she is seeking out Steve in the middle of a military ceremony in the US.

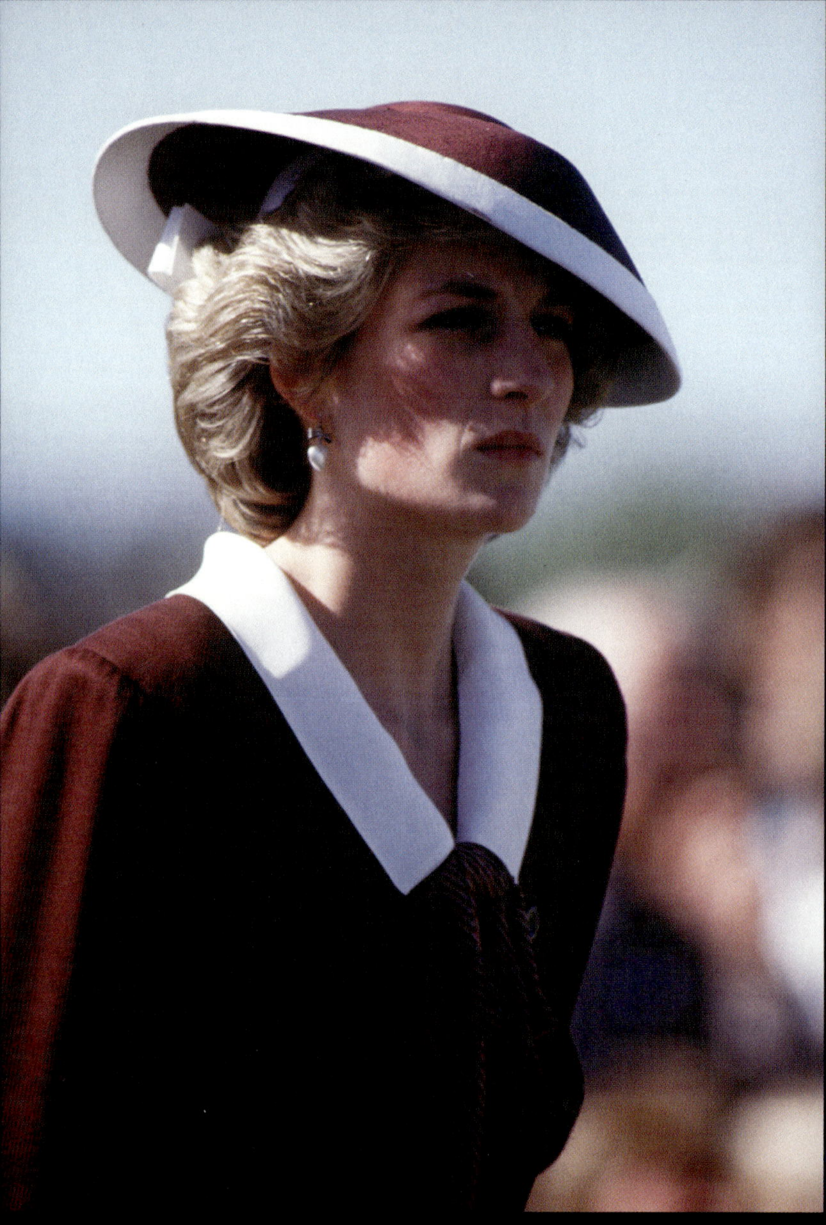

Another fashion spectacular, looking good out of absolutely nothing.

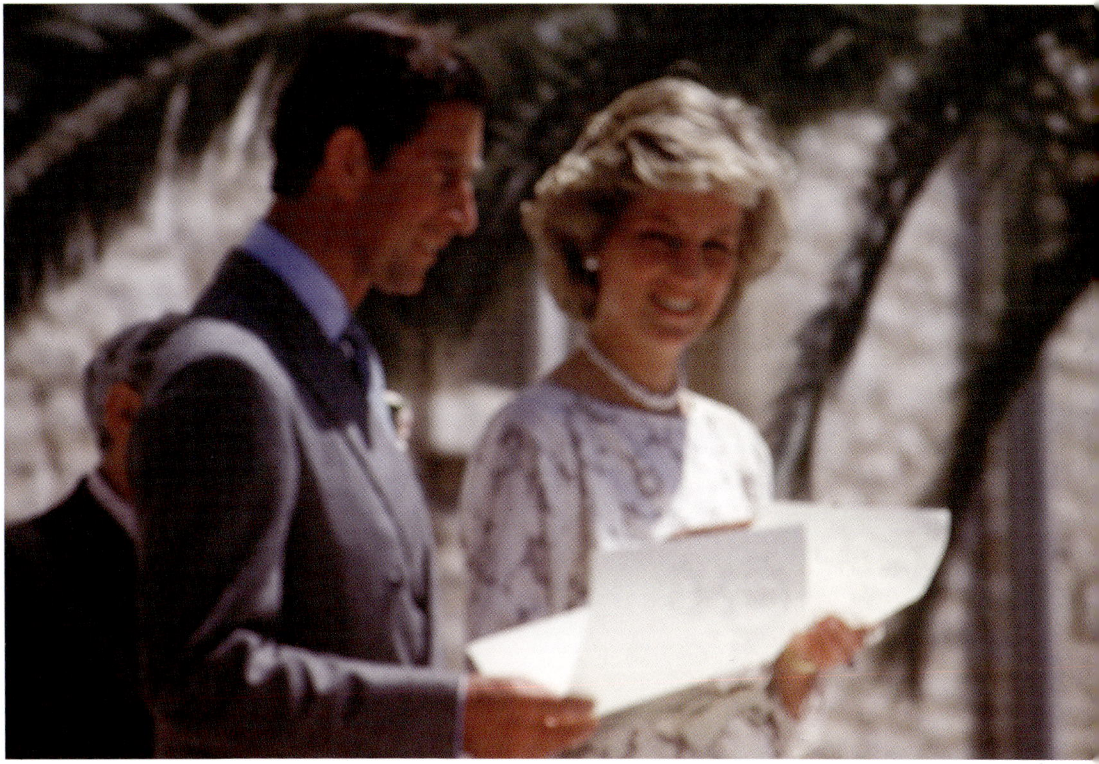

A moment under the Palm trees with Charles reading up about their next public engagement in Spain.

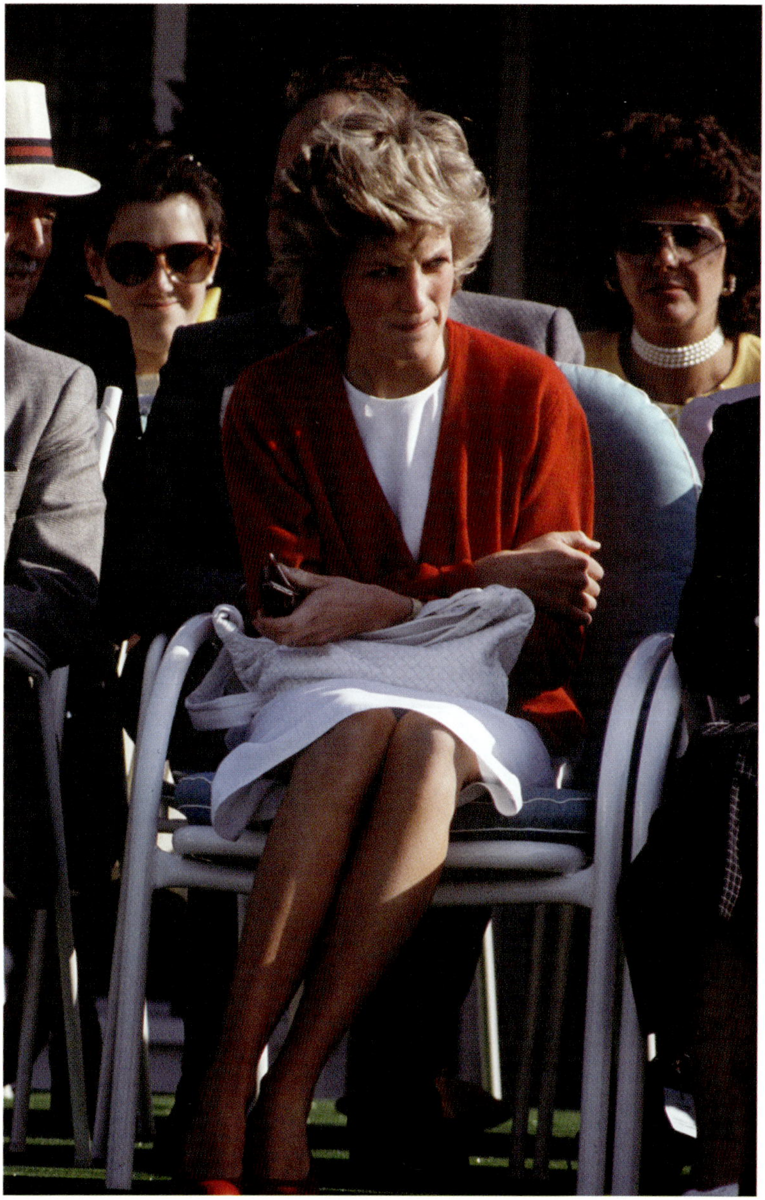

A lot of leg, but then as Charles told her when she was just 19, she did have a terrific pair of pins.

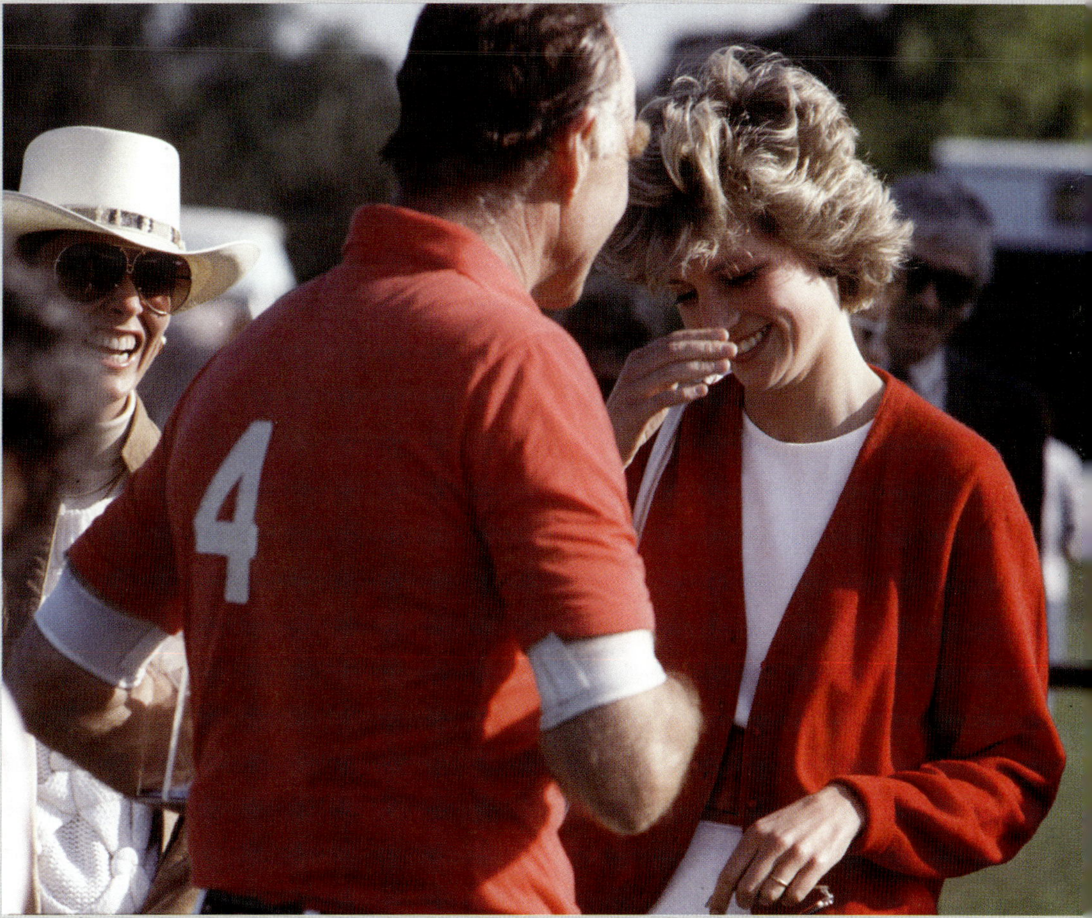

Sharing a funny moment with Major Ron Ferguson at a Windsor Polo Match.

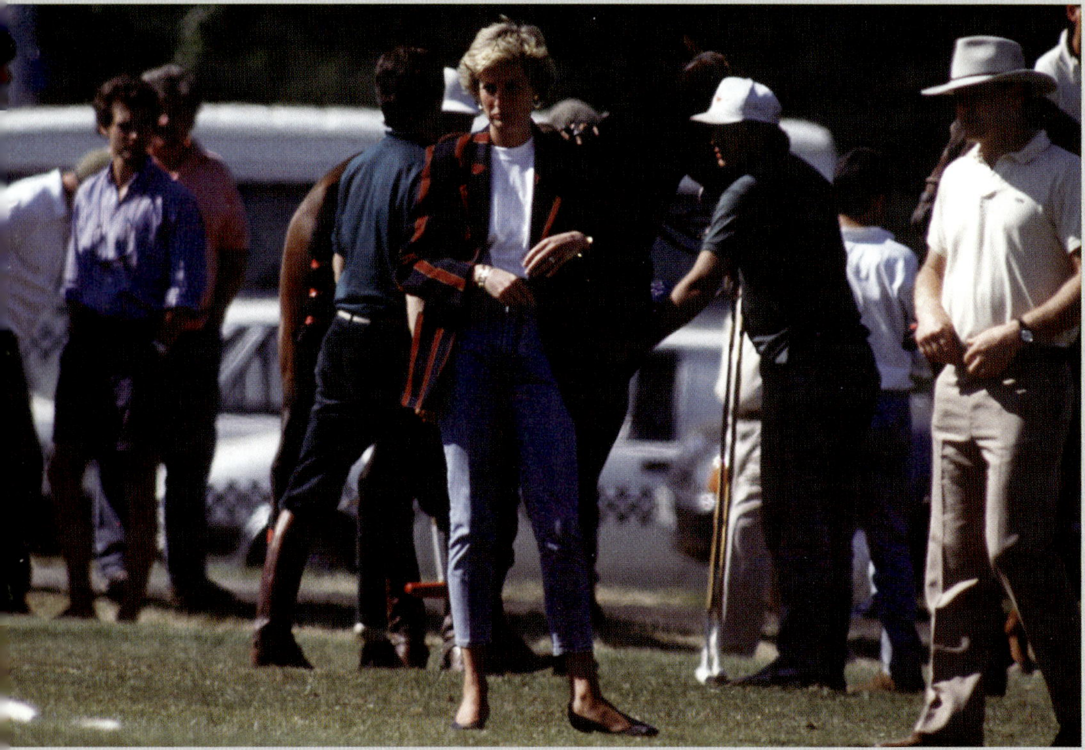

Dressed to kill again at polo. Was anyone looking at the horses?

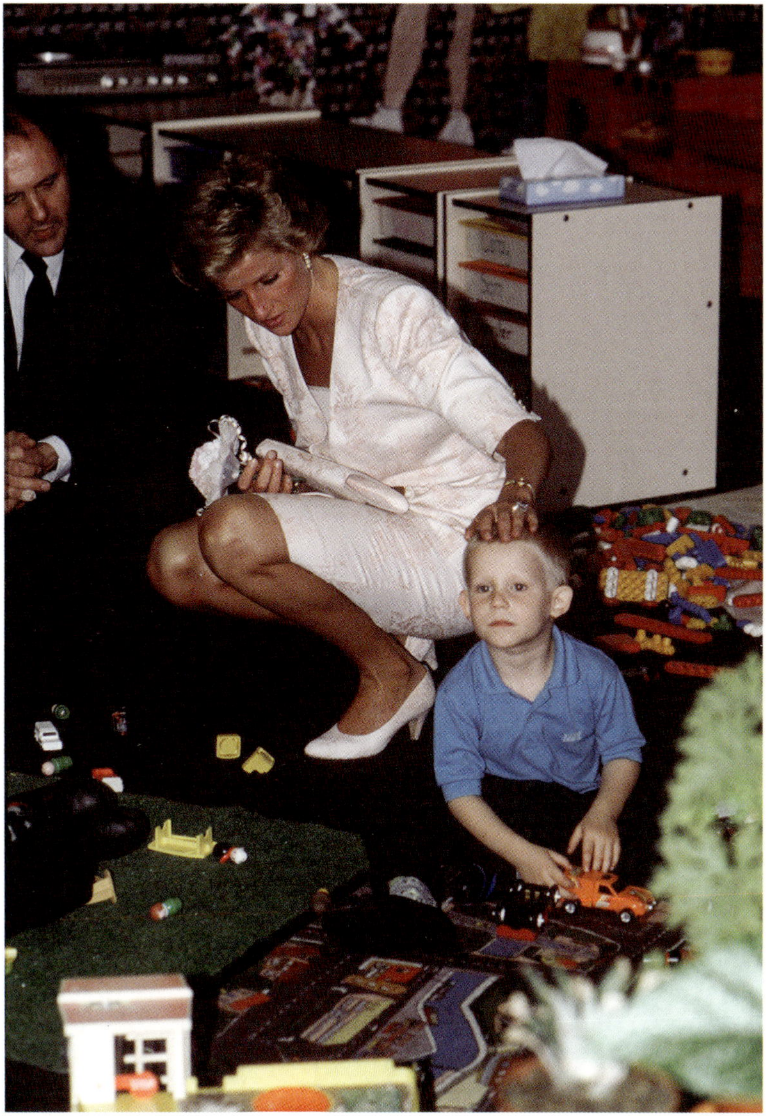

Caring Diana reaching out to a child. No one else in the Royal Family was so completely natural. Caring was second nature to her and totally genuine.

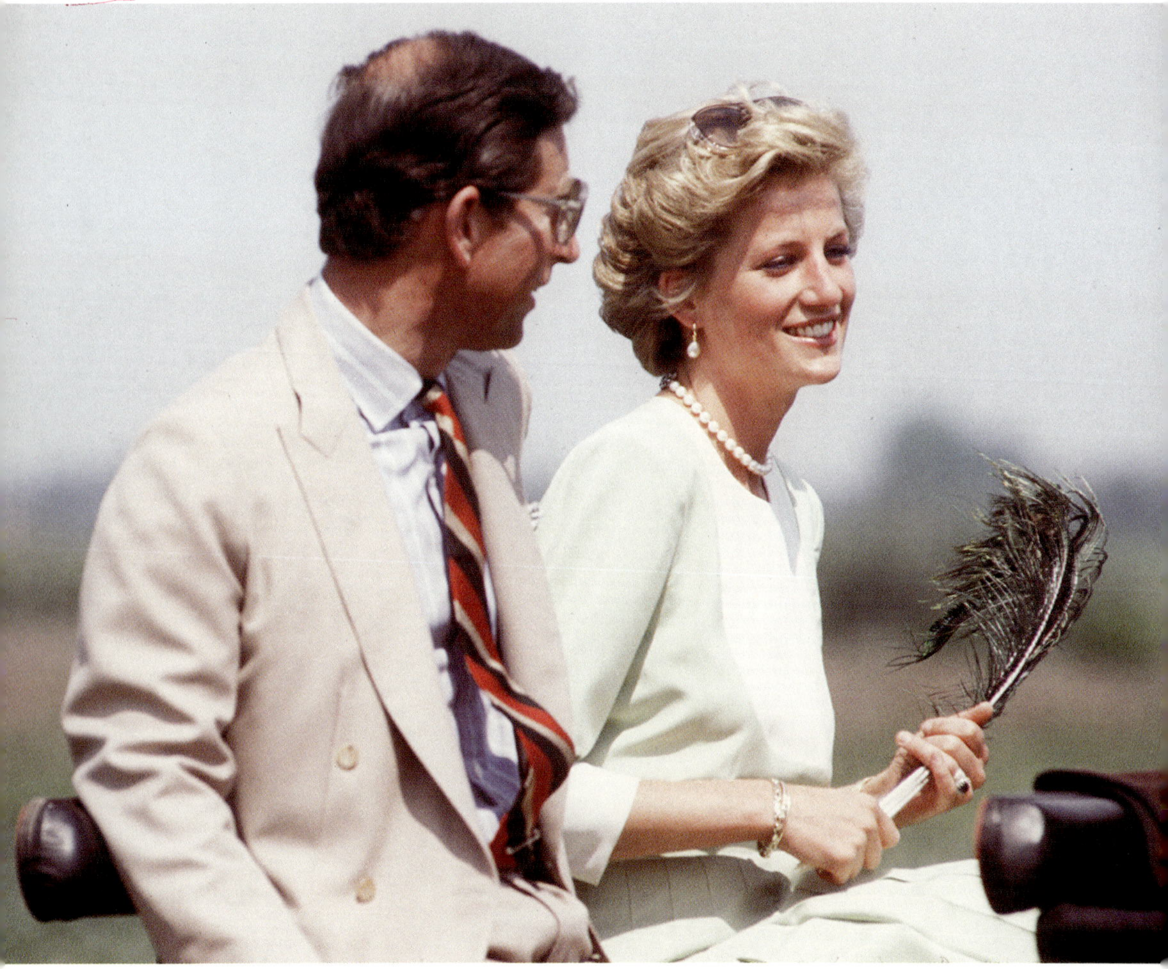

Behind the former Iron Curtain. Diana also became a star of the East the people of Hungary turned out in force for her first visit.

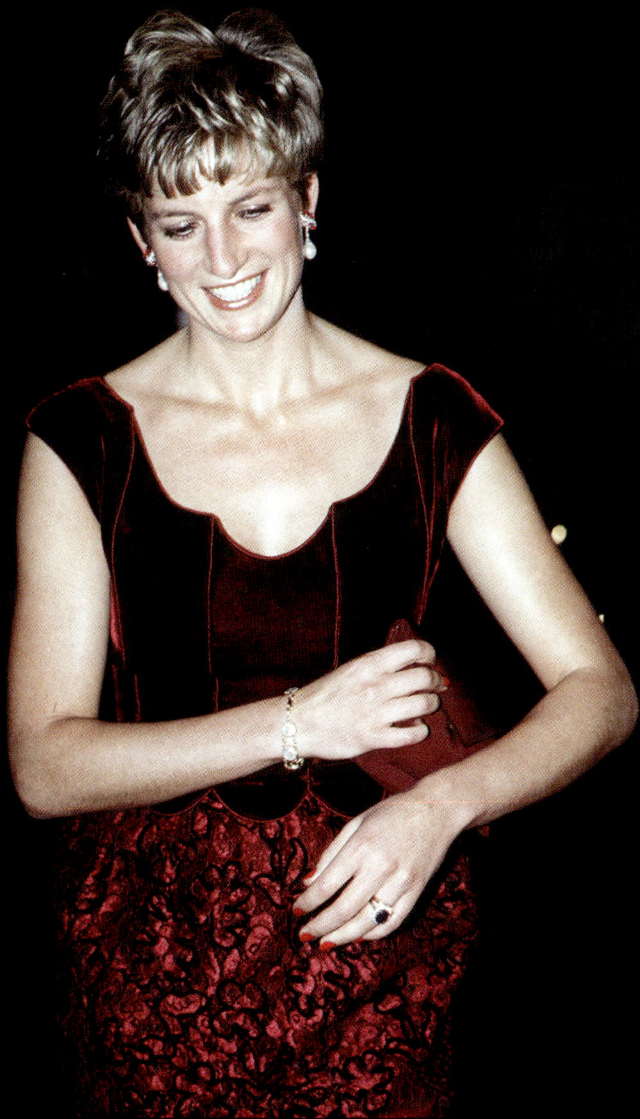

An elegant evening as the star of the show at Her Majestys Theatre in London.

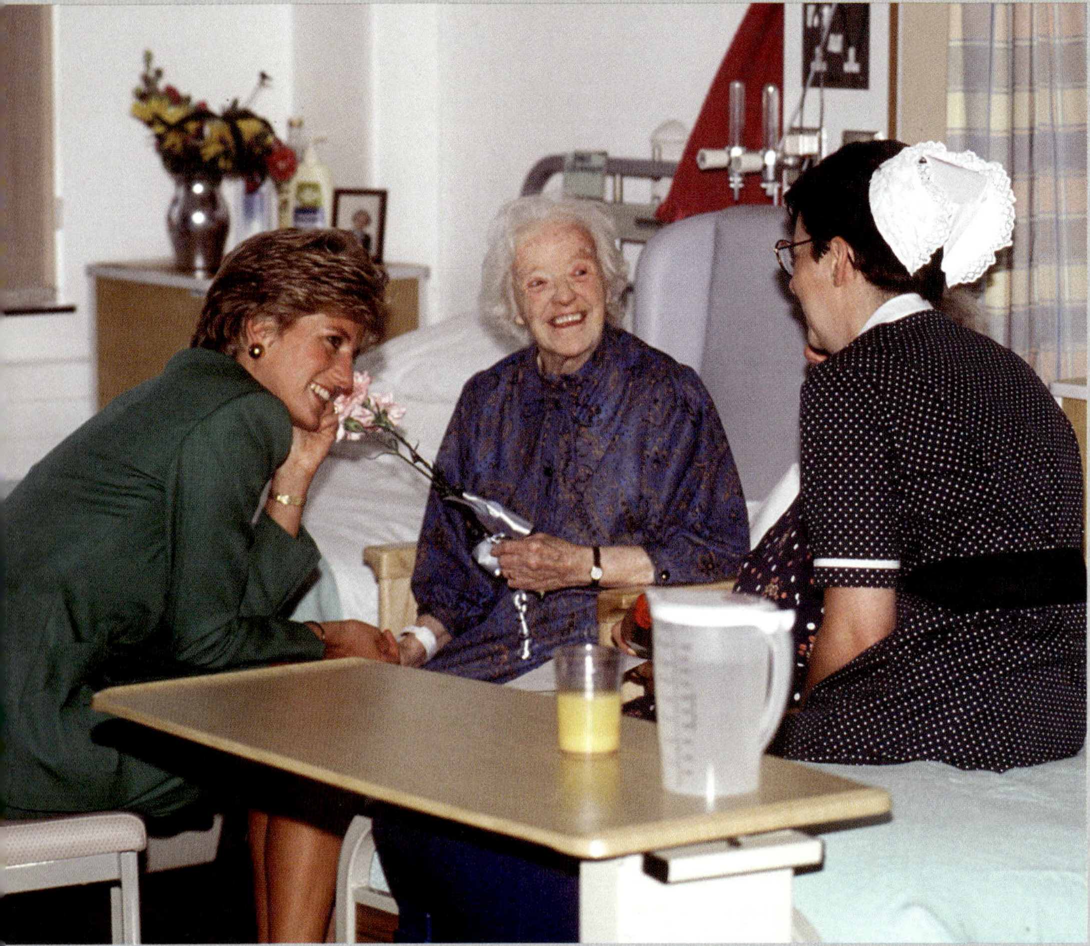

In hospital her bedside manner moved everyone. A doctor said that Diana should be on prescription because she gave every patient a boost.

RIGHT: Garlanded with flowers in Pakistan where rose petals were strewn wherever she walked.

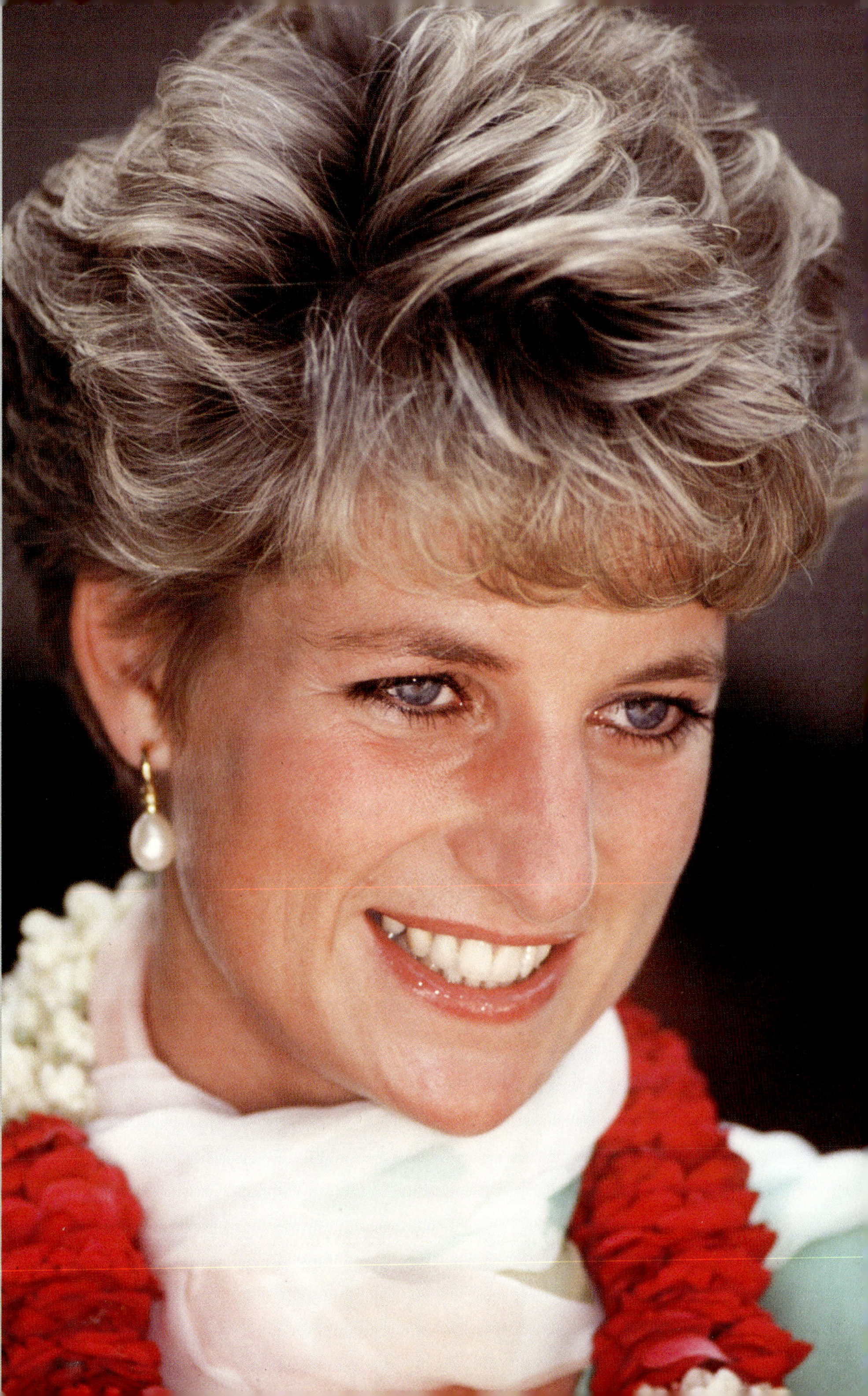

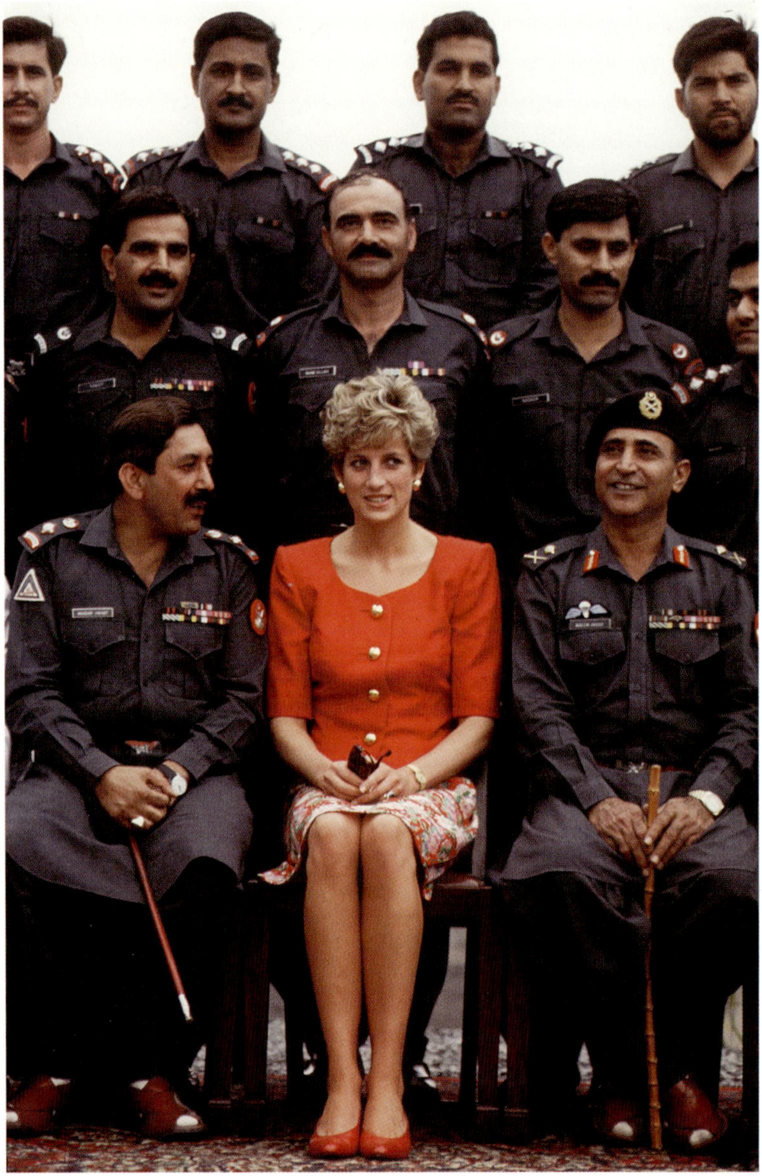

A pin up with the Pakistan Military High Command where the officers acted like little boys in their excitement at meeting Diana.

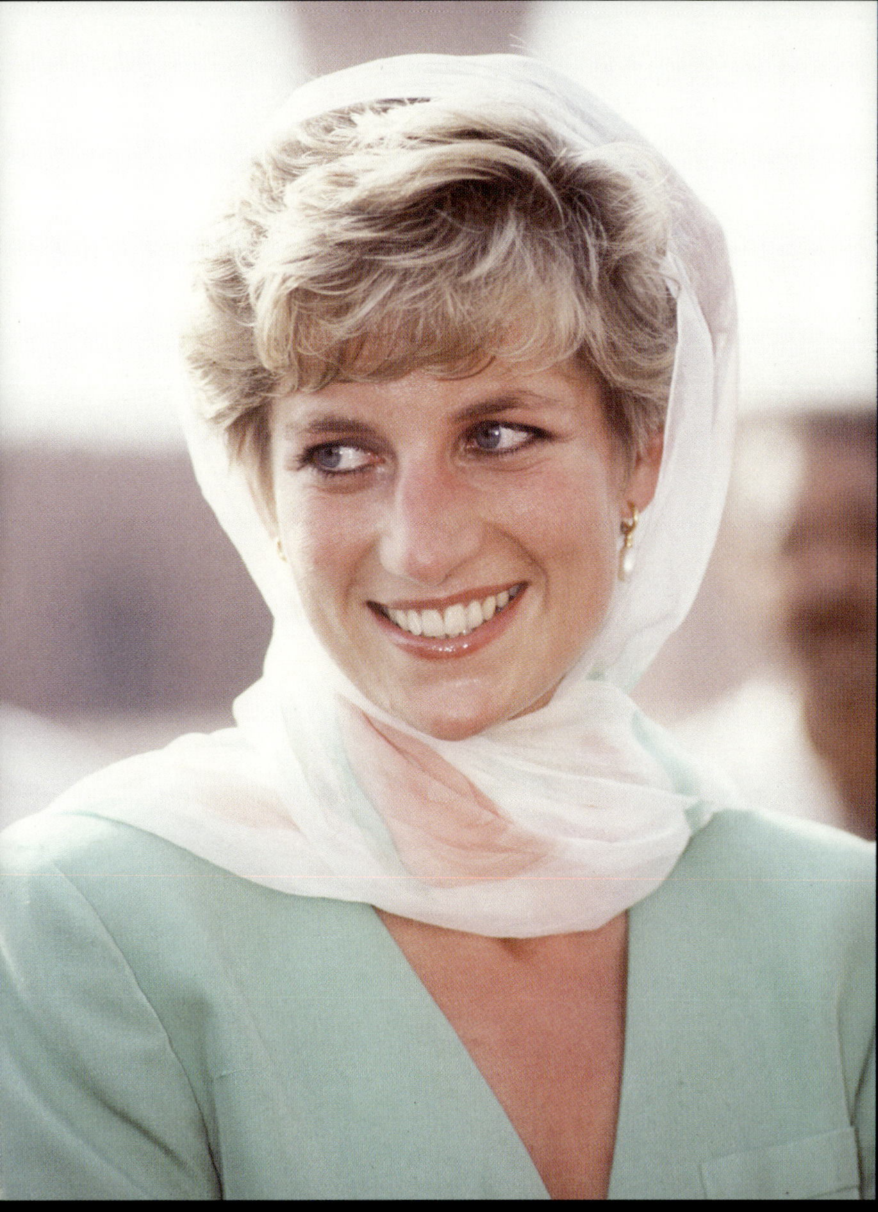

Her blonde hair had to be covered for a religious visit in Pakistan but it only served to frame her beauty.

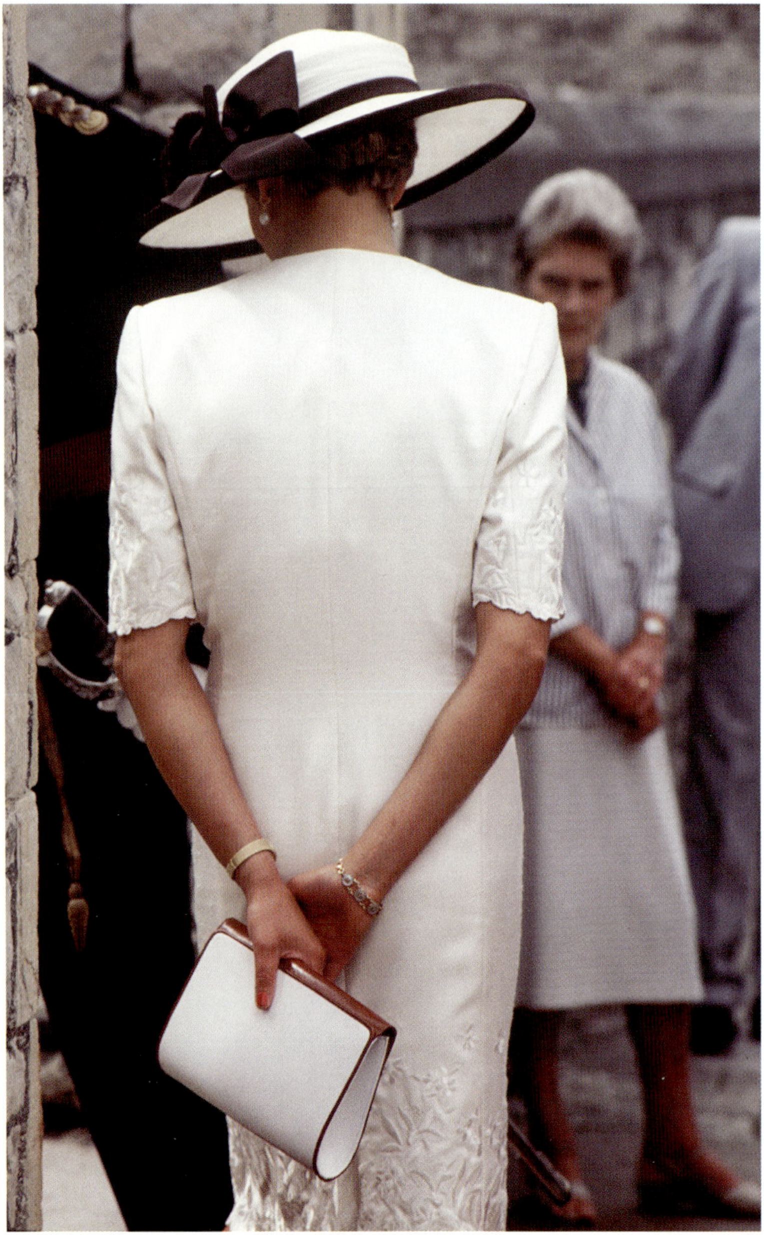

Looking good even from the back, Diana never made a fashion mistake.

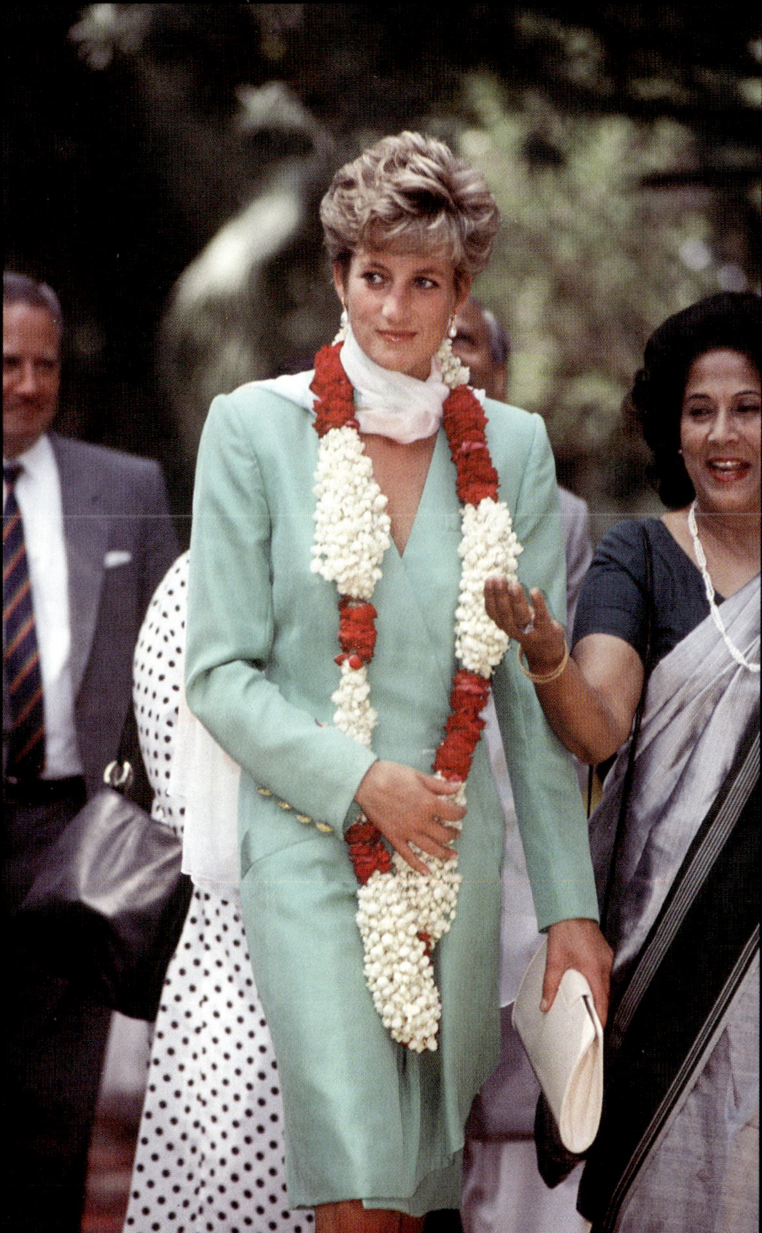

More elegance in Pakistan, a fashion carefully chosen not to offend.

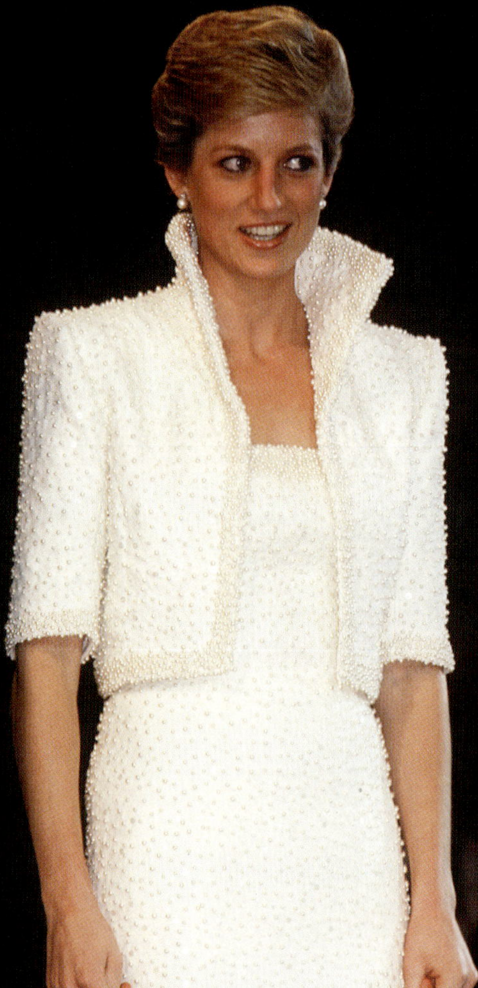

Queen of the Albert Hall fashion awards. She went to present the prizes but became the star of the show.

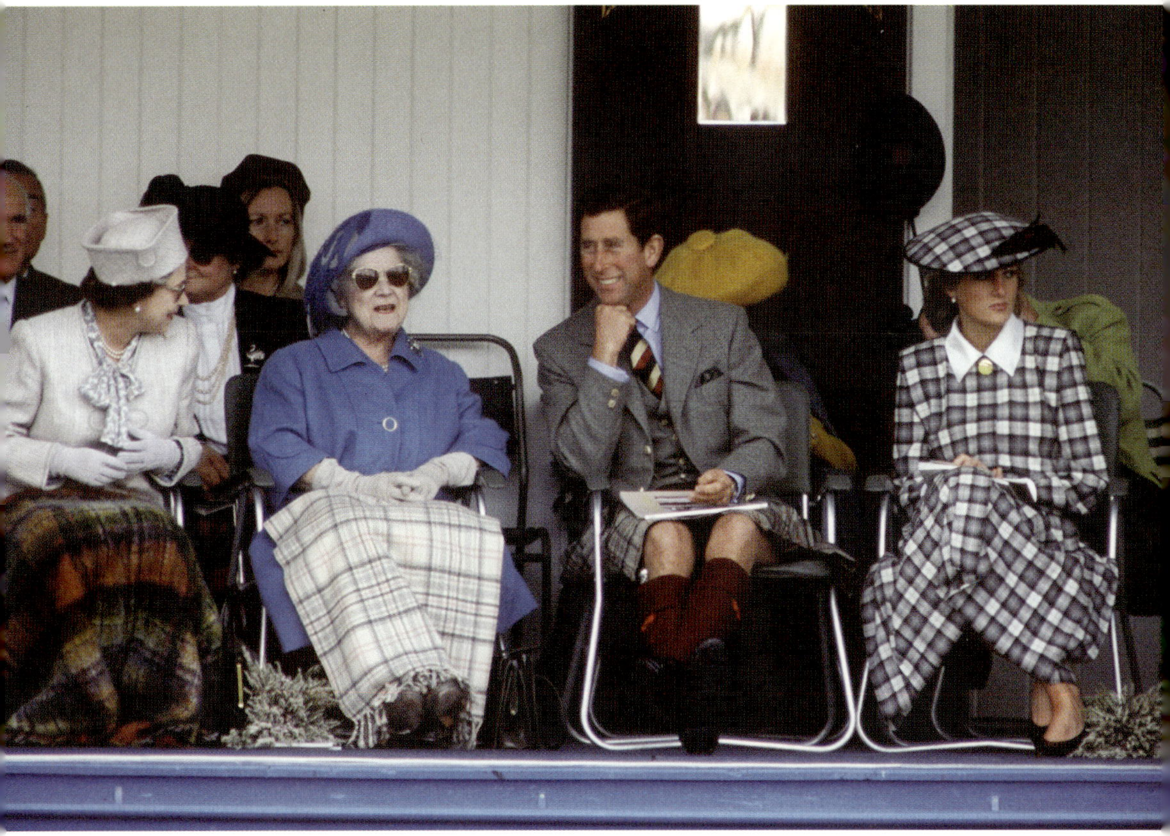

Not her kind of event, freezing but still trying to look happy at the Braemar Highland Gathering. The rest of the Royals loved this event Diana is said to have hated it.

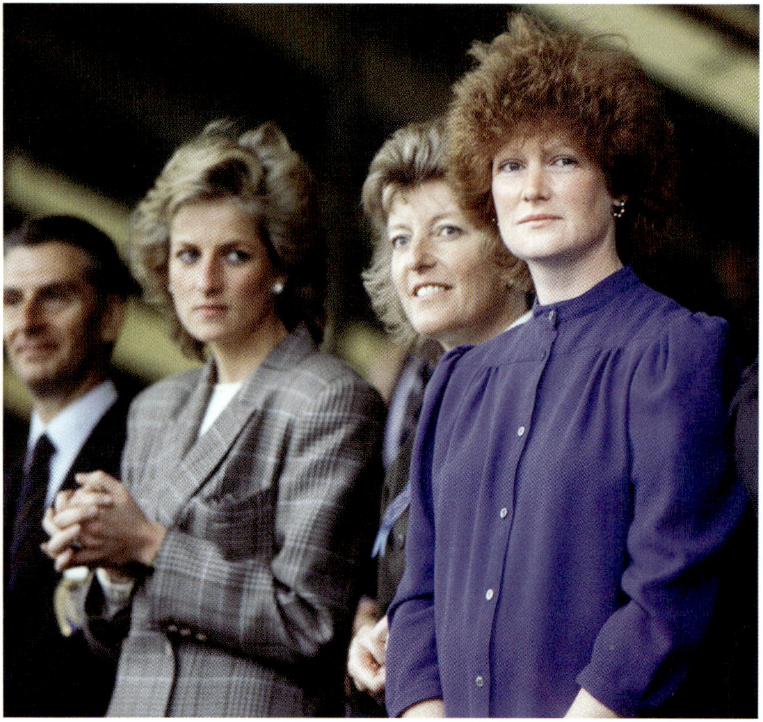

With her favourite sister Sarah at the Windsor Horse Trials, the two had been close all their lives.

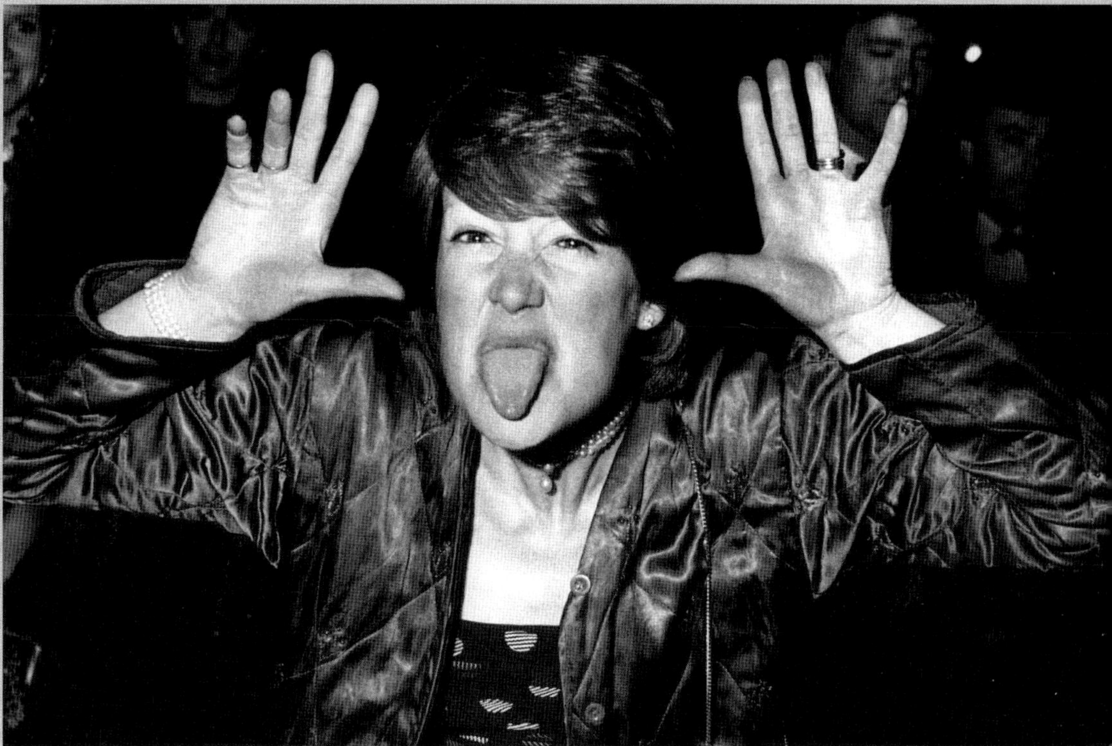

Here's Diana's sister greeting Steve with a cheeky face.

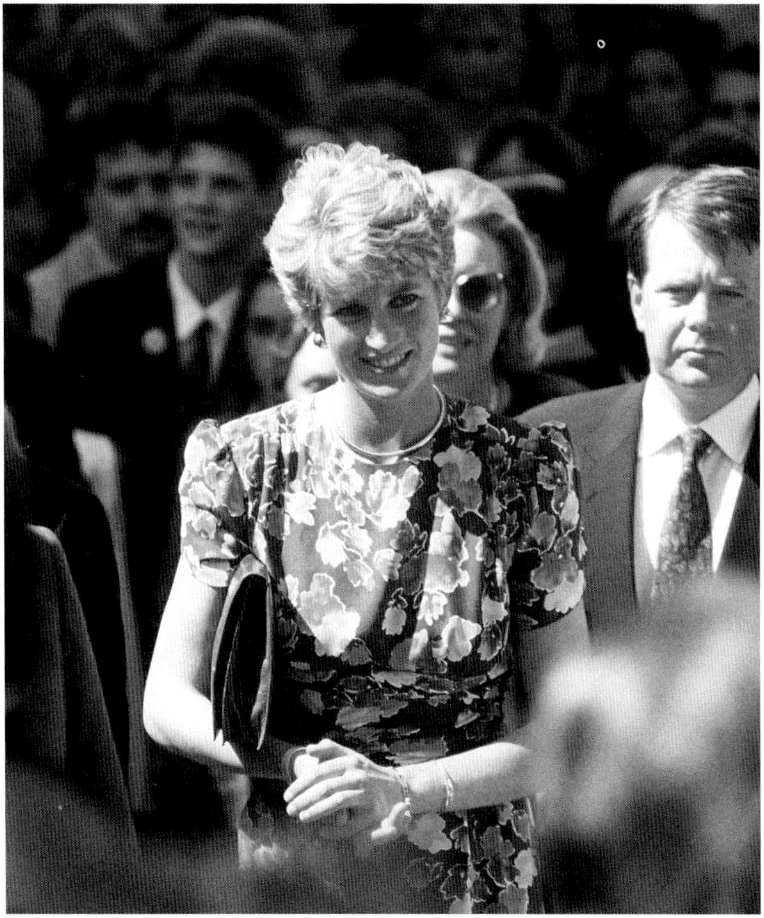

Standing out in the crowd even among the most colourful people in the world the Brazilians, in Rio where they went mad for Diana.

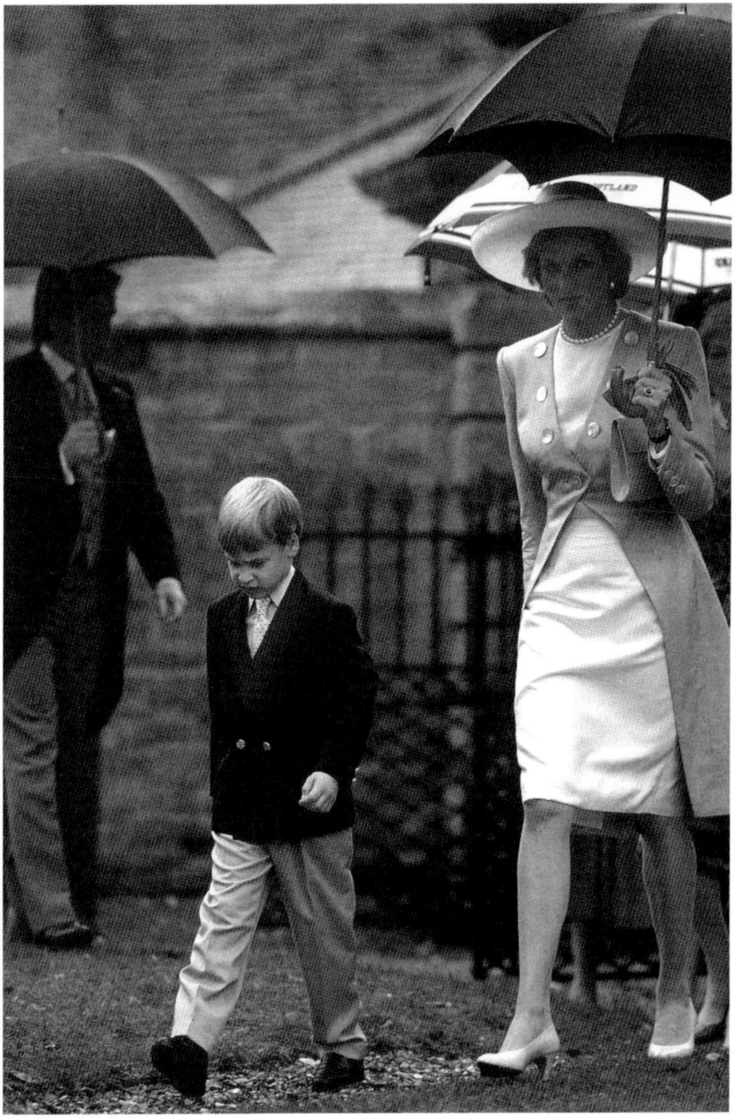

In the rain with William at the ceremony for her brother, Earl Spencer's first wedding.

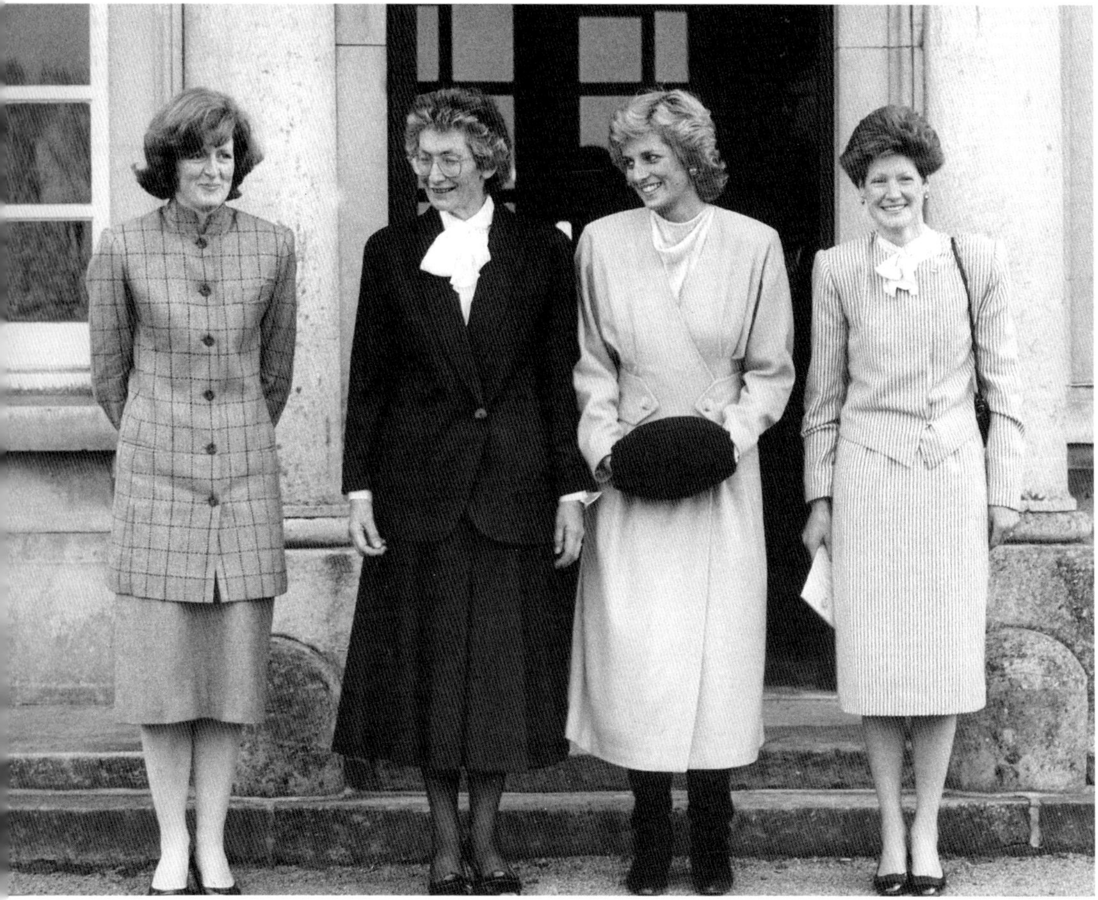

With sisters Sarah and Jane at their old school Riddlesworth Hall.

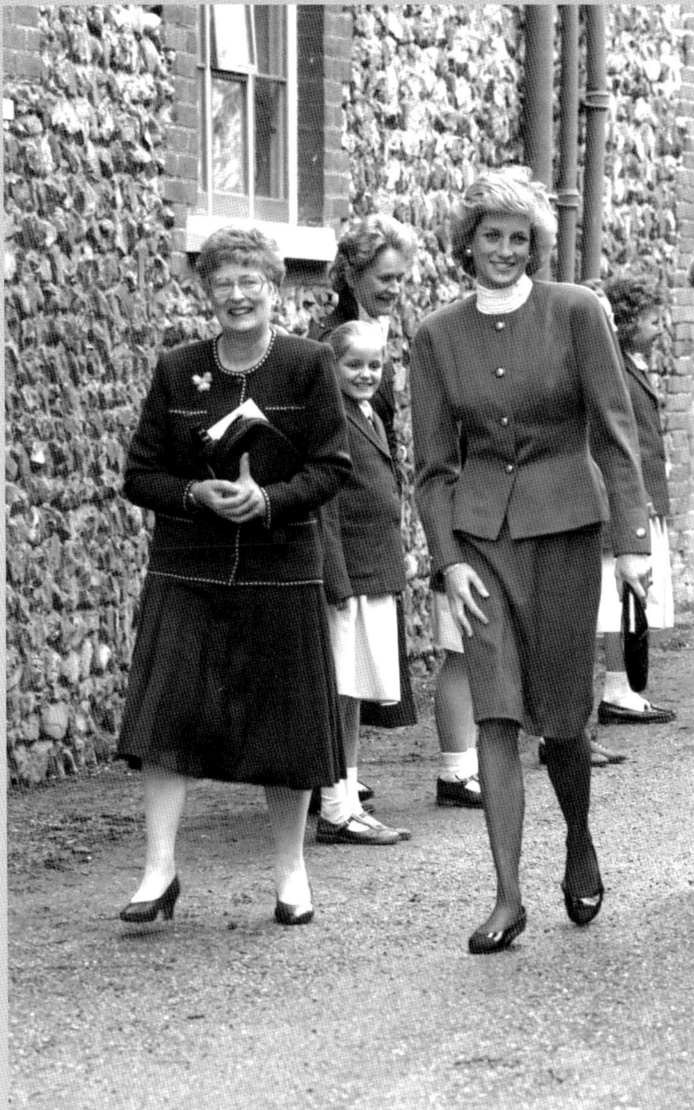

Diana was invited back to her old school Riddlesworth Hall as the most famous old girl.

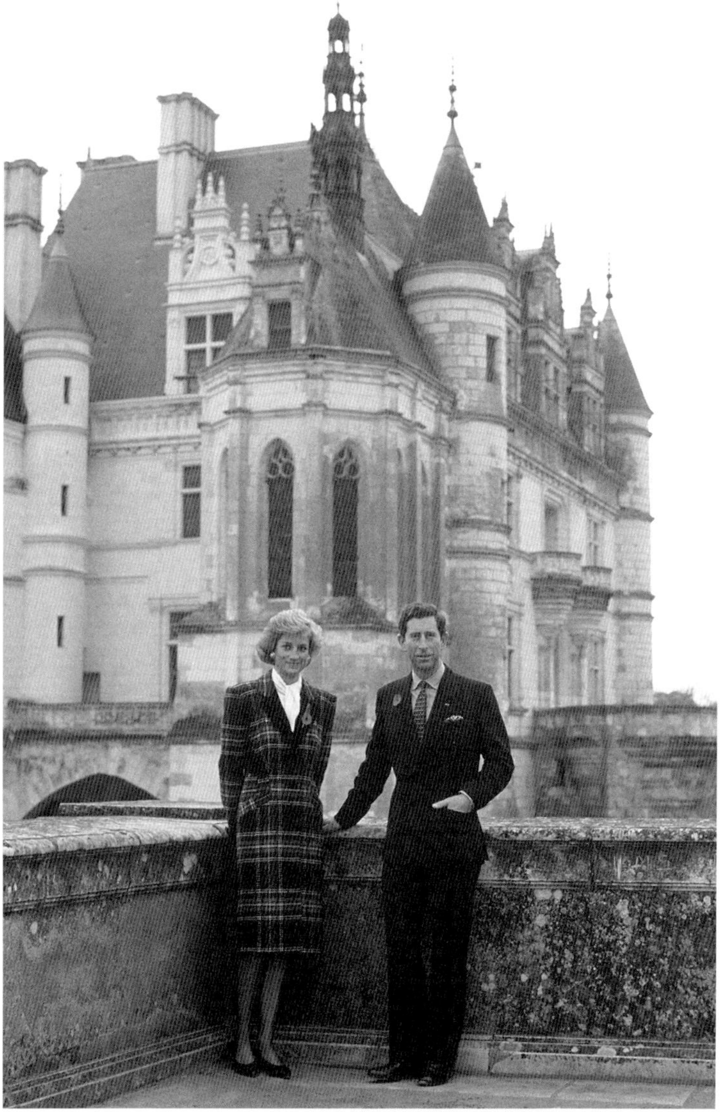

Posing like a couple of tourists again, this time outside an imposing French Chateaux in the Loire.

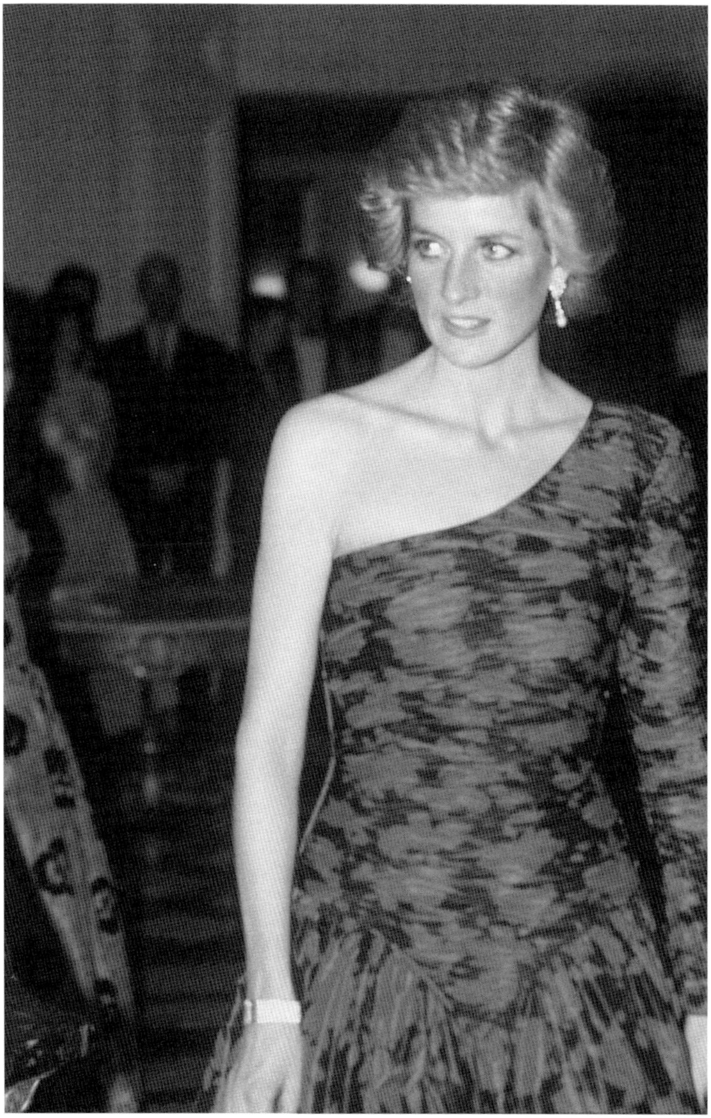

Serious glamour with a daring off the shoulder red dress at a glittering London engagement.

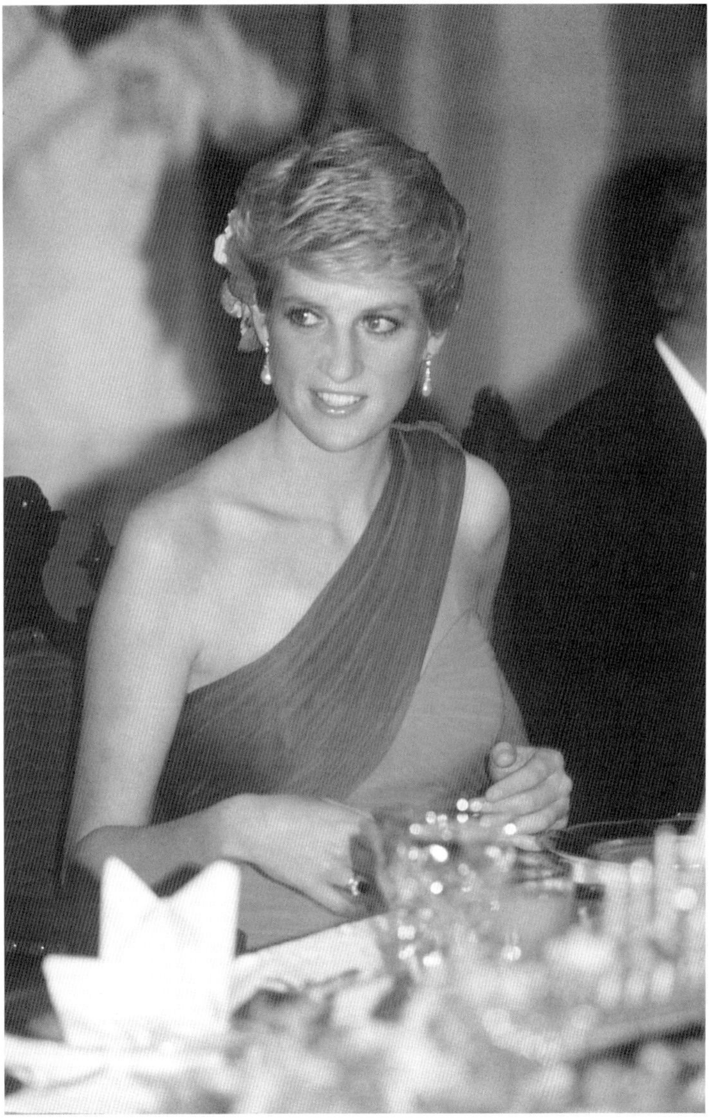

Bare armed and sensational at a banquet in Thailand and where the local press clamoured for every single detail of her clothes which were immediately copied in every back street tailor shop.

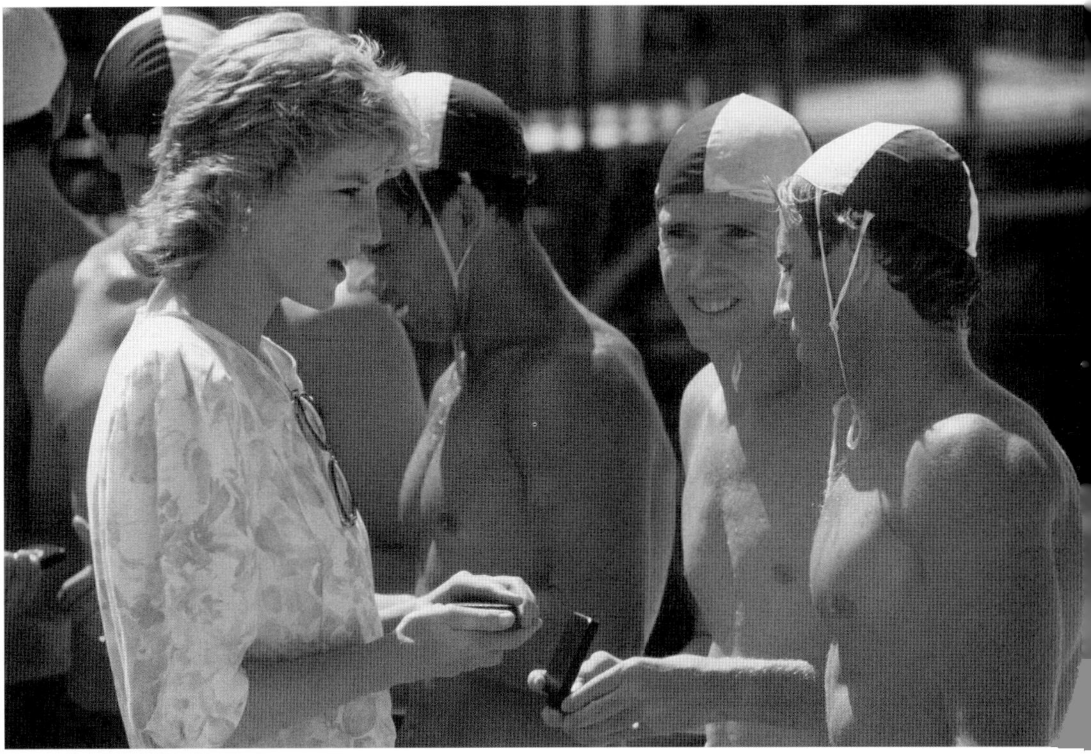

Diana loved this afternoon. She was on Bondi Beach in Sydney admiring the tanned, muscle bound life guards in their tiny speedos.

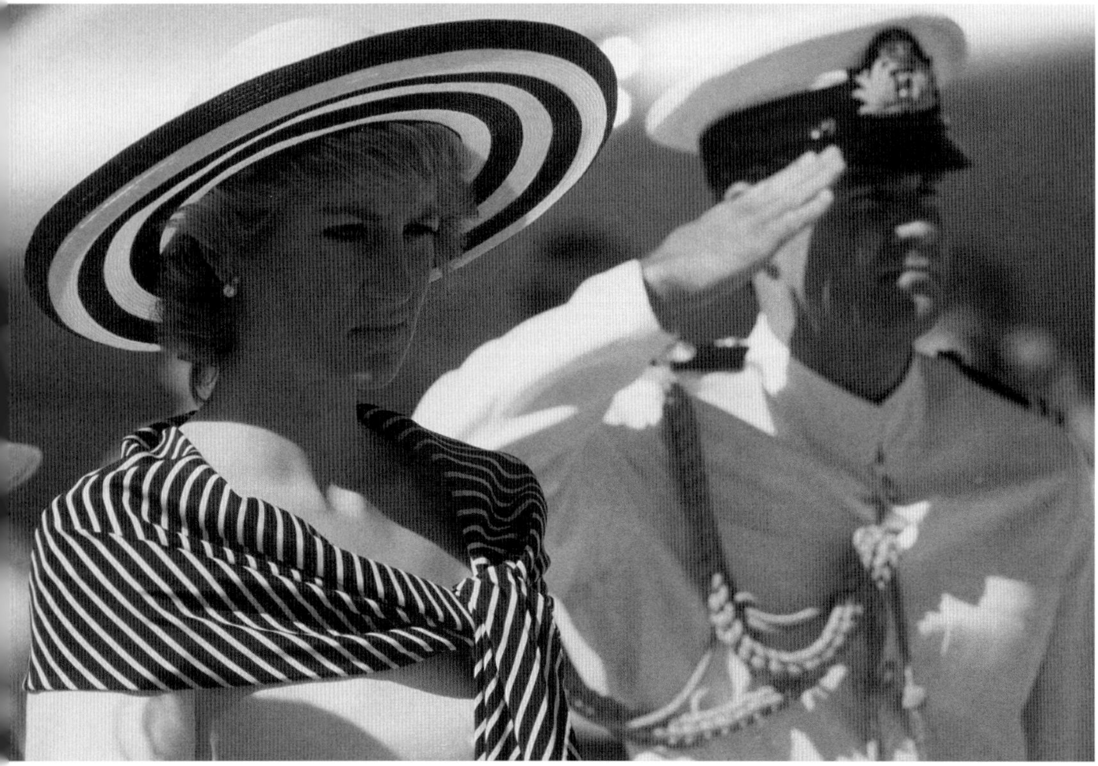

The hat the Aussie press called a 'Flying Frisbee' but the Princess still managed to turn it into a fashion success.

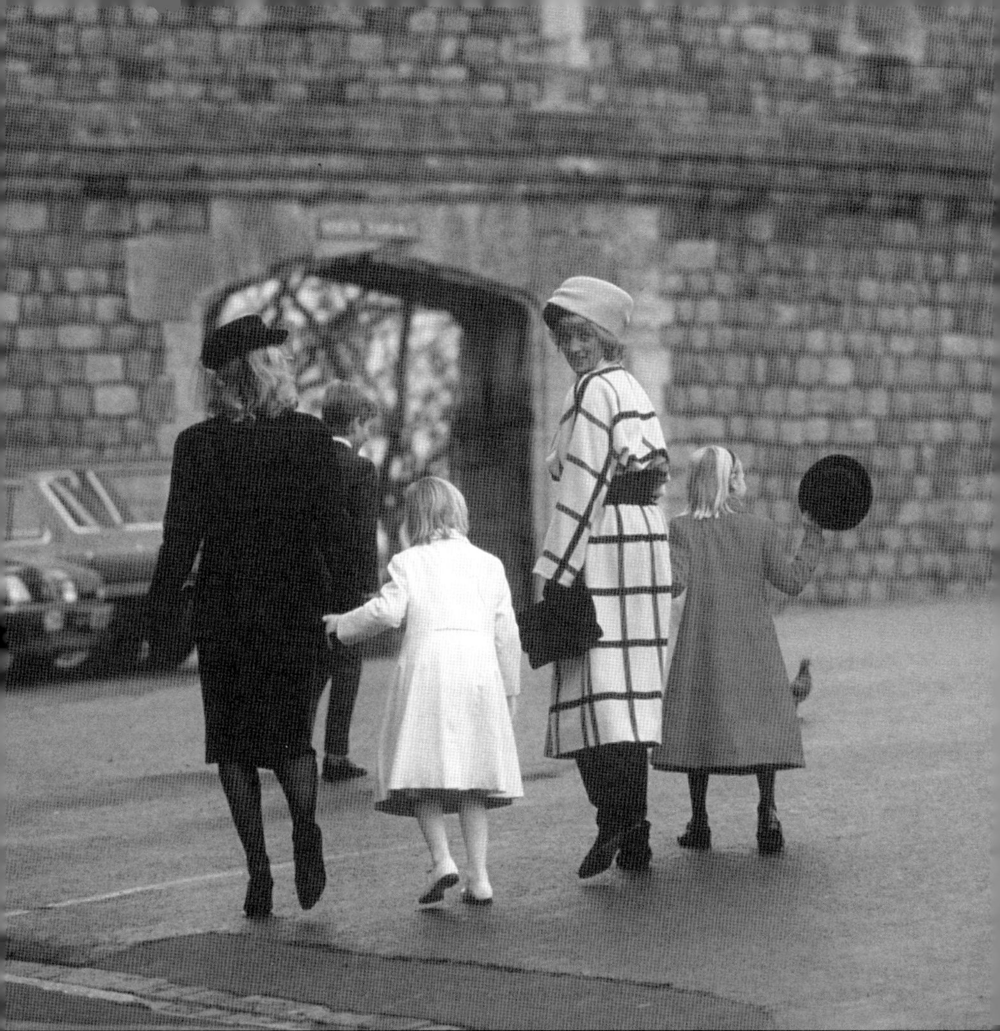

Winter in Windsor and the Princess can't resist one final look back at the camera before going into the lunch with the rest of the Royal family.

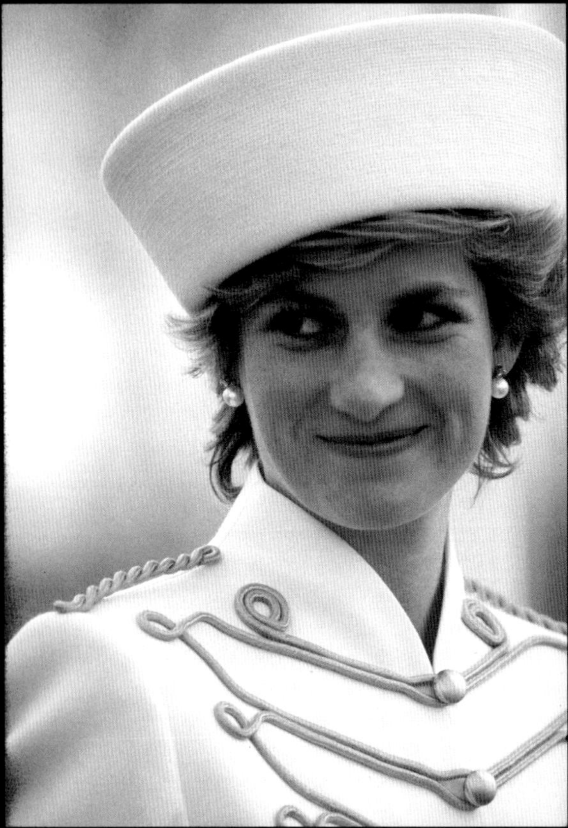

She caused a sensation turning up for a parade at Sandhurst military academy looking like a drum majorette in a braided coat and pill box hat.

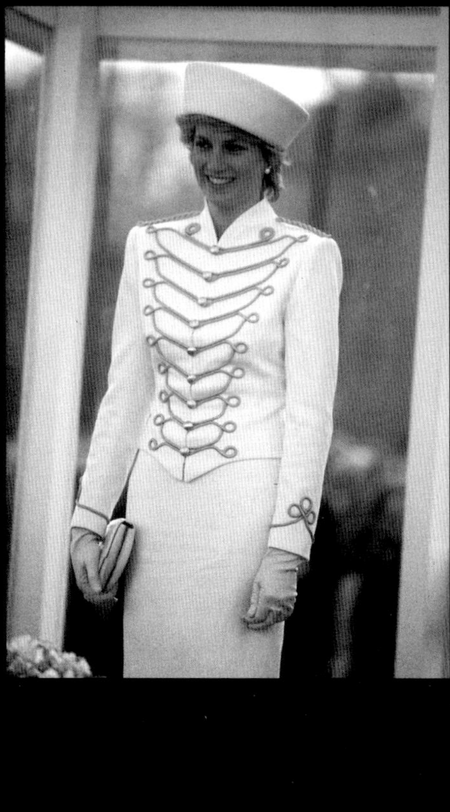

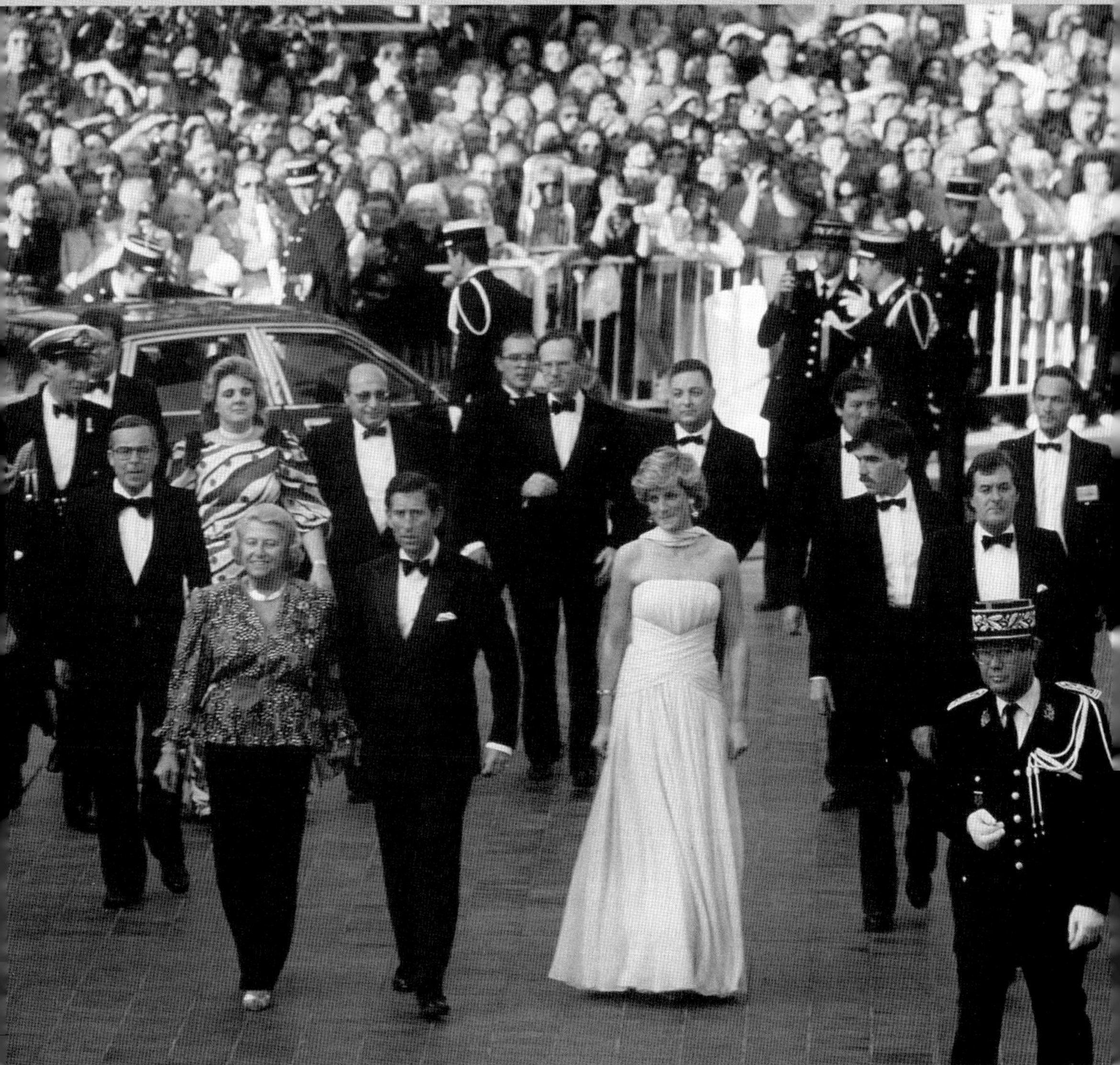

Centre stage at the Cannes Film Festival, bigger than any Hollywood star.

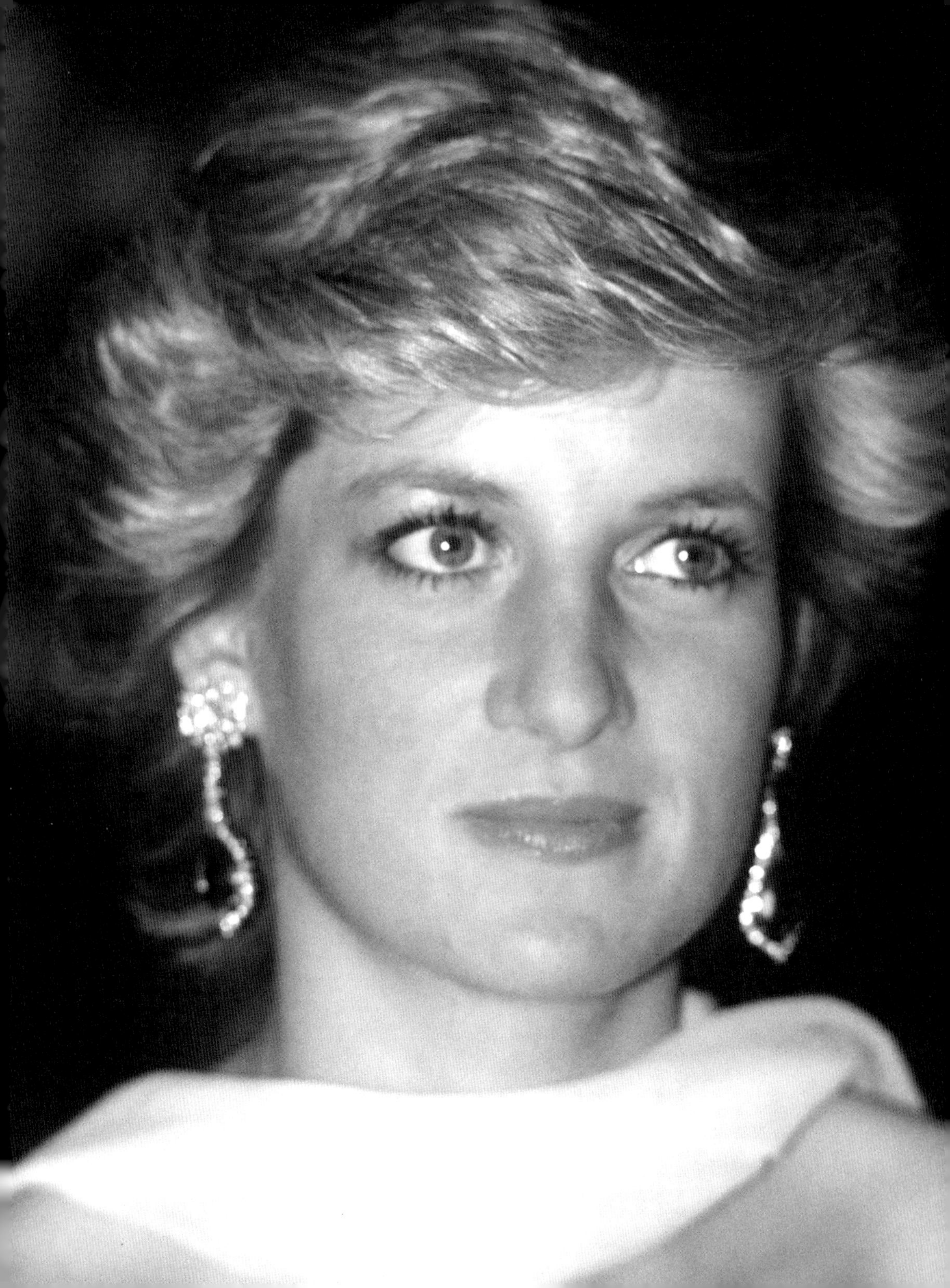

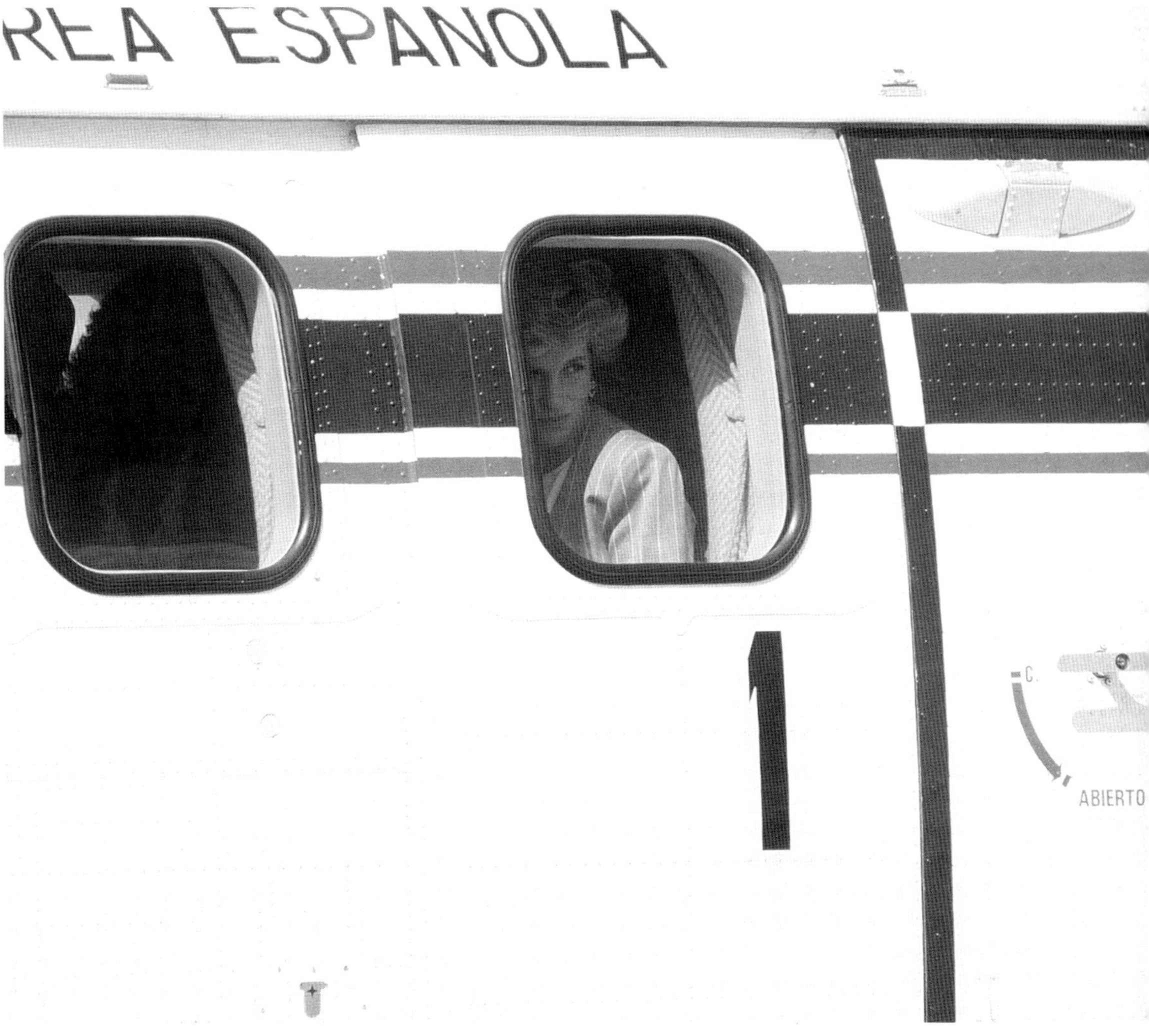

A pensive look from the window of a helicopter in Spain , just before take off. Perhaps it was because Charles (a qualified pilot) was at the controls.

LEFT: Looking fantastic in Cannes. Out glitzing the stars in dazzling sapphires and huge pearl and diamond earings.

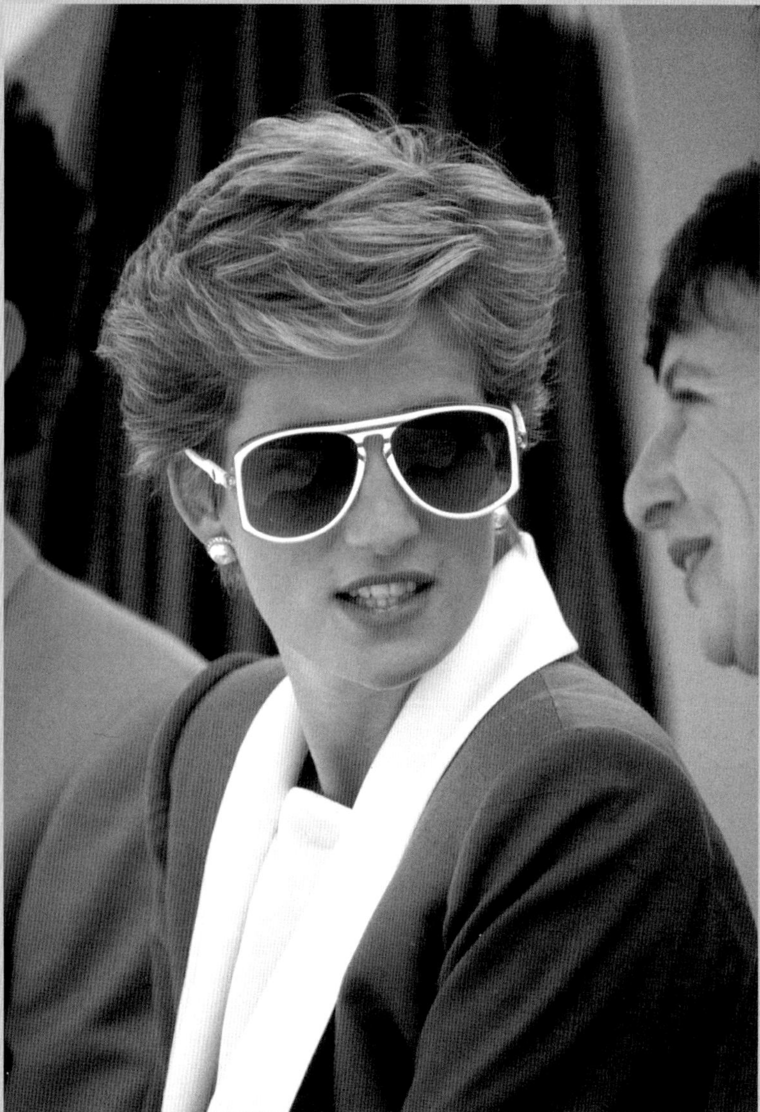

Hiding behind giant sun glasses in Doha, making another fashion statement quickly copied all over Europe.

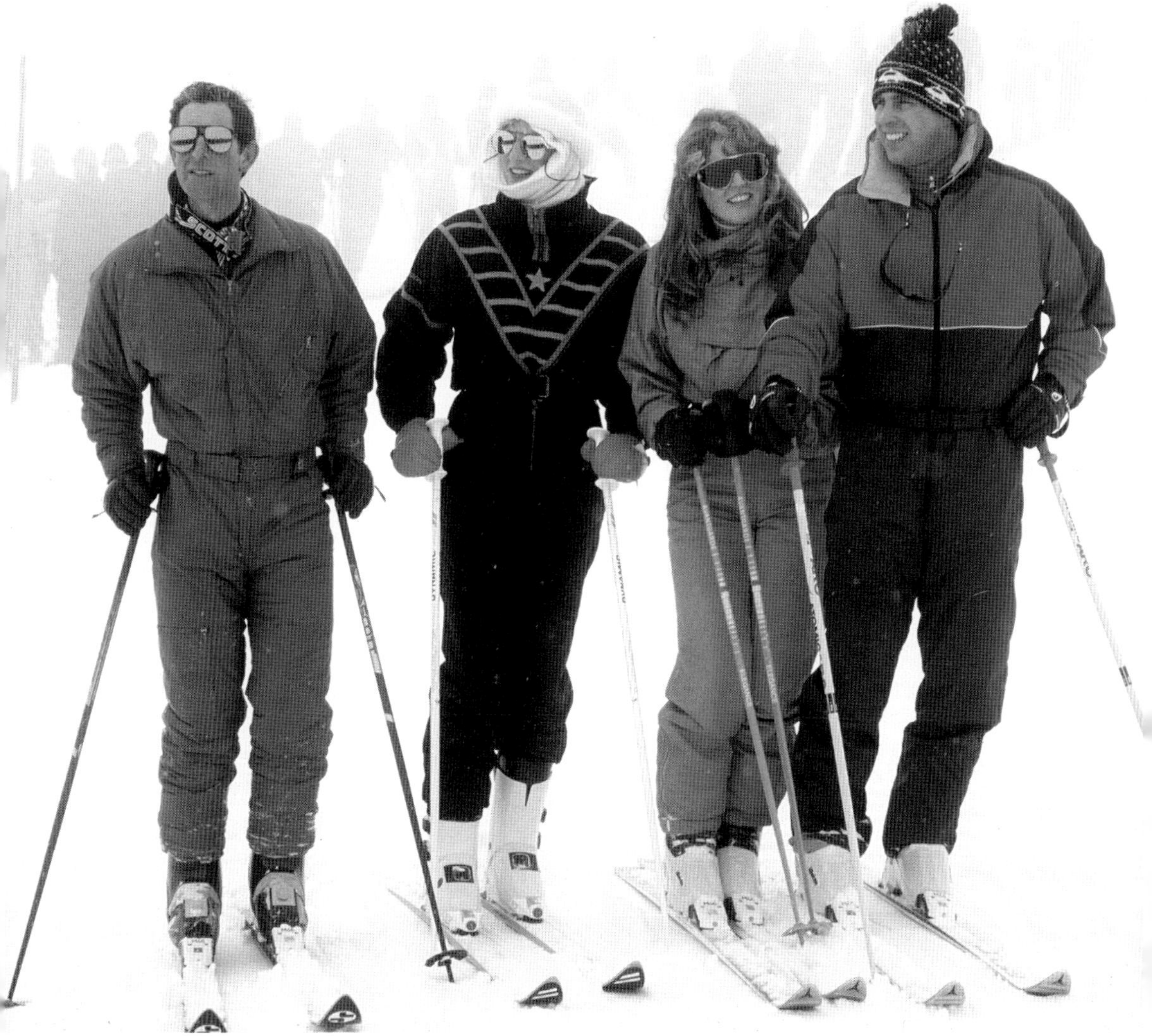

Charles, Diana, Fergie and Andrew, the young Royal skiers in a snowstorm at Klosters in Switzerland posing for the cameras all in trendy one piece ski suits.

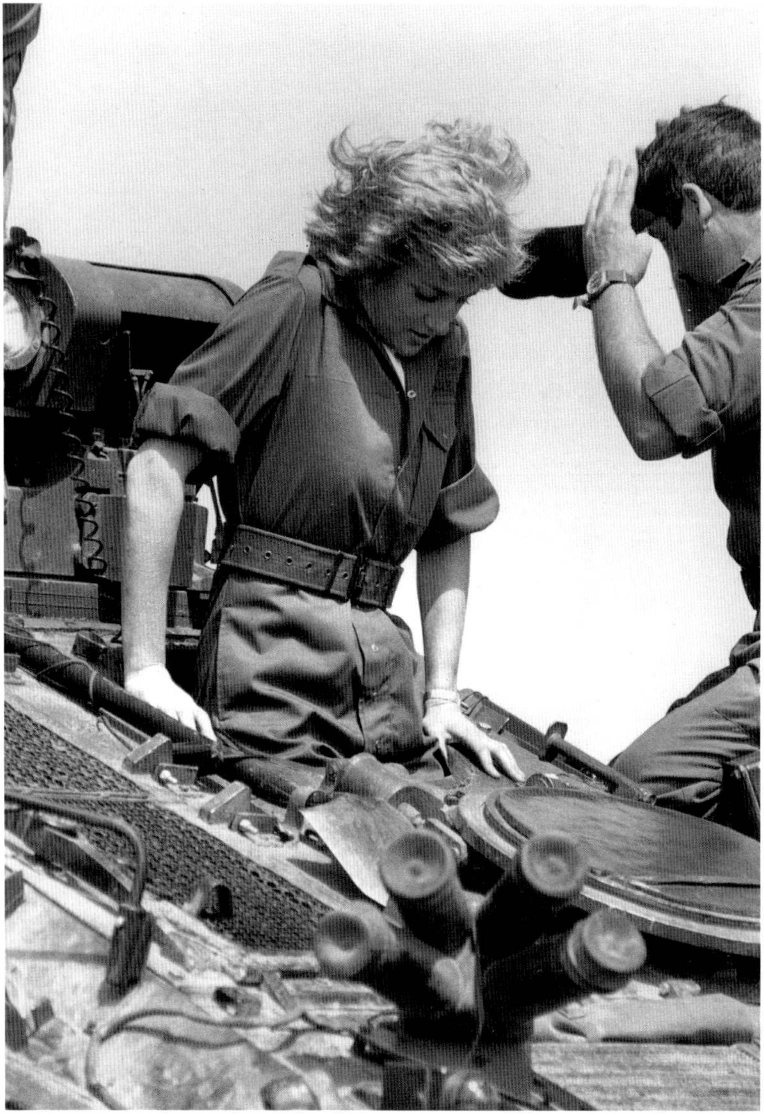

Tanks for the memory, Diana drives an armoured vehicle at an army base and still manages to look good in green overalls.

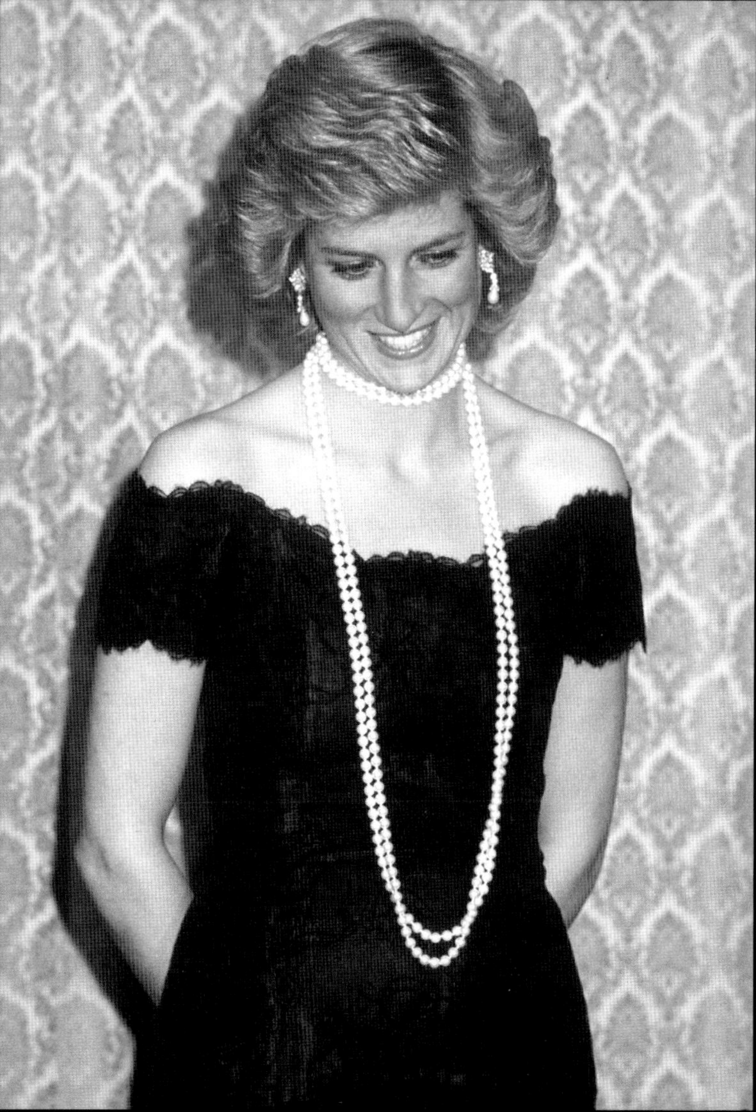

In Germany wearing a simple black dress but highlighting the outfit with a huge double row of pearls (real of course) copied by millions of women all over the world in the following months.

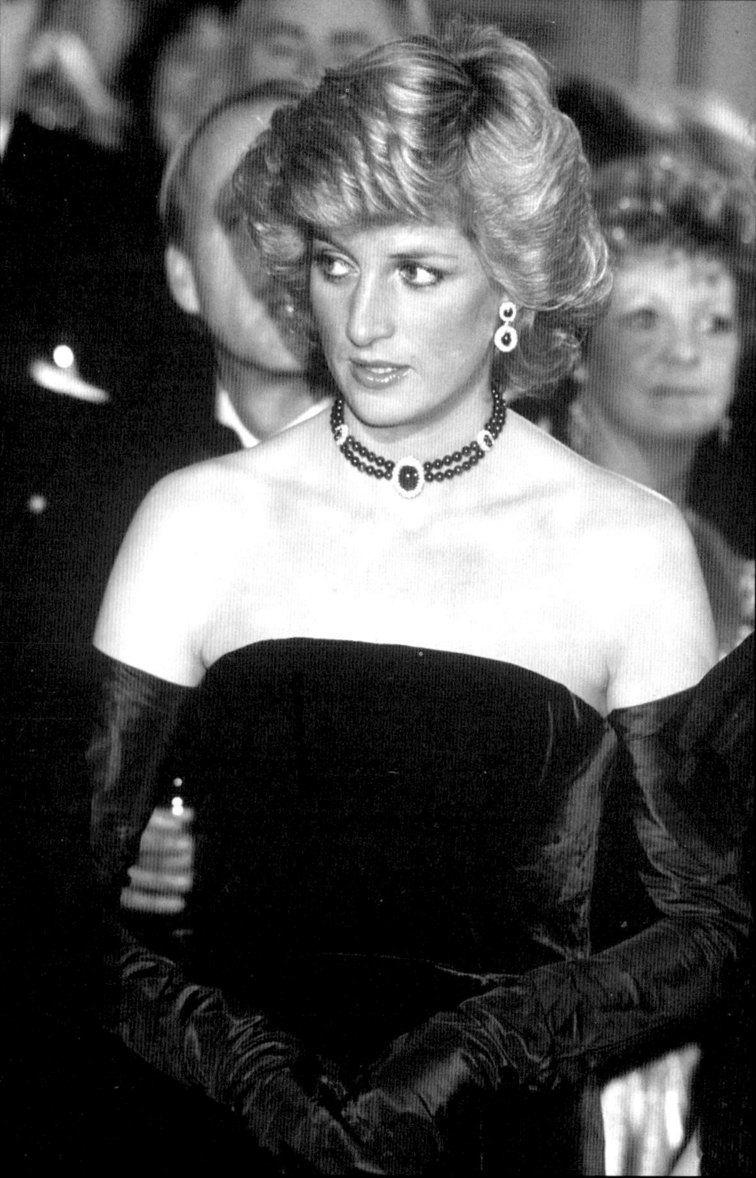

A very sexy black choker studded with pearls. What an eyeful. Instantly the choker was back in fashion.

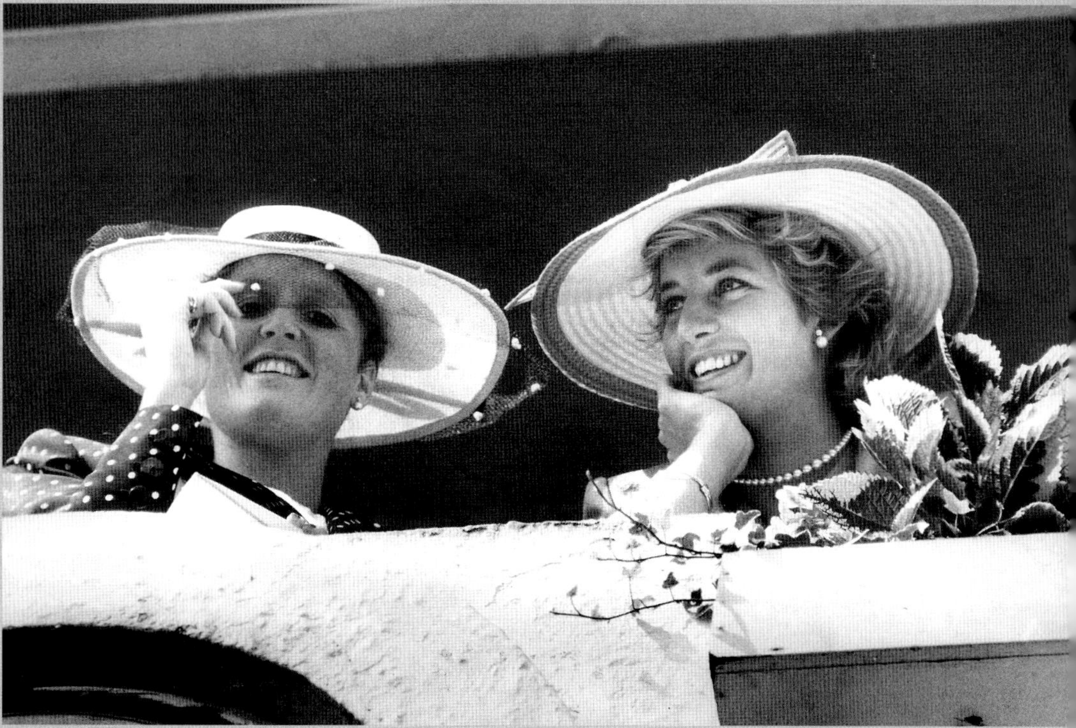

At the 1987 Royal Derby at Epsom, a quiet moment with her friend the Duchess of York.

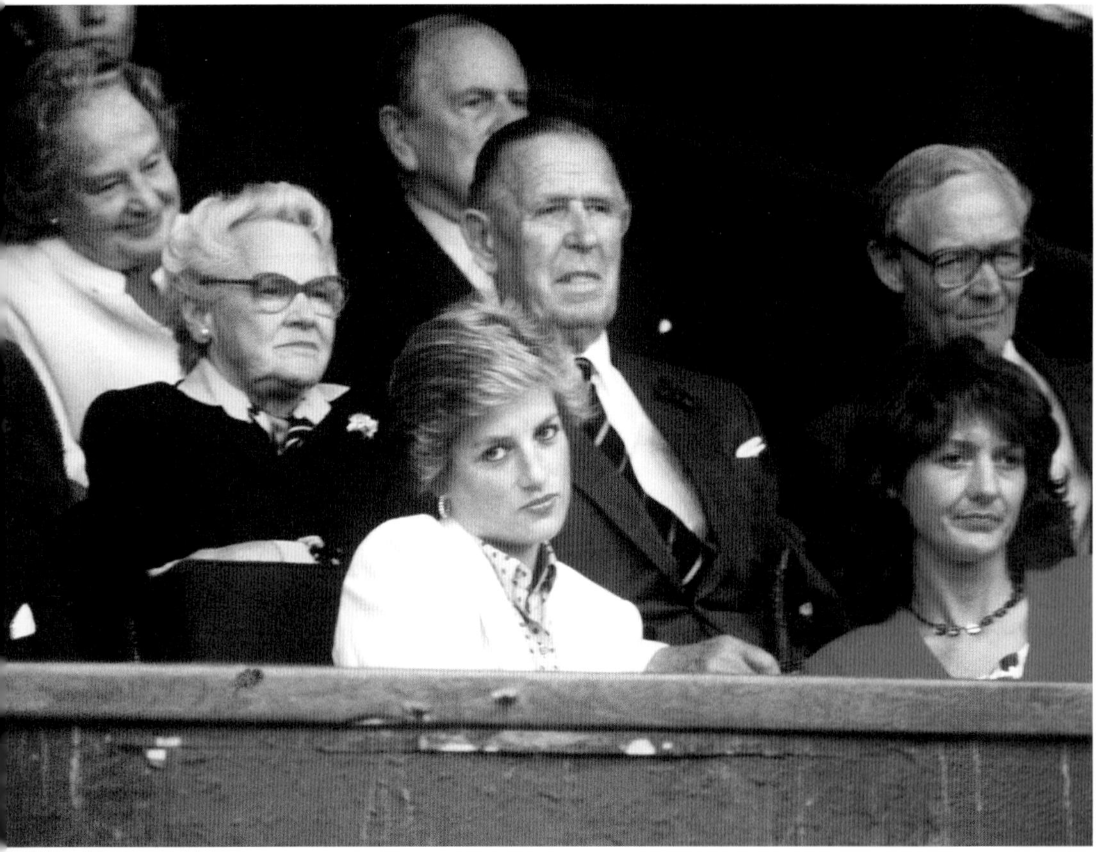

In the Royal Box at Wimbledon looking bored between sets.

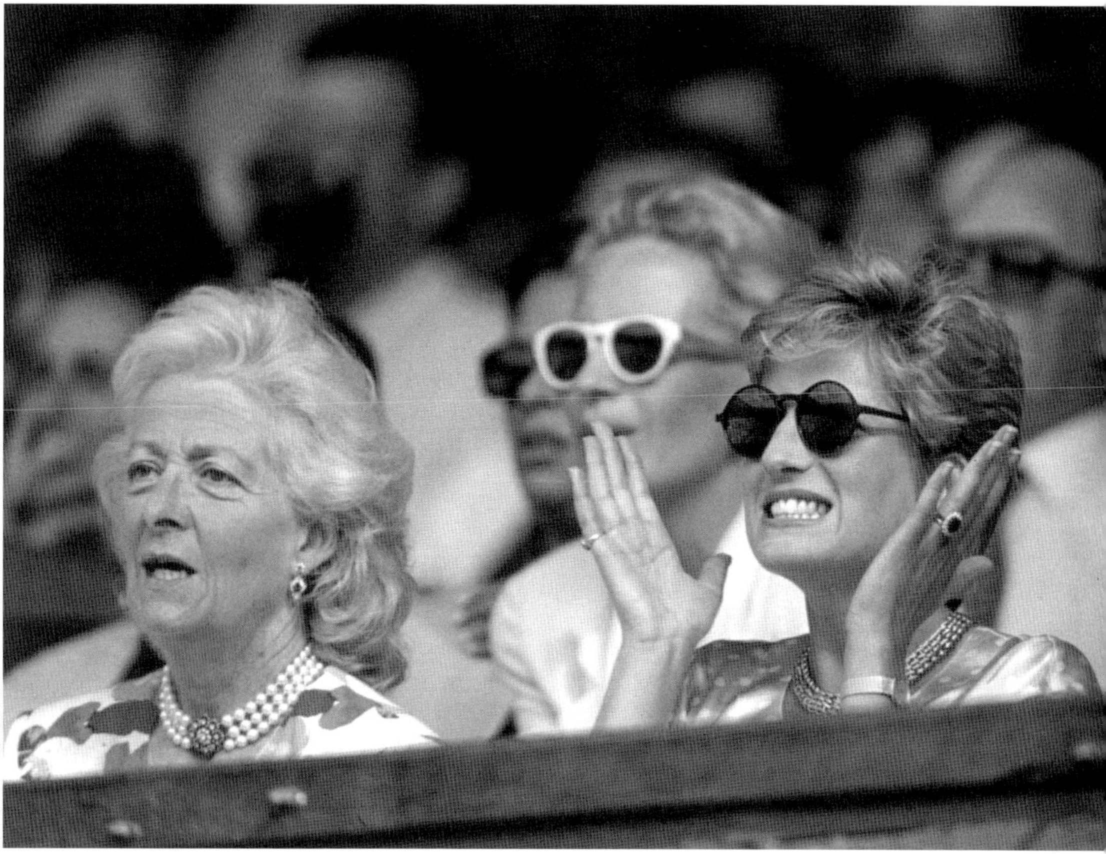

Diana at Wimbledon in happier times with mother Frances Shand Kydd

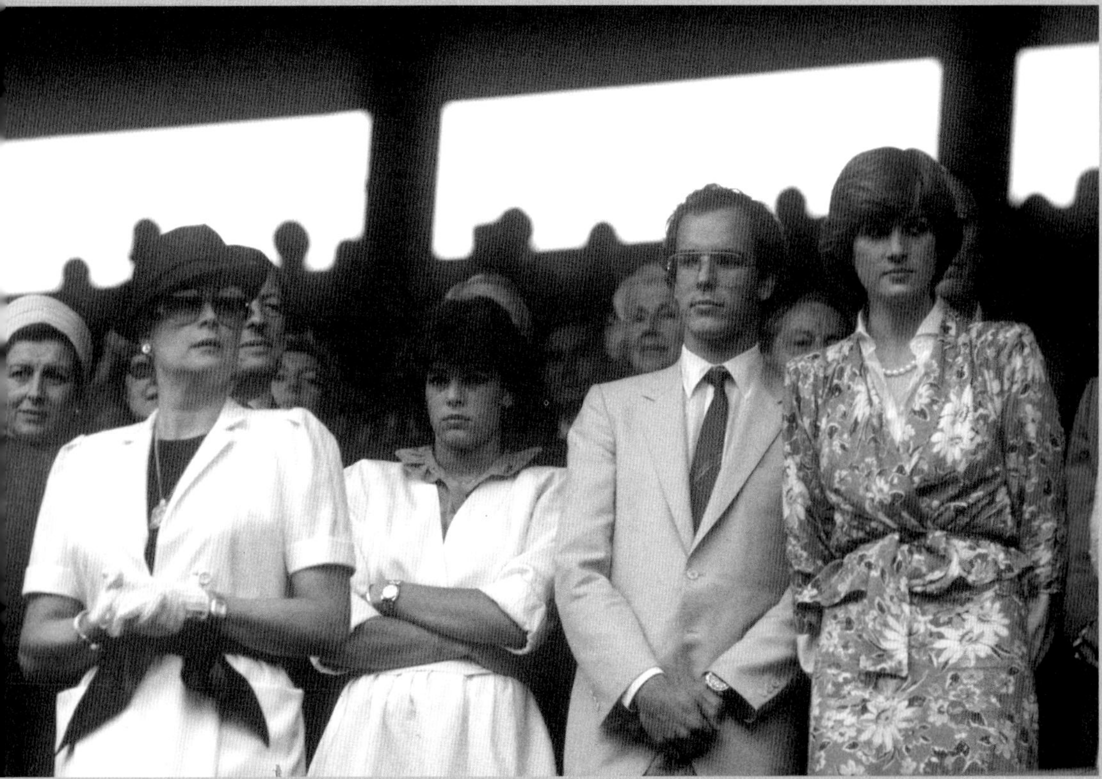

In the box at Wimbledon with former film star Grace Kelly who ironically died in a mysterious car accident. Also there Princess Stephanie and Prince Albert.

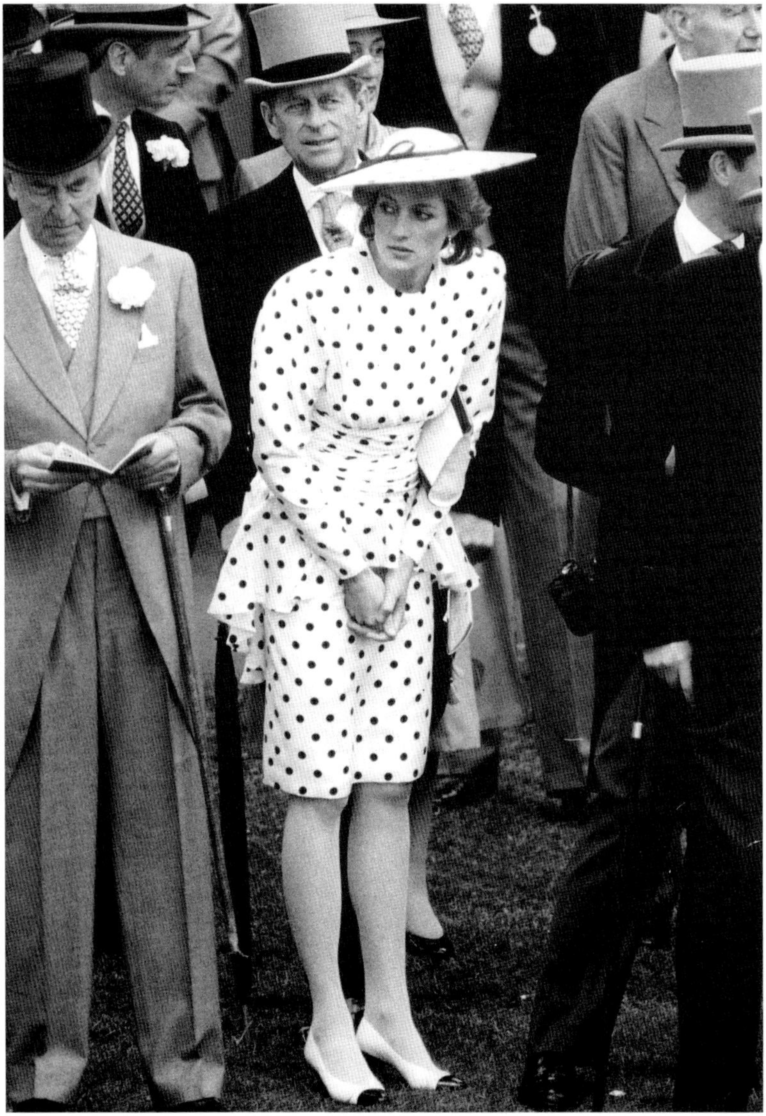

Diana loved Royal Ascot because it was a real chance to show off her keen sense of fashion. Here she is in the Royal Enclosure surrounded by racegoers in top hats but as usual more interested in the people than the horses.

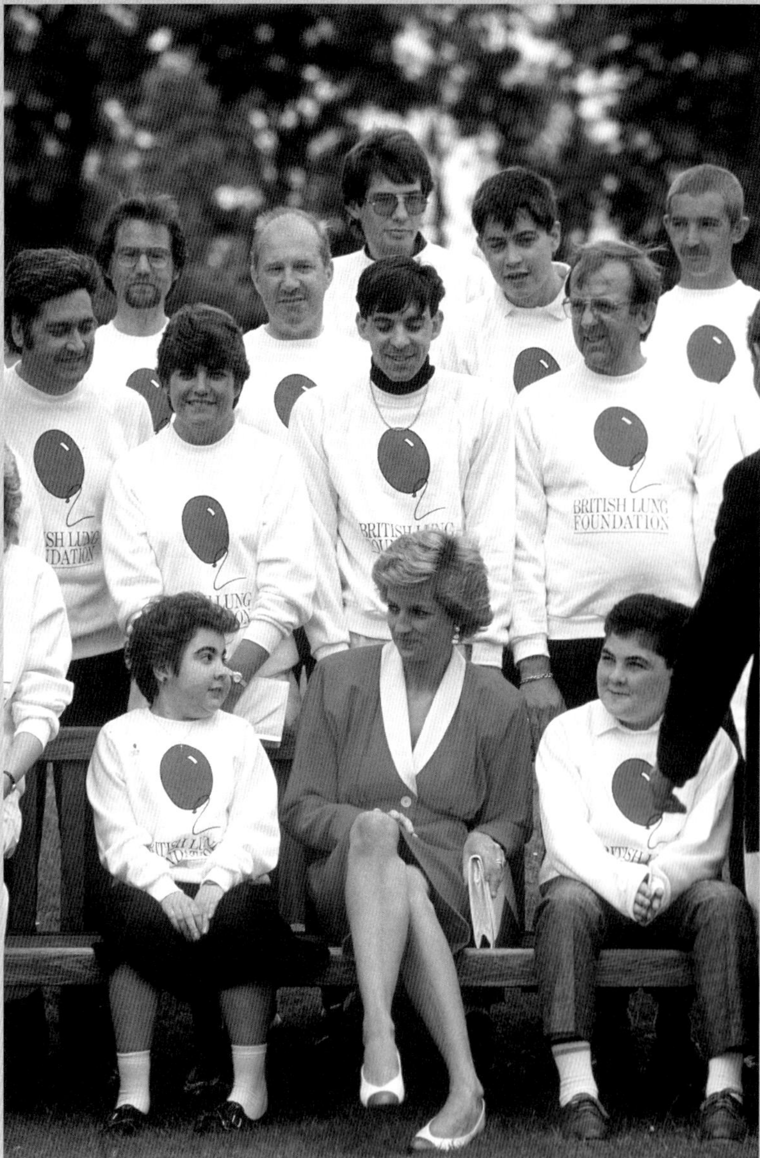

Bringing joy to just some of the patients who received life saving heart transplants at Papworth Hospital.

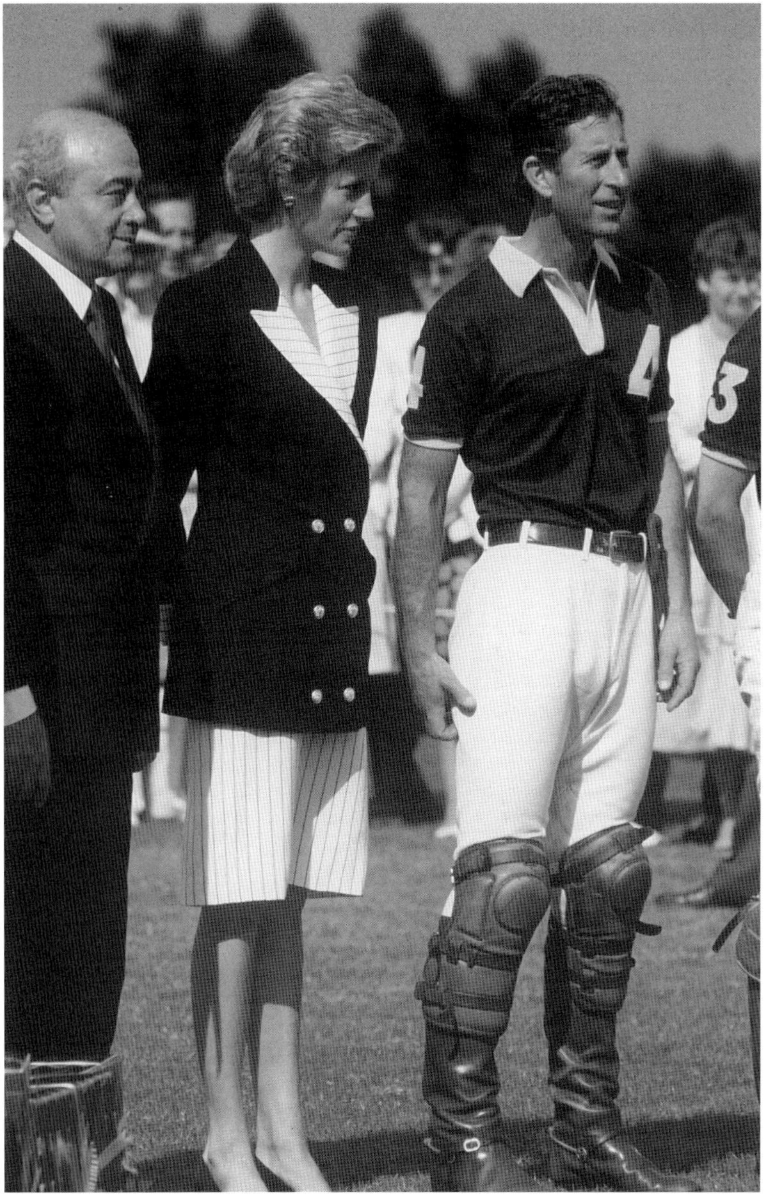

Polo with Charles at Windsor Great Park but this time accompanied by the owner of Harrods Mohammed Al Fayad.

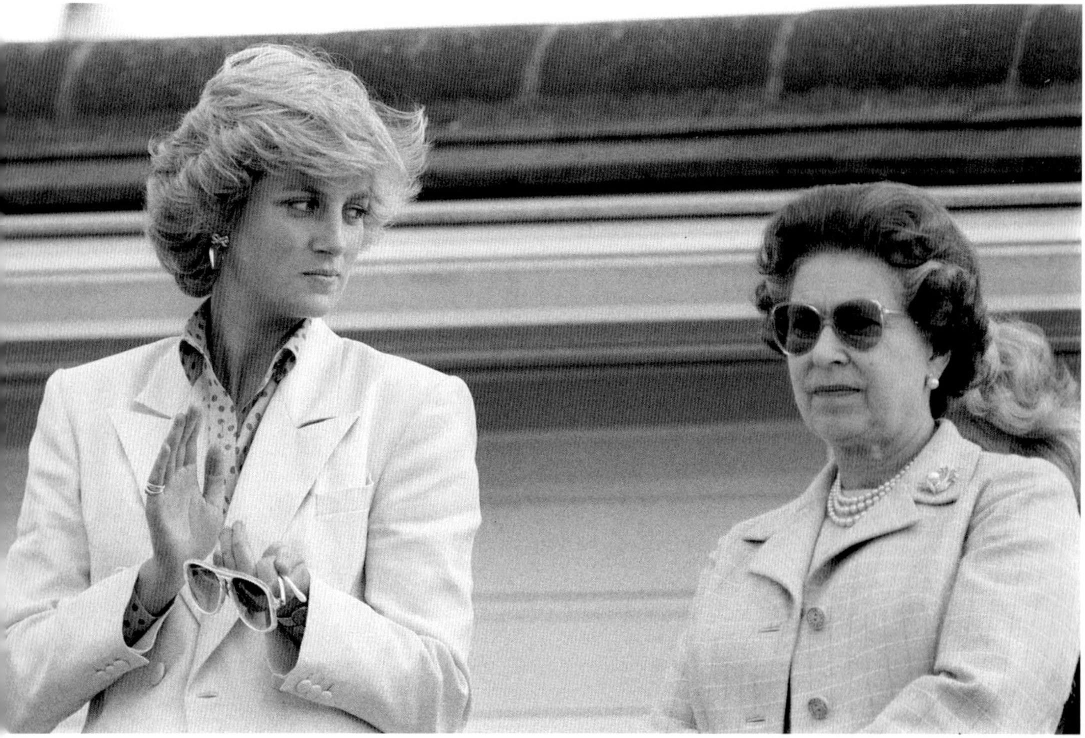

Diana, clearly more than a little nervous in the presence of the Queen at yet another polo match.

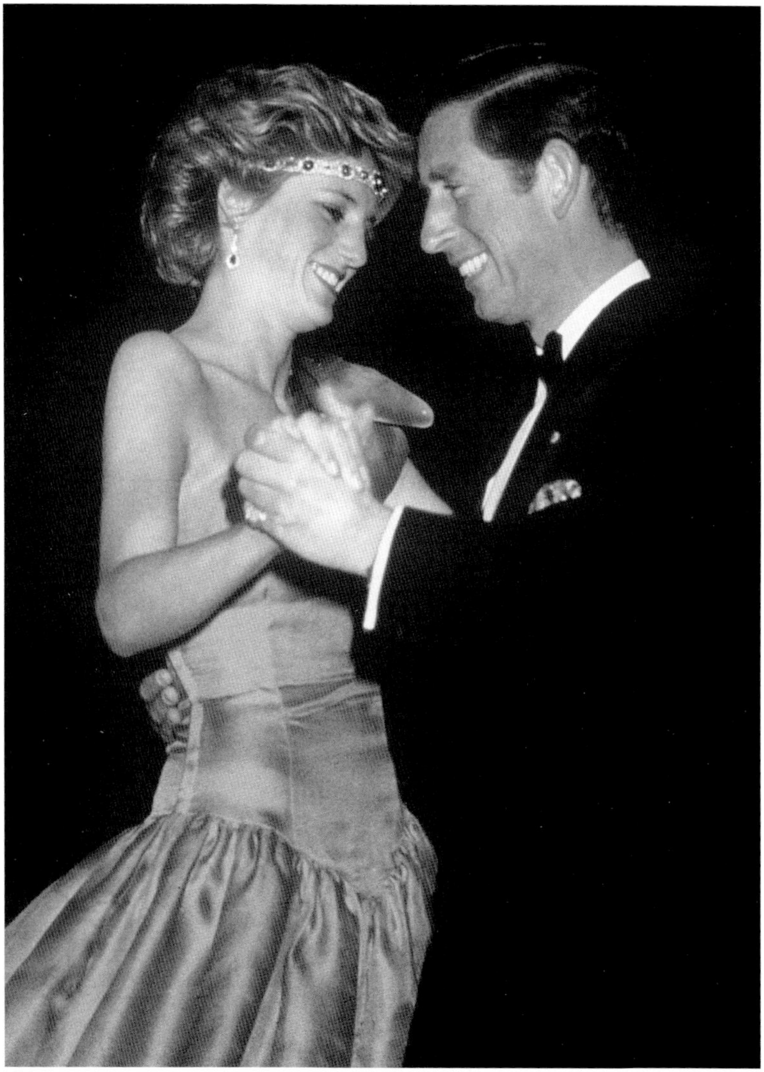

It's the India Squaw look which reputedly made Charles gasp with astonishment the night he took Diana to a ball in Melbourne, Australia. 'You're not going out like that?' asked the Prince. 'Yes I am' said Diana and the world loved her for it. It was a necklace turned into a diamond and sapphire headband glittering in the candle light.

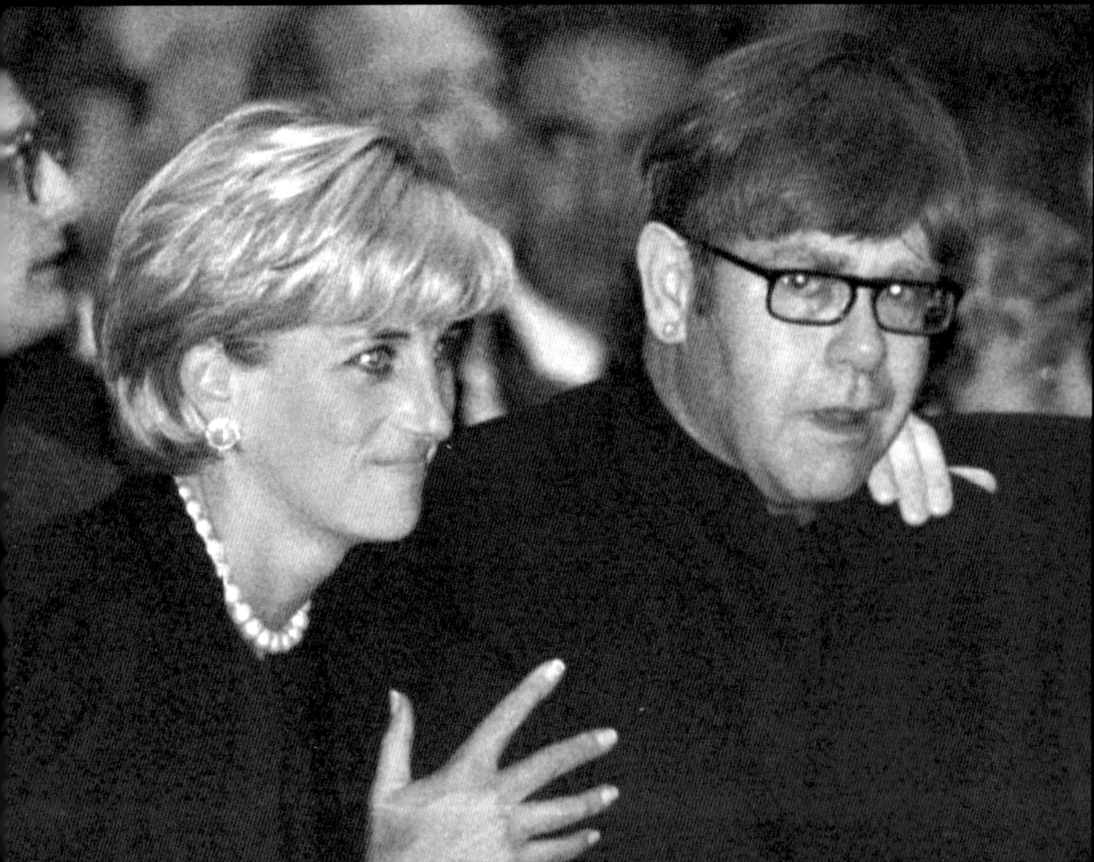

Comforting her friend Elton John who was deeply distressed during the funeral of murdered fashion king Gianni Versace in Milan.

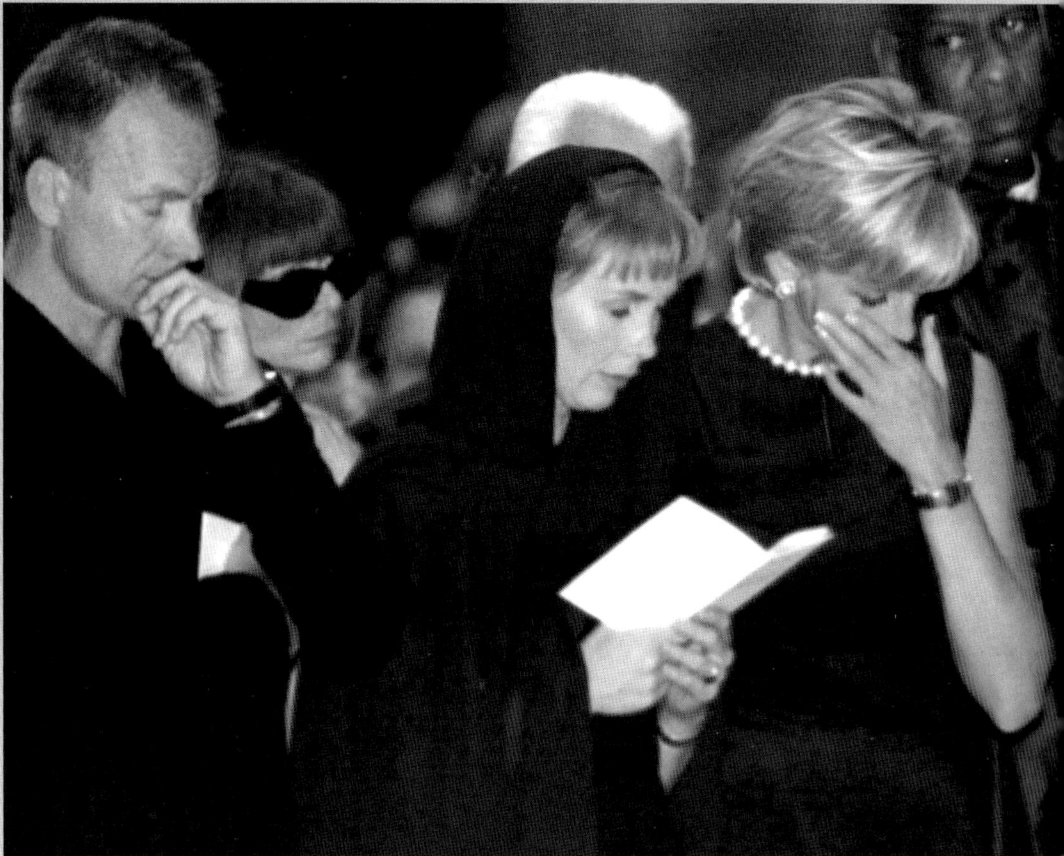

The same funeral with Sting and his wife. Diana may just be shedding a quiet tear for Gianni.

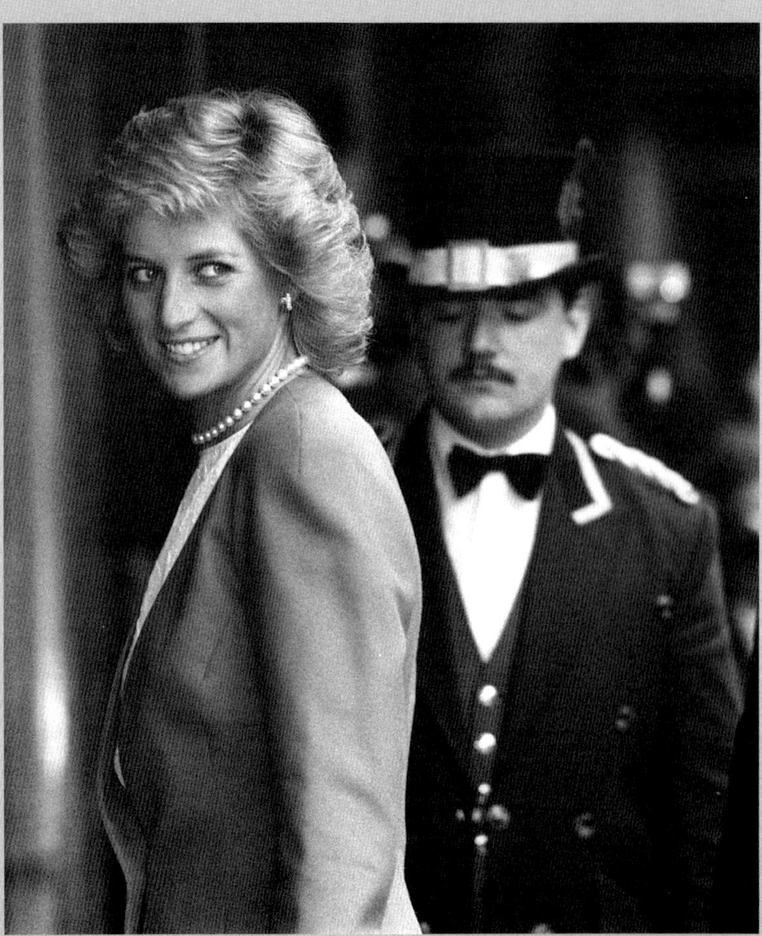

Extremely glamorous. Diana never failed to impress with whatever she wore.

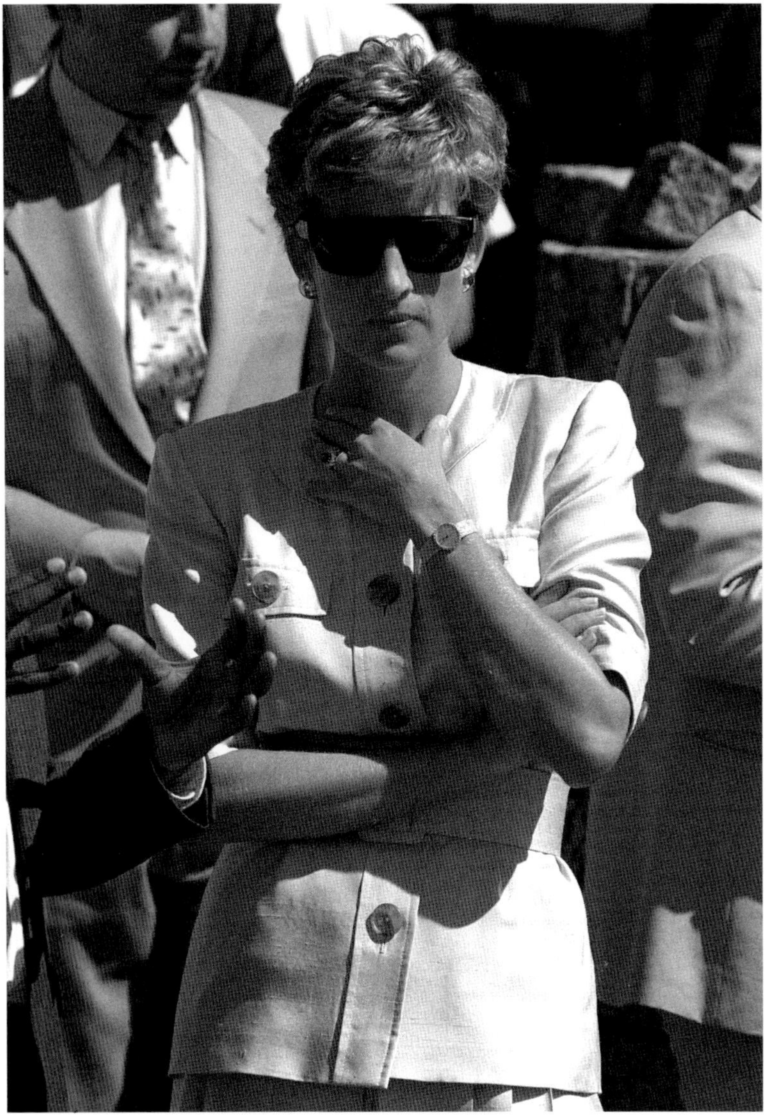

Out of Africa. Even a simple safari suit made her look special.

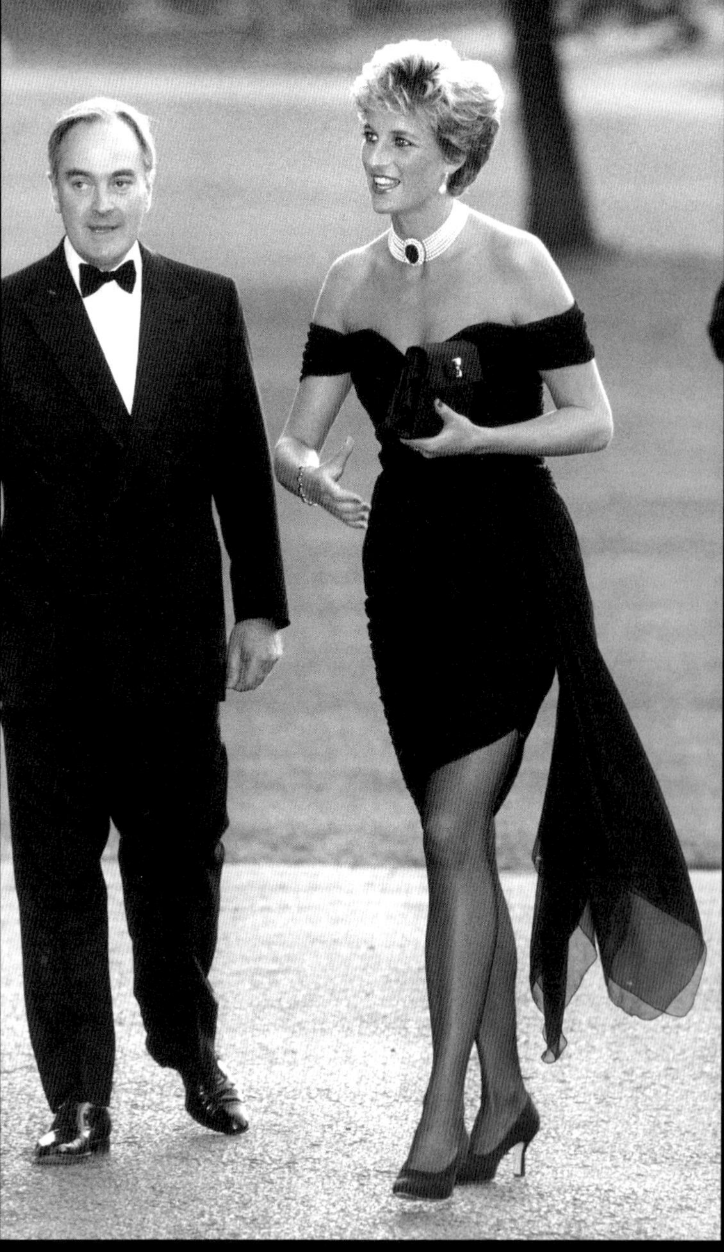

t London's Serpentine Gallery, a simple statement back dress. Mischievous Diana is said to have word this sensation deliberately to pstage her husband who was out in public elsewhere in London that ight. She won.

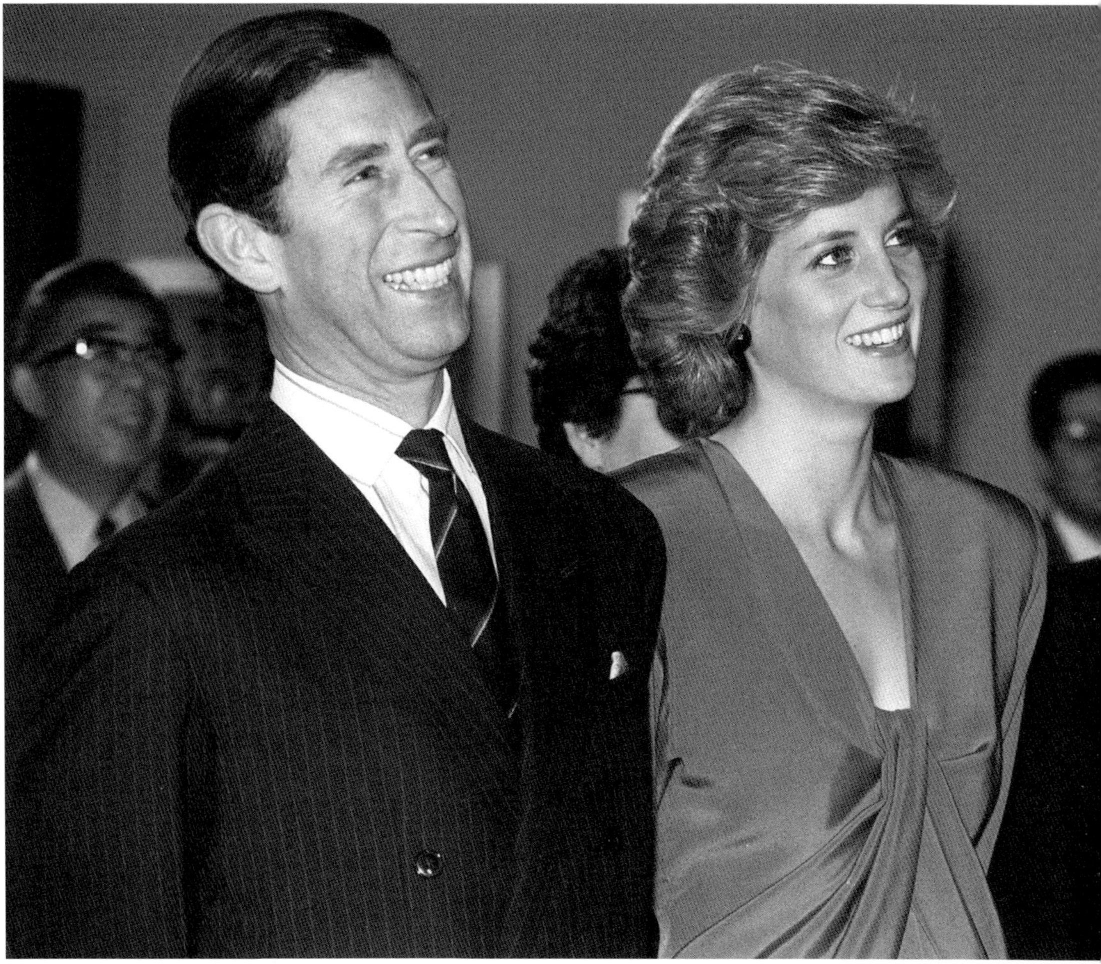

Charles and Diana in happier times in Japan where they were a huge success.

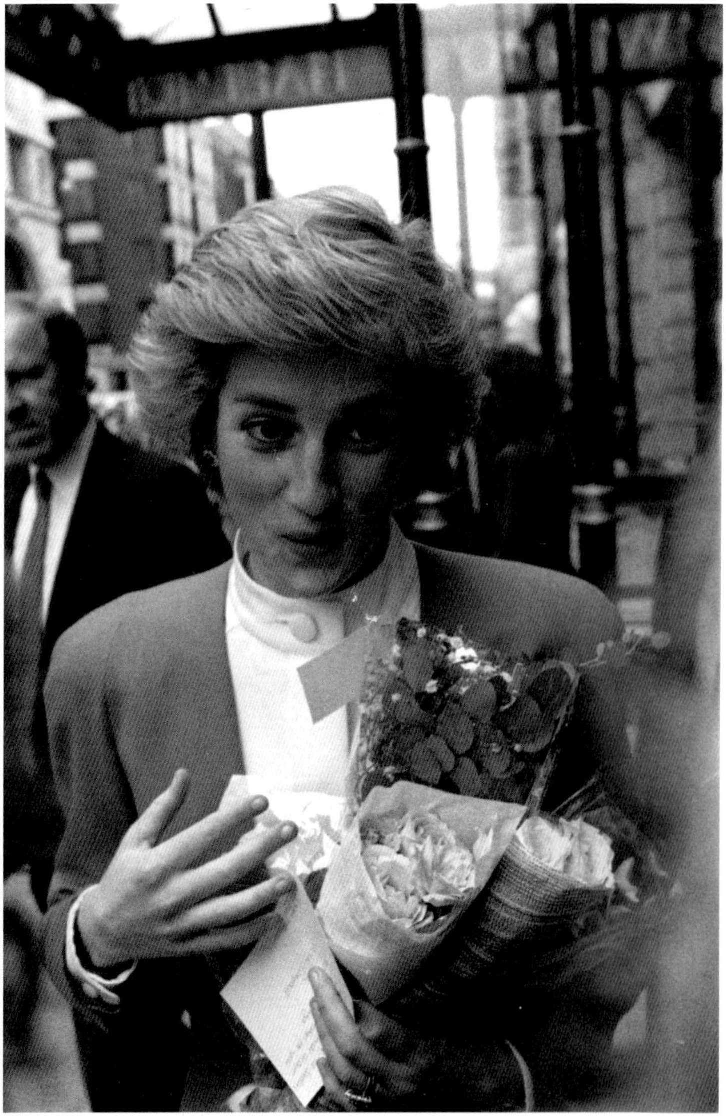

A look just for Steve at a charity do. This lady knew just how to get a photographer's interest.

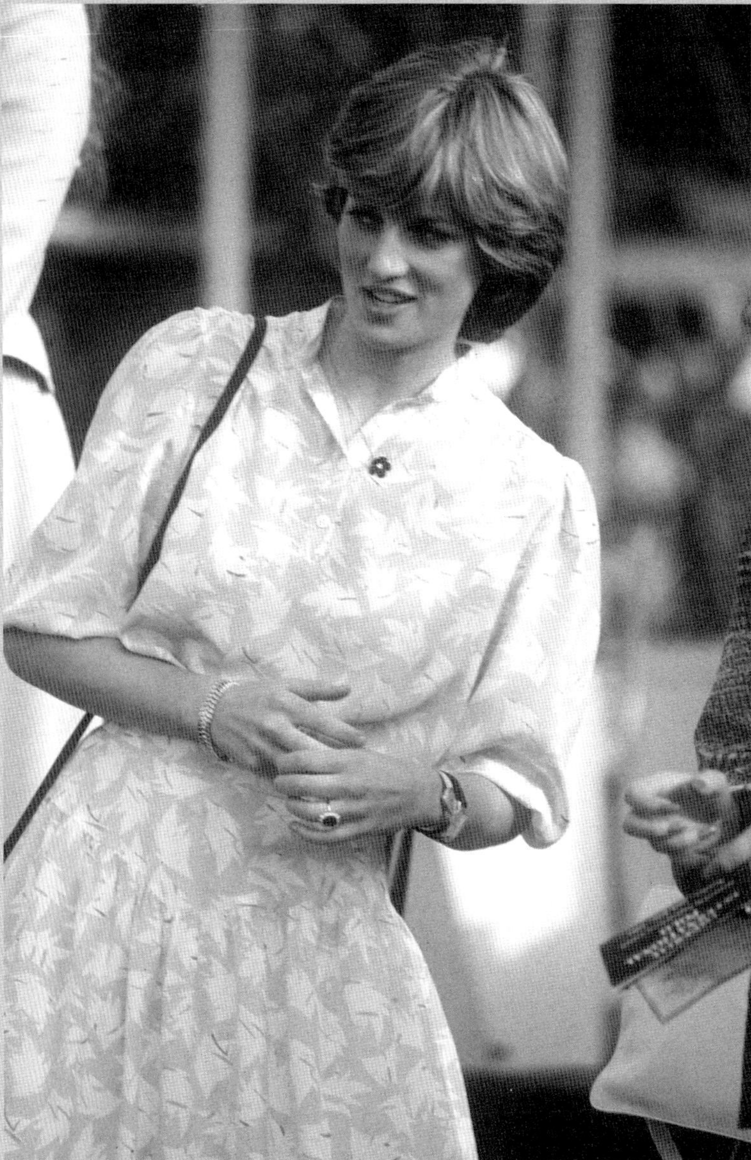

Lady Diana wears her future husband's wristwatch as well as her own while he charges around the polo field. It also gave her another chance to show off that flashy engagement ring.

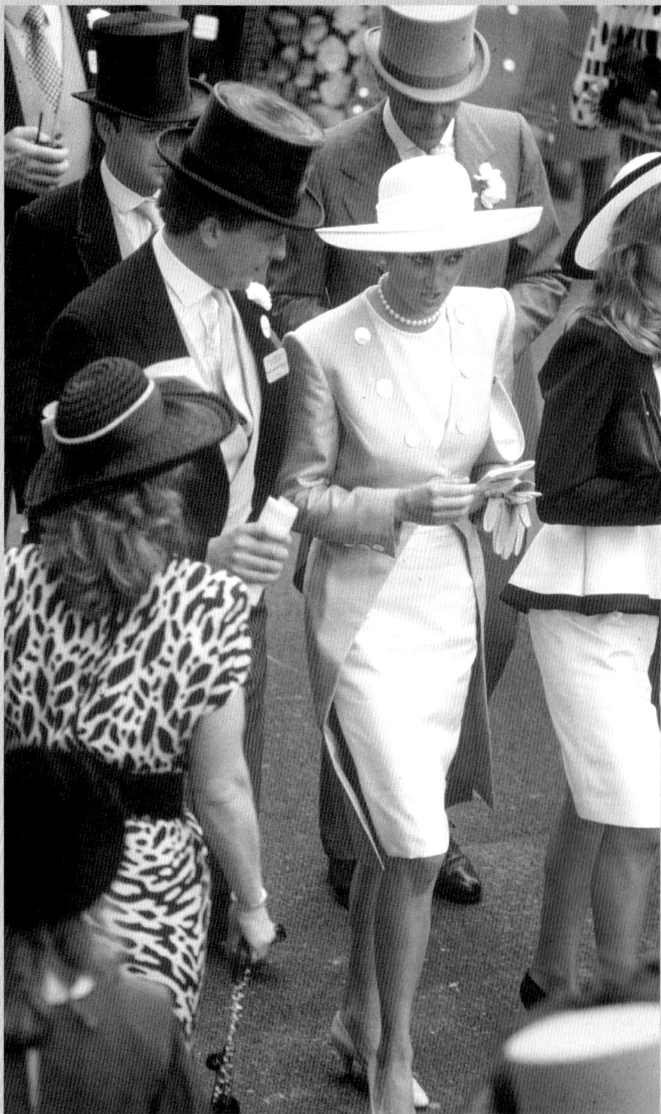

Studying the form (the other fashionable fillies, not the horses) at Royal Ascot.

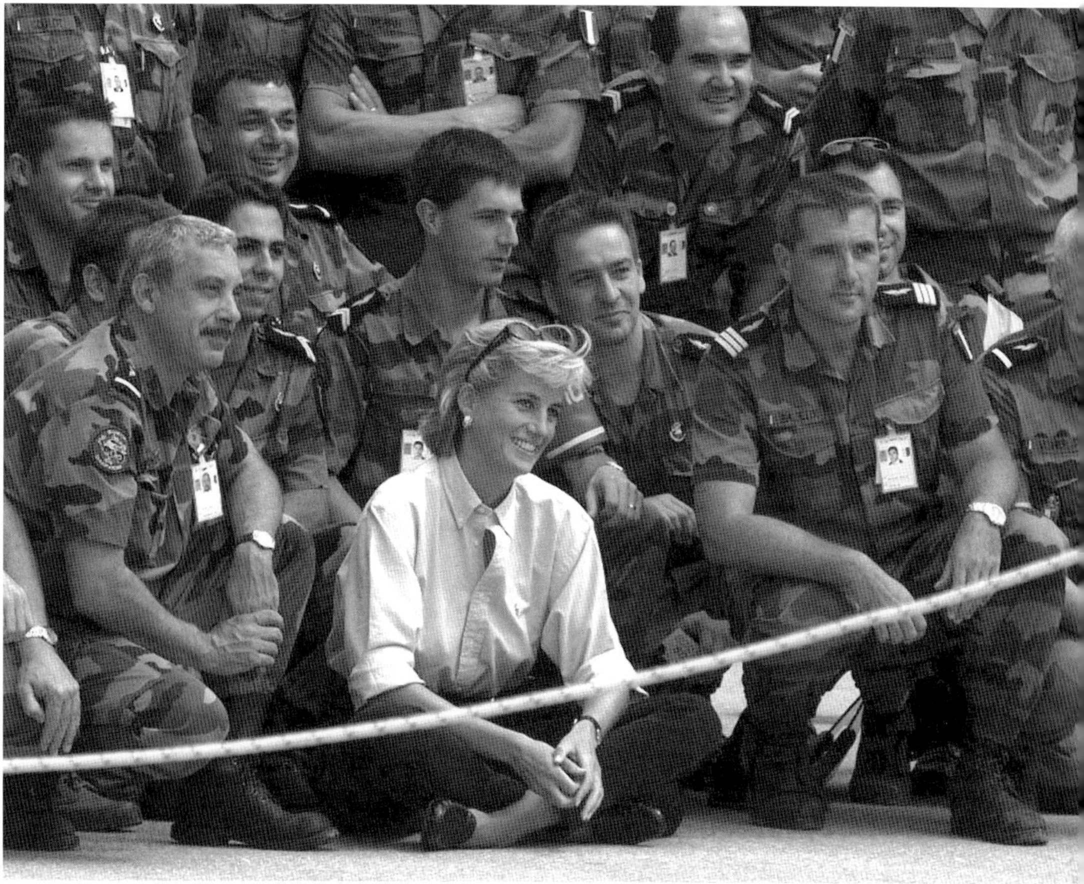

The forces favourite. Diana in simple blouse and slacks is the star of this military show.

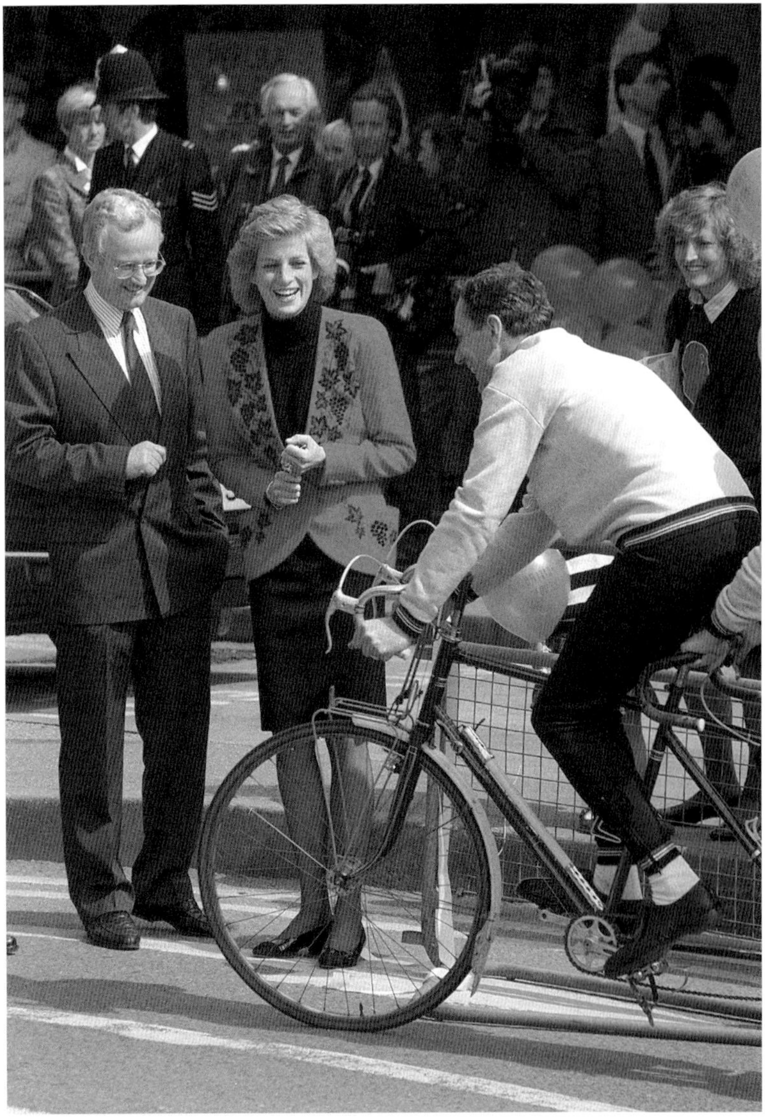

Diana had a keen sense of humour and often found something to amuse her if a public event got a little tiresome.

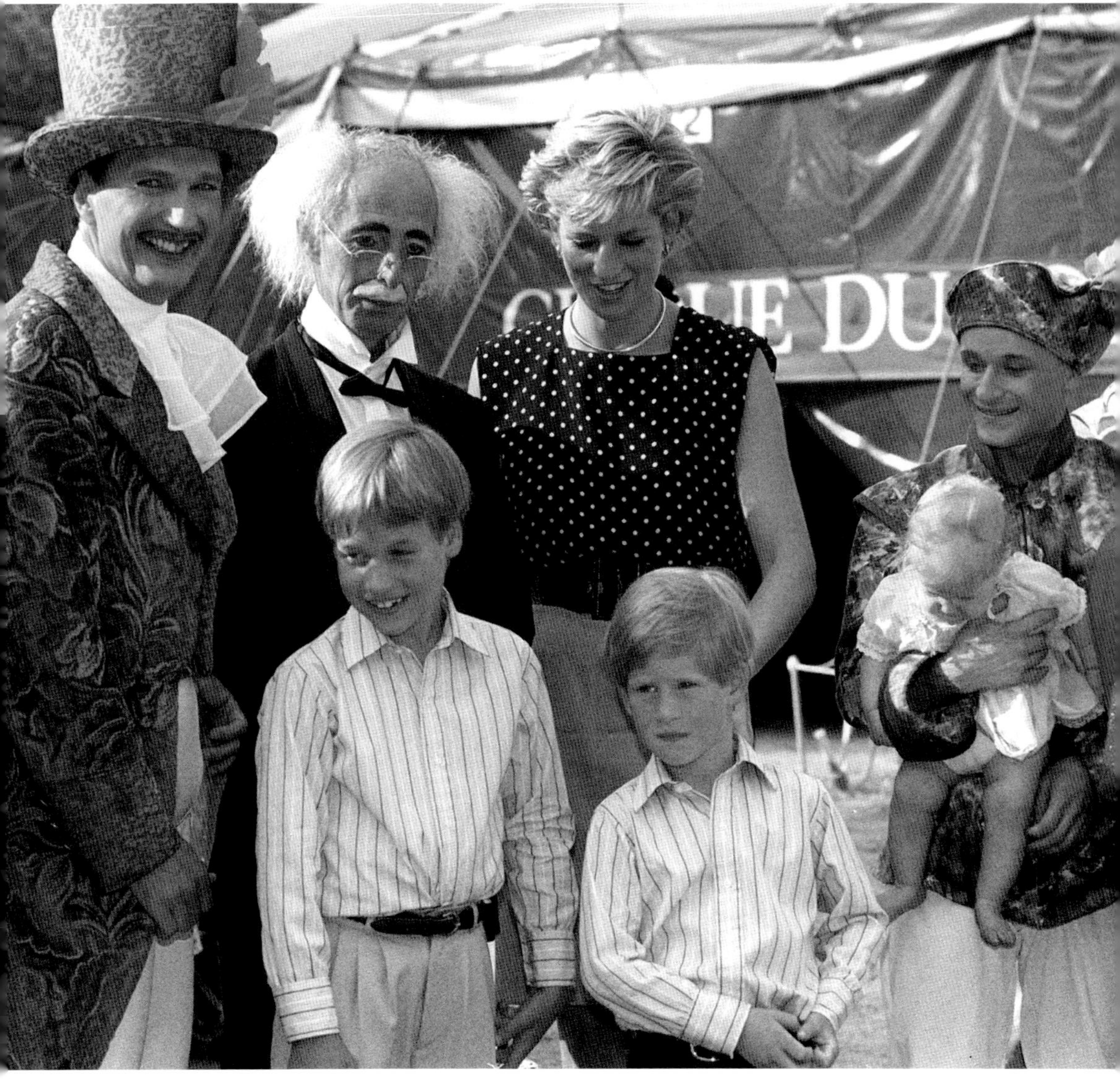

Just like any other mother Diana takes William and Harry for a afternoon at the circus.

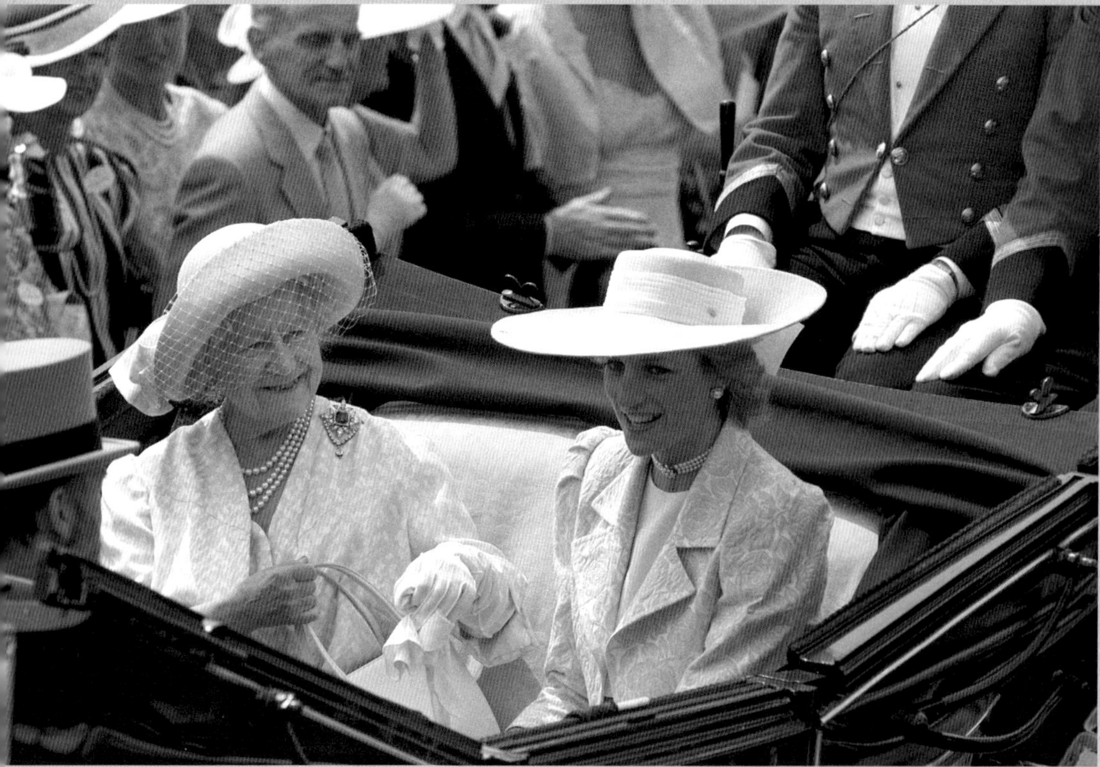

Looking very regal in a horse drawn carriage beside the Queen Mother for the Royal parade at Royal Ascot.

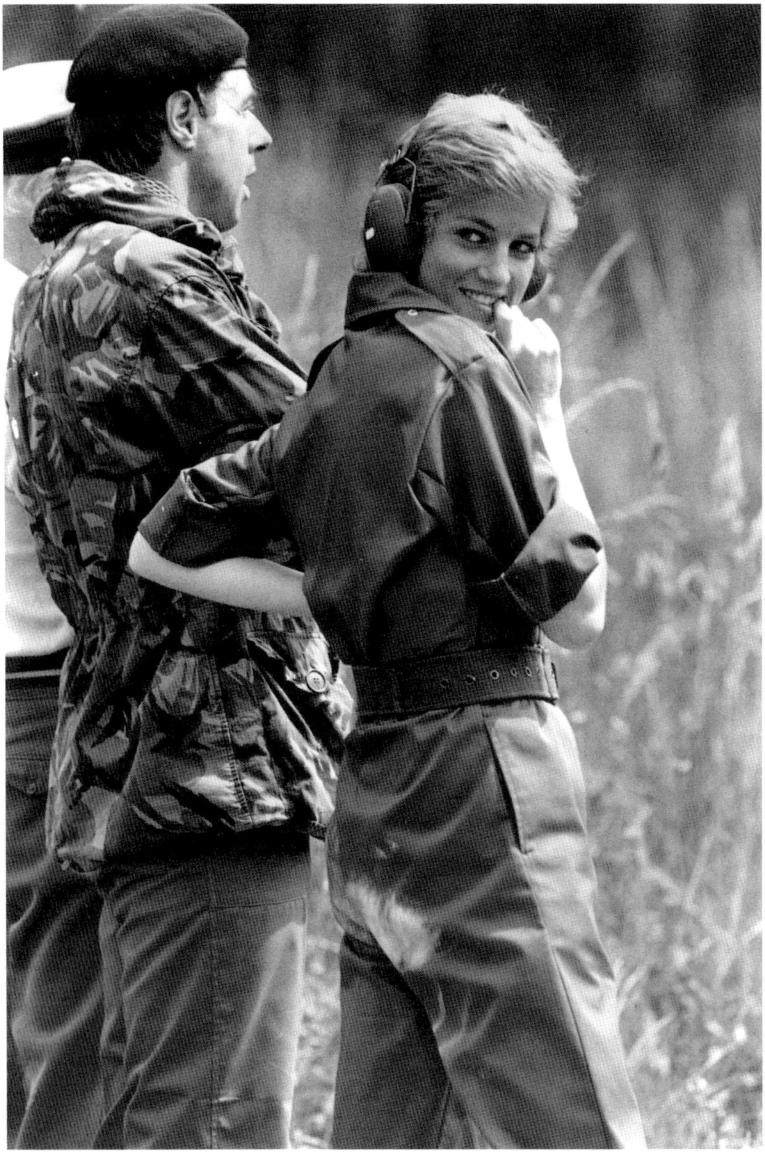

Cutting out the noise on military manoeuvres, Diana still has time for the camera.

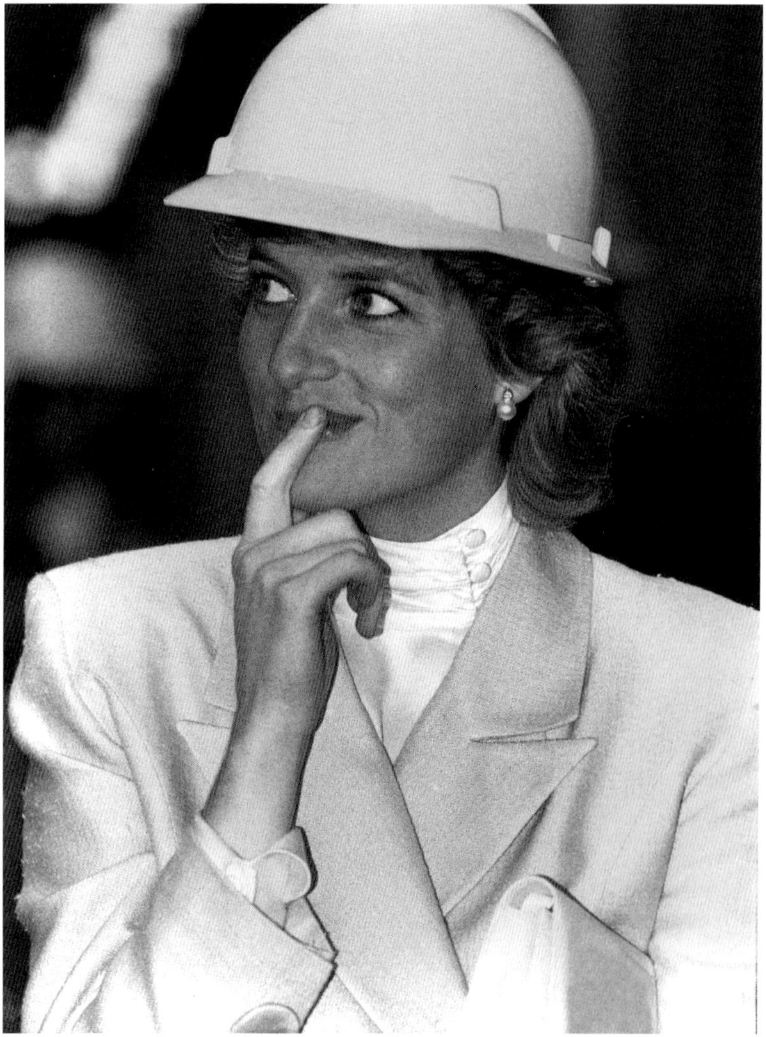

Who do you know who can look stunning while wearing a safety helmet?

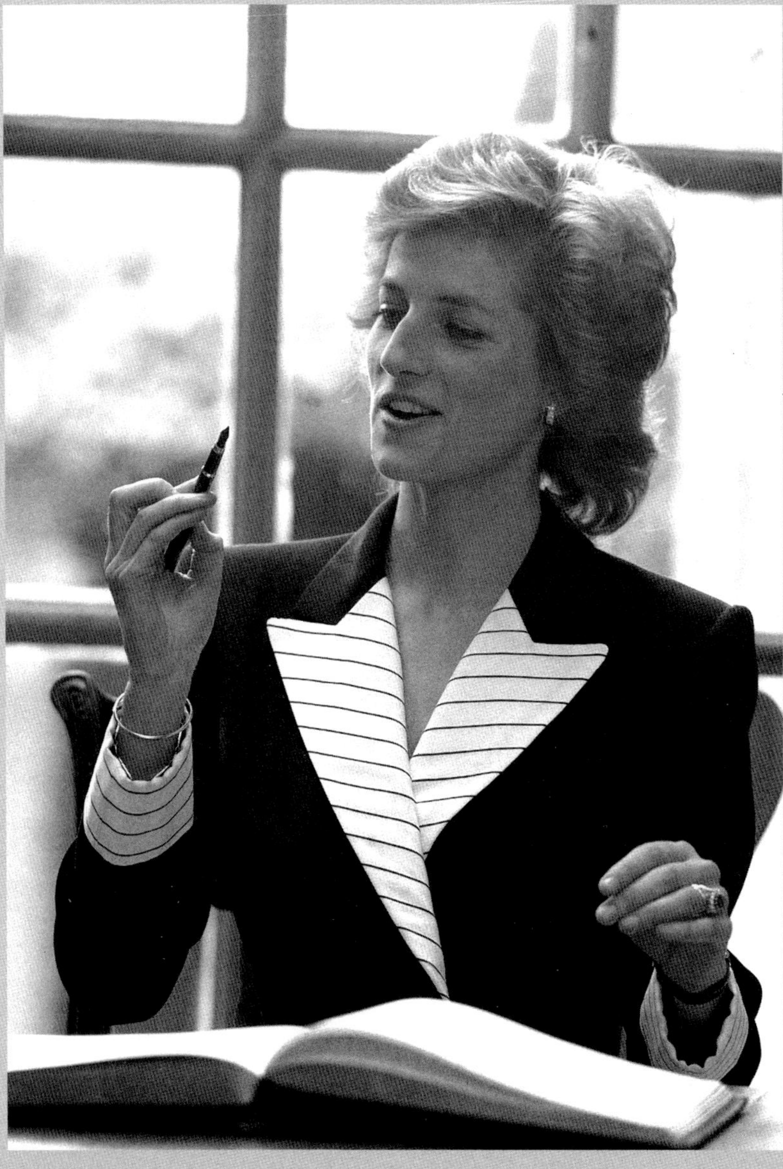

Signing the visitors book with a joke about the pen and looking supremely confident.

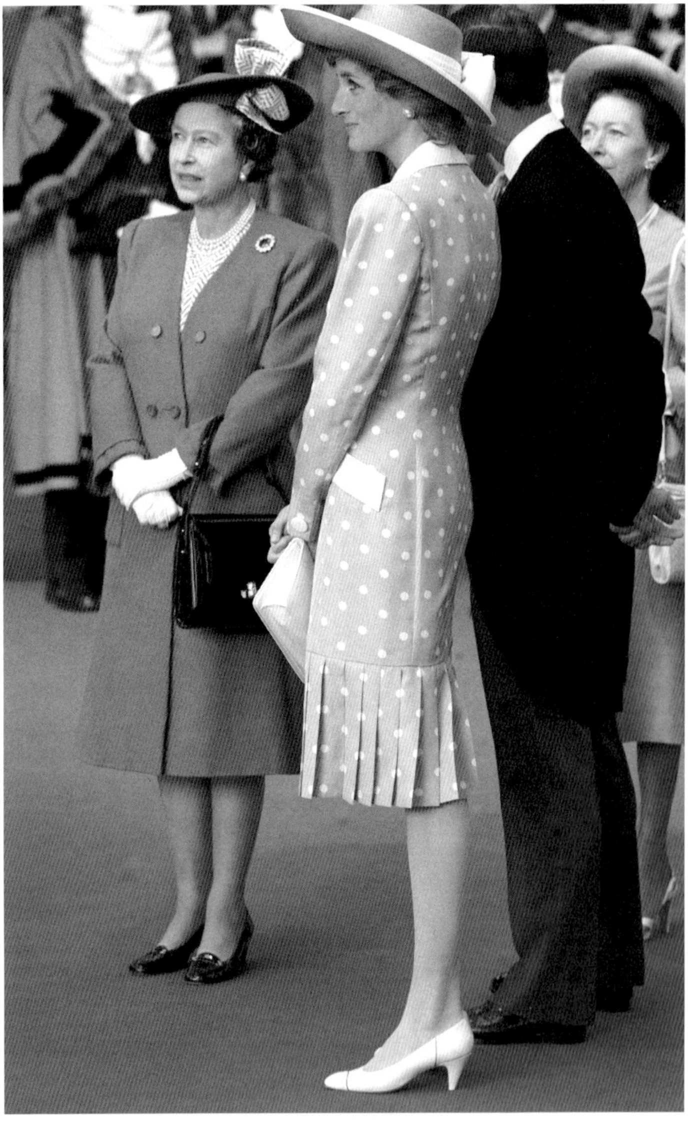

A very nervous Diana attends her first big ceremonial, a welcoming ceremony for a state visit inside Victoria Station, all eyes were on her and not the visiting heads of state.

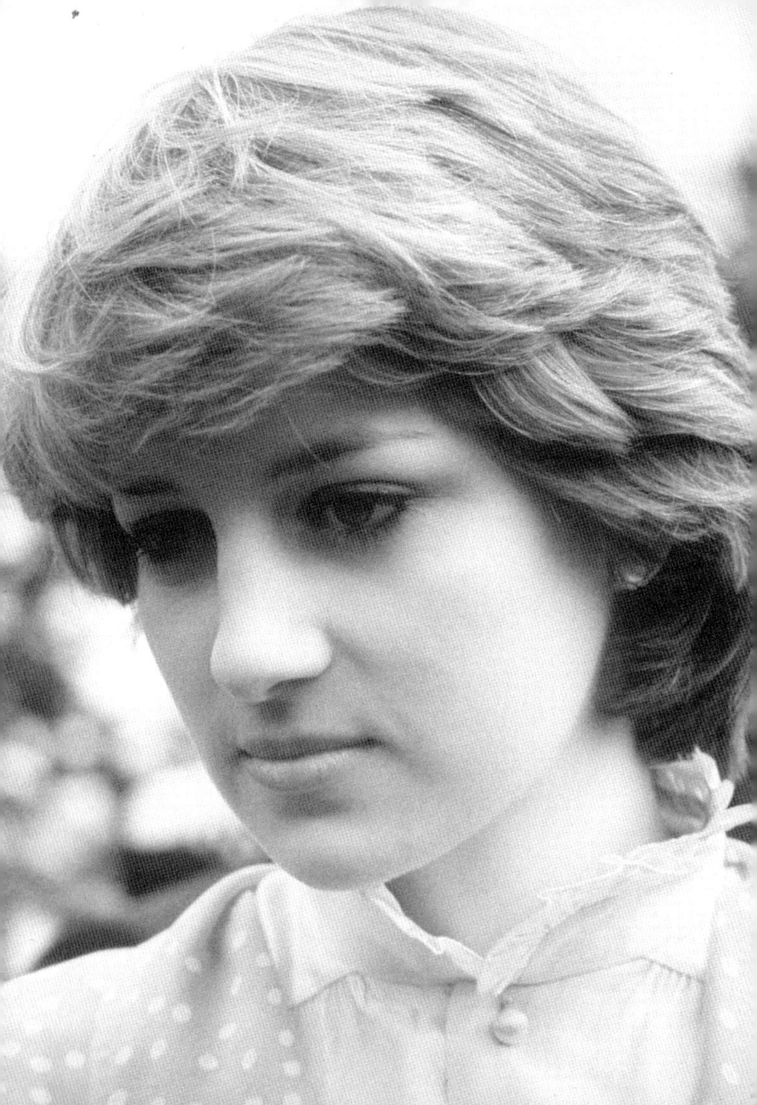

This is how the world will remember that teenager who earned the 'Shi Di' nickname before marrying her handsome Prince and becoming the world's most famous woman.

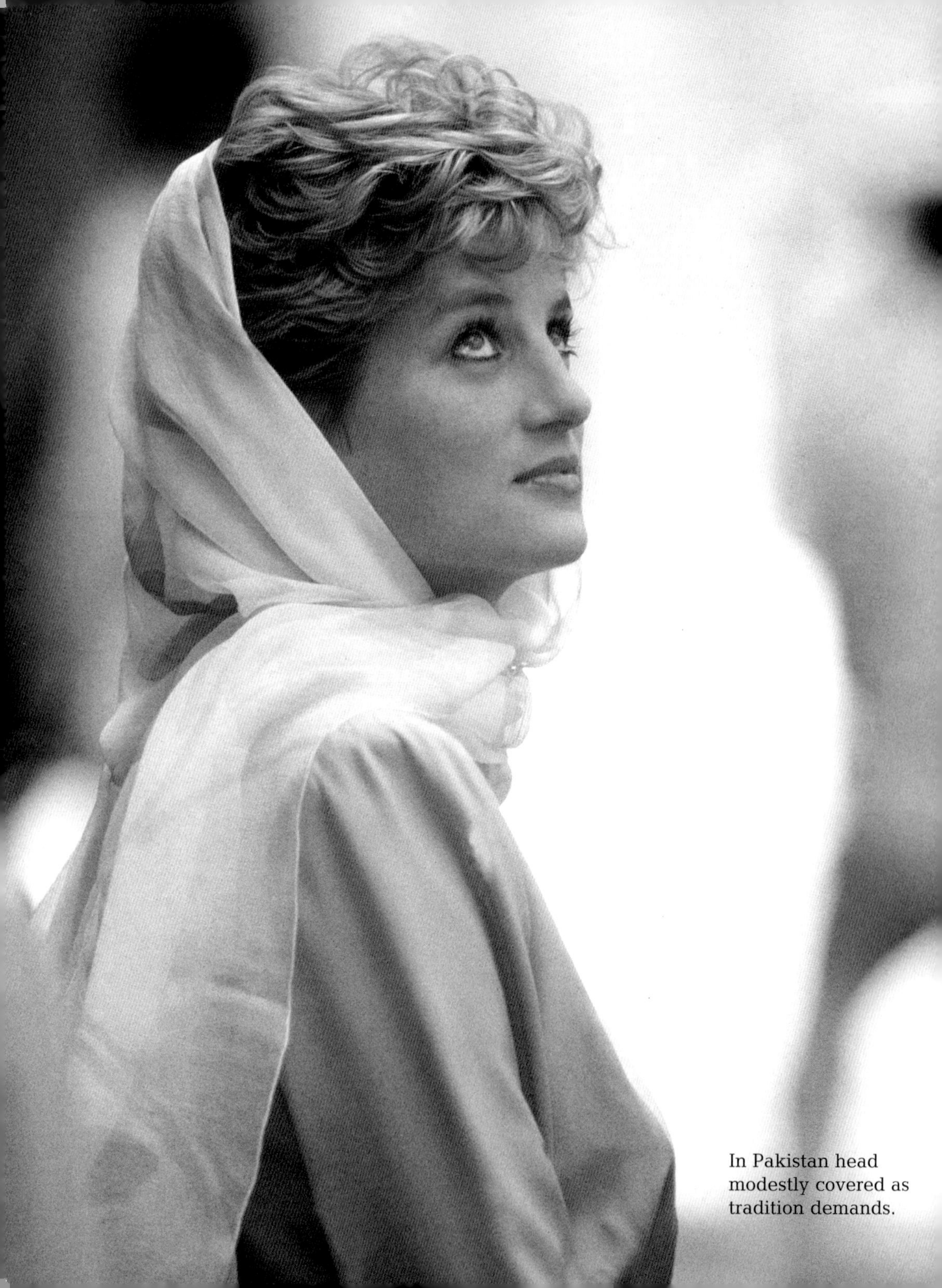

In Pakistan head
modestly covered as
tradition demands.

INDEX

Page 125	Caught in a snowstorm at Klosters in Switzerland.
Page 126	Diana extricates herself from a tight spot.
Page 127	In Germany wearing a simple black dress.
Page 128	A very sexy black choker studded with pearls.
Page 129	Derby Day, with her friend the Duchess of York.
Page 130	In the Royal Box at Wimbledon looking bored between sets.
Page 131	Diana with her mother Frances Shand Kydd.
Page 132	With Grace Kelly, Princess Stephanie and Prince Albert.
Page 133	Diana at Royal Ascot surrounded by racegoers in top hats
Page 134	Bringing joy to the patients at Papworth Hospital.
Page 135	Polo with Charles at Windsor Great Park accompanied by the owner of Harrods, Mohammed Al Fayed.
Page 136	Diana casting a quizzical glance at Her Majesty The Queen.
Page 137	The Indian Squaw look at a ball in Melbourne.
Page 138	Comforting her friend, Elton John.
Page 139	Attending Gianni Versace's funeral with Sting and his wife.
Page 140	Always making the right impression.
Page 141	Out of Africa in a simple safari suit.
Page 142	Upstaging Charles at London's Serpentine Gallery.
Page 143	Charles and Diana in Japan, in happier times.
Page 144	That special look for the camera
Page 145	Diana wearing her husbands wristwatch at Polo.
Page 146	Studying form at Royal Ascot.
Page 147	Wearing simple blouse and slacks at a military show.
Page 148	Diana displaying her keen sense of humour.
Page 149	Diana takes William and Harry for a afternoon at the circus.
Page 150	Looking very regal beside the Queen Mother.
Page 151	Cutting out the noize on military manoeuvres.
Page 152	Making a fashion statement, even in this dinky hard hat.
Page 153	Signing the visitors' book with a joke about the pen and looking supremely confident.
Page 154	Attending her first welcoming ceremony of a state visit.
Page 155	How the world will remember the teenager known as 'Shy Di'.
Page 156	In Pakistan, her head modestly covered as tradition demands.